The Story of the East Lancashire Loom-Breakers in 1826

Lancashire County Books,
1992

William Turner is a local historian born and brought up in east Lancashire. He is the author of two books about the 'Accrington Pals', a local battalion of the 1914–18 war.

Riot!
The Story of the East Lancashire Loom-Breakers in 1826

by William Turner

Published by Lancashire County Books, 143 Corporation Street, Preston
First edition, November 1992

Typeset by Carnegie Publishing Ltd., 18 Maynard St., Preston
Printed and bound by the Bath Press, Bath

ISBN 1-871236-17-7

British Library Cataloguing-in-Publication Data
A CIP catalogue record for this book is available from the British Library

Contents

Acknowledgements v
Foreword vii
Elephants and Chickens 1
Monday – The Beginnings 14
Tuesday – 'A Disposition to Riot' 25
Wednesday – Watch and Ward 35
Wednesday – The Chatterton 'Fight' 41
Wednesday – On Two Fronts 48
Thursday – 'Along by Botany Bay' 55
Dispute and Dishonour 62
The Quiet Which Prevails 71
'A Melancholy Catalogue' 83
'Like a Wicked Noah's Ark' 95
Thomas Emmett – On the Manlius 107
On the Harmony 117
A Lucky Break 129
A Family Story 138
A New Life 145
Surely not in Vain 153
Notes 165
Dramatis Personae 184
Appendix 1 194
Appendix 2 196
Appendix 3 199
Appendix 4 200
Appendix 5 201
Appendix 6 203
Appendix 7 204
Select Bibliography 206

Acknowledgements

IT is impossible to adequately thank all who helped me, directly and indirectly, in my researches for this book. There has been generous and willing help from many people.

Of the many, I particularly thank Mr Chris Aspin of Helmshore for his help and advice at the beginning; Mrs Atherton and Mr D. M. Sailor of Lancaster Castle; Mr W. S. Curtis of the Muzzleloaders Society of Great Britain; Mr G. S. Gill, Curator of the 1st The Queen's Dragoon Guards Museum, Cardiff; Mr Robin Green of Higher Mill Museum, Helmshore; Mr Hubert Hartley, J.P., of Knuzden, Blackburn; Col. (retd.) I. H. McCausland of the Royal Greenjackets Museum, Winchester, and Mrs Jean Price of Botley, Oxford.

My words are considerably enhanced by the excellent maps and artist's impressions of events drawn by Mr Alan Ormerod of Oswaldtwistle, to whom I give special thanks.

My researches also took me, metaphorically, to Australia. My thanks go to Mr R. T. Harbinson, Secretary of the Australian Agricultural Company, Brisbane, Queensland; Mr Dennis Heathfield of Karuah, New South Wales; Pennie Pemberton of the Australian National University, Canberra, for her help with the early history of the Australian Agricultural Company, and particularly Mrs Gill Peasley of Forbes, New South Wales, for sharing with me her researches into the Emmett family tree. Staff at the Australian Genealogical Society, Sydney; the State Library of New South Wales, Sydney and Newcastle (New South Wales) City Libraries were also helpful and patient in dealing with my enquiries by correspondence.

I also acknowledge the help, interest and advice of Local Study Library staff in the following Lancashire County Libraries: Accrington, Bacup, Blackburn, Burnley, Chorley, Clitheroe, Darwen, Haslingden, Lancaster, Rawtenstall, and the Library Headquarters in Preston. I am also indebted to staff at the Central Libraries in Bolton, Bury, Manchester, Oldham and Rochdale; the Lancashire Record Office, Preston; and Wigan Record Office, Leigh.

Invaluable help came from staff at the National Army Museum, the National Maritime Museum, the Public Record Office at Kew and at Chancery Lane, London. Crown Copyright material in the Public Record Office is used by permission of the Controller of Her Majesty's Stationery Office.

I also acknowledge with thanks the financial help of a grant towards costs of research from Mr Chris Aspin and the Higher Mill Trust.

A special note of thanks is naturally due to Mrs Anne McIntosh of Garfield Agency for, as ever, her meticulous typing; Mr Alistair Hodge for his advice and editing skills; and Mrs Zoë Lawson of Lancashire County Books for the advice and assistance that went so well with the cups of hot chocolate.

Finally, I am especially pleased to express my gratitude to Dr Duncan Bythell of Durham University, for reading my manuscript and kindly agreeing to write the foreword.

Foreword

by Duncan Bythell
Senior Lecturer in History, University of Durham

THE Lancashire weavers' riots of April 1826 were one of the most dramatic events in the history of the English cotton industry. Although 1826 was neither the first nor the last occasion on which newly-installed powerlooms were destroyed by angry English textile workers, it was certainly the biggest. For four days, the area bordered by Chorley, Clitheroe, Bacup, and Bury was convulsed as desperate crowds attacked local weaving sheds and smashed over 1100 of the hated machines. The immediate human cost of this brief but spectacular orgy of violence was borne by the six people killed when rioters encountered the military at Chatterton; a further instalment was paid, some months afterwards, by the ten people transported for life, and the thirty others sentenced to prison terms, for their part in the disturbances. The symbolic significance of the 1826 riots – representing vividly the final vain attempt of an old way of life based on the handloom and the domestic workshop to resist by force the 'inevitable march of progress' in the shape of the steam engine and the factory – has long been recognised. Yet the exciting story of what happened during these four hectic days has never been told in detail, and the Lancashire loom-breakers have attracted little attention from historians, compared with the midland Luddites of 1812 and the 'Swing' rioters in southern England in 1830. It is therefore gratifying to the author of this preface, whose 1969 book *The Handloom Weavers* managed to dispose of the 1826 riots in a mere five pages, to be able to commend William Turner's painstaking study, which is based on a thorough examination of the contemporary records. Now, at last, we have an exhaustive, hour-by-hour narrative of the four days of rioting, coupled with a detailed account of the fates of some of the rioters, from an enthusiastic local historian who knows the area and its past intimately.

It is neither appropriate nor necessary to summarise the sequence of events described so eloquently by Mr Turner in the following pages. However, it may be useful to remind the reader, briefly, of aspects of the broader context within which these extraordinary local happenings took place. First of all, how did the Lancashire riots of 1826 relate to the various other episodes of machine-breaking which occurred during the classic period of the British industrial revolution in the late eighteenth and early nineteenth centuries? Irate workers had a long tradition of venting their indignation on their employers' property at times of friction and conflict, and in this sense machine-breaking was sometimes merely one aspect of what Eric Hobsbawm has called 'collective bargaining by riot'. Industrial sabotage did not *necessarily* imply that the machines in question were feared because they threatened workers with unemployment and redundancy, lower wages, or the loss of job control. The simple fact that the machines were the property of an unpopular individual was sufficient to make them fair game, especially when other ways of exerting pressure or gaining redress were inappropriate or unavailable. Nevertheless, the best-known examples of machine-breaking in this period did have genuinely 'technological' overtones – that is, workers feared the damage which a particular machine was causing, or might cause, to their livelihoods, their ways of life, and their communities. Like the earlier Lancashire riots of the 1760s and 1770s against spinning jennies and waterframes, like the Luddite destruction of gig-mills and wide knitting-frames in the woollen and hosiery industries in 1811 and 1812, and like the 'Swing' rioters' hostility towards threshing machines in 1830, the desperate actions of the handloom weavers and their supporters in 1826 were clearly inspired by 'technological' considerations. Yet, unlike the Luddites, who acted in small conspiratorial groups at dead of night and whose campaign extended over several months, the Lancashire rioters operated in large crowds and in broad daylight. The determined men and women who attacked the weaving sheds made no attempt at secrecy, and the outbreak, which seemed to start spontaneously and to spread by imitation, subsided as quickly as it had begun. In this respect, the east Lancashire riots of 1826 had more in common with those in the southern agricultural districts to be visited by 'Captain Swing' four years later than they had with those in the east midland counties which had been haunted by 'General Ludd' fourteen years before. It is also worth remembering that, as with the agricultural labourers in 1830, it was not only the weavers directly threatened by the new powerlooms, but also other members of the communities whose well-being was at risk if their staple industry collapsed, who were sufficiently incensed in 1826 to take the law into their own hands to this remarkable extent.

Secondly, there are the particular problems of time and place. Why did people want to destroy powerlooms in 1826 (rather than earlier or later) and why was it in this part of upland Lancashire (rather than in Manchester and its surrounding towns, where the bulk of the early powerlooms were in fact located) that the disturbances took place? The timing of the riots is not difficult to explain: the cotton masters only became interested in using powerlooms during the massive export boom of the early 1820s, and their new weaving sheds were still being built and equipped – often as extensions to their already-existing spinning mills – in 1825 and 1826, when the boom broke. The self-same boom which encouraged the masters to invest in powerlooms also saw the final burst of prosperity for the local handloom weavers, who found their services were in at least temporary demand until the new machines were up and running. But when boom turned to slump at the end of 1825, the handloom weavers immediately faced at best starvation wages, or at worst complete unemployment. Under these circumstances, they naturally saw the new looms not only as the cause of their present plight, but also as a permanent threat to their future well-being and long-term survival. But why was it the weavers of Rossendale and its neighbourhood, rather than those of Manchester, Oldham, or Bolton, who now decided that desperate straits called for drastic remedies? To answer this question would require a lengthy digression, which cannot be attempted here, about the peculiar social and economic structure and cultural heritage of the small upland weaving villages from which most of the rioters came. Crudely, however, we may suggest that wage earners in the bigger south Lancashire towns were already, by the 1820s, familiar both with factory work and with the wider range of employment normally available in complex and expanding communities. In addition, they operated within a relatively sophisticated political milieu and in a pattern of relatively orderly and formal industrial relations. Conversely, the small Pennine weaving villages, whose populations had mushroomed during the previous half-century, had remained almost entirely dependent economically on the handloom, whilst politically they had enjoyed considerable freedom from the subtle controls normally exercised in other rural districts by parson and squire and in the big towns by the commercial and professional bourgeoisie. Imbued with a strong sense of community, independent-minded, but at the same time unsophisticated, ill-organised for collective bargaining, undisciplined, and inadequately policed, these Lancashire hill-billies behaved predictably when they suddenly realised that every aspect of their way of life was threatened with imminent destruction. Had their urban cousins joined them in rioting, as the authorities evidently feared they might, the outbreak of 1826 would have been more serious, and order would have taken longer to restore; but with hindsight, it seems that such a development was by this time highly improbable.

Thirdly, there is the question of the long-term legacy of the 1826 riots. Were they just a four days' wonder, quickly forgotten, or did they have a lasting impact, not so much on the districts involved, as on informed public opinion in the country at large? For the authorities, both locally and nationally, riots of this magnitude were yet another reminder of the difficulty of maintaining law and order through an uneasy partnership of amateur magistrates and professional soldiers: the case for having a permanent civil police force throughout the country was greatly strengthened by events like these, although it was not until 1839 that legislation to encourage the setting-up of county constabularies was passed. Nevertheless, overt coercion was not necessarily seen as the only – or even the best – way of ensuring that similar riots did not break out again. A widely canvassed explanation for the rioters' conduct was that they were 'ignorant', 'deluded', and 'misled' in believing that crude physical violence could solve their problems and in failing to appreciate the benefits which society as a whole gained when property was secure and when enterprise and intelligence were encouraged and rewarded. One young Manchester doctor, James Phillips Kay, alarmed and impressed by the awful implications of the 1826 riots, concluded that the solution lay not in repression, but in enlightening the whole population, through properly-controlled formal schooling, about the 'correct' rules of personal conduct and about the basic principles of political economy. Abandoning medicine for a career in public administration in the 1830s, Kay became one of the founding fathers of the English system of state education as it developed after 1833; and in later life, as Sir James Kay-Shuttleworth of Gawthorpe Hall, Padiham, he became a landowner and local worthy in the very district where the riots had taken place. The impact of the great loom-breaking on his social thinking is evident from the fact that in 1860 he published, anonymously, a virtually unreadable three-volume novel, *Scarsdale, or Life on the Lancashire and Yorkshire Border 30 Years Ago*, which was set against the background of the events of 1826. And when, in his public speeches in the 1850s and 1860s, Kay-Shuttleworth reviewed the moral and social 'progress' which he had witnessed in Lancashire during his lifetime, he often contrasted the lawlessness and ignorance exemplified by the rioters with the good order, prosperity, and class-harmony which now prevailed. In explaining why no more powerlooms were broken in Lancashire after 1826, Kay-Shuttleworth had no doubt that the schoolmaster had been more influential than the policeman.

The rioters of 1826 failed to prevent the introduction of the powerloom into the Lancashire cotton industry. Nevertheless, the painful transition from hand to power took another generation. Whilst the number of powerlooms increased dramatically over the 1830s and 1840s, especially in the larger towns, the process was irregular and uneven because of the recurrence of boom and slump. For over twenty years in many of the small upland villages in the handloom belt of north-east Lancashire, weavers were faced with a stark choice: either to stay put, bring-up their children to the handloom, and eke out a precarious living by maximising the number of workers per family; or to move down into town and send their children into the factory even if they were unable or unwilling to do the same themselves. During these two decades of harsh material poverty, many of the weavers looked for relief to a reformed Parliament, and threw their energies into the Chartist movement in the hope that this would secure either a tax on powerlooms or a system of state-enforced minimum wages. But the Chartists' democratic demands were consistently rejected, and the post-1832 Parliament, far from offering sympathetic legislation which would help handloom weaving survive, seemed determined, through such measures as the 1834 Poor Law, to make life harsher still. Only in the 1850s did a new solution appear in some of the old weaving villages. It was a solution which required collective self-help rather than state intervention, and it involved joining the factory masters rather than beating them. During the 1850s, a combination of the joint-stock legal form with the ideology of co-operation led to the establishment in north-east Lancashire of a number of village weaving sheds, owned and run by public companies, whose worker-shareholders had pooled their meagre resources in order to create work and wages for themselves and their families. Like the riots of 1826, the story of the co-operative mills of the 1850s has been neglected by historians. Yet both these episodes in the development of the Lancashire cotton industry deserve to be remembered, because each, in its own way, is a tribute to the insistence of the poor but proud men and women who were our ancestors on their right to fight their own battles and solve their own problems. Those of us who, in more comfortable times, enjoy the privilege of writing their history have a duty to ensure that their efforts – even when judged 'misguided' or 'unsuccessful' – are not forgotten. William Turner's definitive account of the 1826 riots is another timely reminder of the irrepressible determination of ordinary people to make their own history, no matter how much inconvenience they might cause to their 'betters' in the process.

CHAPTER ONE

Elephants and Chickens

THE handloom is one of man's most ancient and simple inventions. The rudimentary beginnings of weaving originated seven thousand years ago in what are now India and Iraq. The first loom was made of sticks wedged into the ground to hold threads in tension whilst the weaver interlaced other threads at right angles to form a cloth.

In Asia, Africa and the Americas, wind-breaks, mats and primitive fishing nets were woven on a frame using grasses or reeds. For prehistoric man the loom ranked with the spear and the axe as the means of providing the necessities of life. The basic principle and structure has not altered since those times. Weaving is the most ancient of man's arts.

By the Middle Ages, the weaving of woollen cloth on relatively sophisticated handlooms was, in Britain, second only to agriculture as an occupation. Until the advent of the Industrial Revolution the handloom, particularly in Yorkshire, Lancashire and the West Country, was the mainstay of life for hundreds of thousands of men, women and children. Its importance is seen in the present-day 'heirloom', which originated as the family loom passed from generation to generation. 'Spinster' derives from the custom of an unmarried woman spinning yarn to weave her household linen before marriage. The word 'loom' itself derives from the Old English *geloma* – 'tool'.

From the twelfth century woollen cloth production centred on Flanders and was exported all over the known world. The first cotton cloth made in Flanders was a coarse cloth with a cotton weft and linen warp known as 'fustian' – so named from the Egyptian town of Al-Fustat (now part of modern Cairo). Cotton weaving came to England in the sixteenth century when Dutch and Flemish weavers, refugees from religious persecution, came to East Anglia. They later settled in south and east Lancashire and established, as a domestic or 'cottage' industry, the manufacture of fustian cloth. By the end of the century cotton weaving and spinning began to oust the traditional domestic woollen industry of Lancashire.

During the seventeenth and eighteenth centuries cotton handloom weaving spread to most parts of north west England, Ulster and southern and western Scotland. In north west England most handloom weavers lived south of the River Ribble and in the areas bordering on northern Cheshire and Derbyshire and the West Riding of Yorkshire. Other smaller areas centred on Carlisle and the Borders.

By the middle of the eighteenth century Lancashire began to produce plain white calico (so called from its origins in Calcut, India). Local specialities, however, were cambrics, muslins and ginghams. Blackburn became noted for 'Blackburn Checks'

A Map
of the County Palatine of
LANCASTER
(1826)
LONSDALE
HUNDRED
Ulverston
Dalton
Lancaster
Area of Map
Garstang
AMOUNDERNESS
HUNDRED
Preston
BLACKBURN
HUNDRED
Clitheroe
Colne
Burnley
Accrington
Blackburn
Oswaldtwistle
Haslingden
Rawtenstall
Bacup
LEYLAND
HUNDRED
Over Darwen
Helmshore
Chatterton
Edenfield
Chorley
Summerseat
Rochdale
Bury
Crompton
Shaw
Bolton
Ormskirk
SALFORD
HUNDRED
Oldham
Wigan
WEST DERBY
HUNDRED
River Irwell
Manchester
Liverpool
Warrington
A.Ormerod 1991

(with a linen warp and cotton weft) and 'Blackburn Greys' (plain with a linen warp shot with cotton). Manchester specialised in stripes, Preston in checks. Fustian, the garb of the working man (in contrast to woollen broadcloth, the cloth of the middle classes) came from Bury and Rochdale. Burnley and the Rossendale Valley produced fustian and calico, together with woollens and worsteds.

The rough hilly moorlands of east Lancashire in the area bordered by Blackburn, Burnley, Bury and Rochdale had a relatively sparse population and a thin, inadequate soil. Communications were difficult, the market towns small and separated by barren moorlands. The area, and the Rossendale Valley in particular, in the eighteenth century was, and always had been, poverty stricken. The Commonwealth Church Survey in 1650 recorded the three hundred families in Haslingden and the three hundred in Newchurch in Rossendale (the main centres of population in the valley) as 'lamentably poor – too poor to support a minister'.[1]

A hundred years after the Commonwealth, in the eyes of some, they were not surprisingly, considered 'ignorant and barbarous'. Their dark ways and rough pastimes are indicated by the guidelines of worship of early Baptists in the area. The Lumb Baptists (that is, of Lumb, a small hamlet in the valley) in 1753 condemned the local practice of resorting to 'augurers, witches, wizards and to them that have familiar spirits'. Baptists were warned 'not to drink, nor to attend races, cock-fights, bull-baits, nor play with cards or dice'.[2]

The isolation, poverty and harsh climate produced, in east Lancashire, as in Rossendale, a hardy rough folk who were blunt in manner and speech. They were clannish and suspicious of strangers yet were hard working and subtle of wit. There were, however, those who were self-taught instrumentalists and singers who delighted in the music of Handel, Mozart and Haydn. Others were botanists and horticulturists. There were poets and writers and readers of the classics.

The typical handloom weaver of Lancashire was an independent artisan and most of his working life centred on his farm or cottage. He owned his loom and worked his own hours to supplement farming or other work. (David Whitehead, a Rossendale manufacturer, recalled how, in his youth, he had to milk morning and night and weave fustian the rest of the day.[3]) The preliminary operations of carding and spinning the yarn ready for weaving were performed by the women and children of the household. The discipline of work was relentless. A single loom needed the efforts of five or six people to prepare the yarn. No-one was too young to earn his or her living and all worked long hours to earn the necessities of life. As William Radcliffe, a former handloom weaver, described his early life: 'My mother taught me (while too young to weave) to earn my bread by carding and spinning cotton, winding linen or cotton weft for my father and elder brothers at the loom, until I became of sufficient age and strength for my father to put me to the loom'.[4] (Such training laid the foundation for Radcliffe's own career in the industry as a manufacturer and developer of the powerloom.)

During the latter part of the eighteenth century there was an ever expanding market for cotton goods causing a demand for cotton yarn. A number of Lancashire handloom weavers and spinners began to experiment with improved methods of production. Four inventions in particular revolutionised the life of the handloom weaver.

In 1733 John Kay, a native of Walmersley near Bury, invented the 'flying shuttle', a device which speeded the process of 'plucking' the shuttle, with its weft, backwards and forwards across the warp of the cloth. Weaving could now be done twice as fast. By the 1760s its general use by handloom weavers created an increase in the demand for yarn. About 1769 Kay's son, Robert, invented the 'drop-box', by which the weaver could use several shuttles using different coloured threads without substituting one shuttle for another by hand.

As trade developed the means had to be found to maintain the supply of yarn. The Royal Society offered a prize of fifty pounds for 'the best invention of a machine that would spin six threads of wool, flax, hemp or cotton at one time and require but one person to work and attend to it'.[5] James Hargreaves, a handloom weaver of Stanhill, near Oswaldtwistle, solved the problem. In 1770 Hargreaves himself described in his specification for patent number 962, 'I had brought to perfection a method of making a wheel or engine . . . in order for spinning drawing and twisting of cotton to be managed by one person only . . . [to] spin, draw or twist sixteen threads at one time'.[6] Hargreaves' Spinning Jenny increased enormously the output of yarn, albeit the machine was used within the weaver's home.

Richard Arkwright, a Preston barber, in 1769 patented a device for spinning by rollers, by which a cotton thread strong enough to make a fine warp was produced. Pure cotton goods (linen warps were now no longer necessary to strengthen the cloth) were now possible. Arkwright's Water Frame revolutionised the cotton industry. 'The jenny simply multiplied human hands, whilst the water frame was a substitute for human skill.'[7] The water frame helped begin the factory system. Large buildings, water power and considerable investments were now required.

The next development concerned with spinning was the spinning mule developed by Samuel Crompton of Bolton. His 'mule', so called because it used the best features of the jenny and the water frame, was in use by 1779. It made an even stronger and finer thread. Within ten years automatic mules fitted with several hundred spindles were developed and in use. By 1800 the factory mule had replaced the domestic jenny. In the mid eighteenth century the handloom had outrun the spindle. Arkwright and Crompton reversed this. It was only a matter of time before yarn production increased a thousandfold.

In 1784 the Reverend Edmund Cartwright was on holiday, from his Leicestershire parish, in the cotton spinning valley of the River Derwent in Derbyshire. Cartwright heard from cotton spinners that when Arkwright's patent expired there would be such a glut of cotton yarn that weavers would not be able to keep up. From this Cartwright, himself of an inventive turn of mind, developed the idea of the powerloom.

Introducing the powerloom to the cotton industry was not easy. In 1792, after many experiments and trials, Messrs Grimshaw, cotton manufacturers of Manchester, built a factory at Knott Mill to hold four hundred powerlooms. The mill was promptly burned down by a mob of handloom weavers, and was not rebuilt.

The new powerloom was imperfect, even crude, and efforts to improve it continued for some 25 years, but Cartwright had initiated the inexorable move towards full mechanisation of weaving which led indirectly to the gradual yet painful extinction of the handloom weaver.

Meanwhile, throughout the late eighteenth century and early nineteenth century, the new machinery existed – though perhaps not harmoniously – alongside the handloom. The economic and social way of life of the handloom weaver continued. Even though they used the Kay's flying shuttle and the drop-box there was still an ample supply of yarn – to the extent that a thriving export trade developed.

Trade expanded and the high earnings and the constant demand for labour attracted many to the trade. In remote hamlets and folds, in villages large and small, in isolated farms on the moors, Irish immigrants, farm labourers, the unskilled poor, set up looms. Some yeoman farmers turned to weaving full-time. '. . . every lumber room, even old barns, carthouses and outbuildings of every description were repaired, windows broke through the old blank walls and all fitted up for loom shops.'[8]

The so-called 'golden age' of the handloom weaver began. For some twenty years until the deep trade depression of 1812, the weavers were in a 'state of wealth peace and godliness'. William Thom, a handloom weaver, recalled: 'Four days did the weaver work – for them four days was a week as far as working went – and such a week brought the skilful worker forty shillings. Sunday, Monday and Tuesday were of course Jubilee. Lawn frills gorged freely from under the wrists of his fine blue, gilt-buttoned coats'.[9] After so much poverty the new wealth was well celebrated. 'Their dwellings and small gardens clean and neat – the men each with a watch in his pocket and the women dressed to their own fancy.'[10]

In the Pennine uplands of east Lancashire there worked, generally speaking, three types of handloom weaver. Firstly, the most common, the self-employed, high status artisan who worked by the piece for a choice of masters. Secondly the young journeyman weaver who worked either for a small manufacturer (a weaver/employer) in a handloom factory, or loom shop, with several other weavers, or in his own home for a single master. Thirdly the yeoman farmer, or smallholder, working part-time on his loom.

The three groups were eventually to merge into one – that of an outworker, who worked in his own home on his own loom, or a rented loom, and who wove up yarn to the specification of the larger manufacturer or his middleman. The manufacturer received back the finished length of cloth and paid the weaver a price from which he bought the yarn for the next piece.

This 'putting-out' system, inherited from the days of woollen manufacture, operated throughout east Lancashire. Putters-out were often ex-weavers. William Radcliffe spoke of his 'golden age', about 1785: 'Any man who was industrious and careful might then from his earnings as a weaver lay by sufficient to set himself up as a manufacturer – I was one of the few'.[11] Only a relatively small outlay was required to embark on a new career.

The putter-out could either be a middleman dealing with spinners for yarn and manufacturers for the finished cloth, or be an agent on a commission basis for a Manchester mercantile house. The handloom weaver, particularly in remote and moorland areas, had neither time nor transport to get his own yarn or sell his own cloth direct. The manufacturer therefore controlled the market. Manufacturers could be either a one-man business dealing with a dozen weavers or a corporate business dealing with several thousands. No matter on what scale, a manufacturer's profits were secure. The capital costs of the handloom were borne by the weaver. The burden of 'slack trade' was passed on to him by the manufacturer as he adjusted wages in accordance with price variations.

Henry Sudell, a Blackburn manufacturer with a score of agents, indirectly employed over two thousand weavers. He 'accumulated enough wealth, influence and authority to determine prices throughout east Lancashire'.[12] He was ostentatious in his wealth.

In 1799 Sudell built a country house at Mellor, near Blackburn. He stocked the surrounding park with deer and wildfowl and kept a pack of hounds. 'His entry into Blackburn was almost a state occasion. He was equipped with a magnificent carriage drawn by four carefully matched horses, with postilions in a livery of crimson and gold, and all caps were doffed at his approach.'[13]

The relationship between the independent handloom weaver, 'blunt in manner and speech', and the putter-out or his agent of often the same origin, was not, to put it mildly, always cordial. Putters-out were renowned amongst weavers for their parsimony and unscrupulousness and stories of their dealings passed into folklore.

Thomas Newbigging of Rossendale recalled, in 1891, an old handloom weaver 'Betty', telling him how her father took his finished piece to the putter-out and then asked him for a penny for a muffin to eat on the way home. The putter-out replied, 'Eh mon! If I were to gie thee a penny it would be giving all't profit our maister gets for a cut [piece]! [They were probably making a clear guinea at the time.] They're nearly working at a loss now, by ev'ry cut thar't weyving! Nay, id'dle never do to gie thee pennies in that reckless way, lad!'[14]

Betty herself took her cuts in on a raw cold morning. 'Hello, Betty, here so soon? Wern't you feart [afraid] o'meeting t'deil [devil] as you come oar't moor?' 'I said "Nowt o't soart. I wur noan feart o' meeting deil up on't moor for I knew the hangments weel I'd find deil when I geet here!" '[15]

Even in the so-called golden age of handloom weaving life was hard and poverty never far away. The high wages attracted too many not concerned with skill and pride in their craft, but in the easily learned weaving of comparatively low quality calico and fustian. Formal apprenticeships lapsed and handloom weaving became principally a semi-skilled trade with unrestricted entry. The high status of the independent artisan weaver was degraded. Handloom weaving, as a trade, became fated to suffer a progressive deterioration in status and standards.

Too many weavers and too many manufacturers led to cut-throat competition. Because the small manufacturer had little capital (the principal part was invested in the yarn they put out to weavers), they had no reserves in the periodic 'hard times'. Acting on the theory that low prices encouraged a demand for goods, they reduced prices to dispose of cloth to the warehouses and immediately passed on the reduction to the weaver.

Weavers were defenceless against the more ruthless manufacturer and found themselves under-cutting each other yet working longer hours for less pay – so began a vicious circle which led to distress and consequent unrest and violence. The years 1799, 1807–8, 1811–12 and 1816–21 were particularly severe and weavers protested in vain that their grievances be redressed.

In 1799 an Association of Weavers in Bolton published a manifesto protesting against wage cutting and declared: 'A peaceful demeanour shall always guide our actions, and we trust a candid public . . . will afford us the support we merit'.[16] This, sadly, was too optimistic. In 1807 a 'monster' petition from Lancashire weavers to Parliament protested against wage reductions and asked for a legal minimum wages policy. The request was rejected in May 1808 on the grounds that too many were in the trade, warehouses were overstocked and a minimum wage would only encourage this to continue. There was therefore no case for interfering with the natural cycles of trade.

This rejection was a turning point in the attitude of the handloom weavers towards the government. A strike followed and 10,000 to 15,000 weavers demonstrated on successive days on St. George's Fields, Manchester. The demonstration was dispersed by the military with one man killed and several wounded. The later vindictiveness of the authorities was shown by the imprisonment, 'for uttering malicious and inflammatory words', of a popular manufacturer Joseph Hanson, who supported the minimum wage principle. The effects of this ill-advised prosecution were long and injuriously felt. It introduced that bitter feeling of employed against employer which was later manifested in 1812, 1817, 1819 and 1826.[17]

Periods of prosperity seemed to be ever short-lived. Every time trade declined and wages fell the weavers petitioned the government for justice and relief from their distress. In 1811 yet another monster petition signed by 40,000 weavers was dismissed with yet more compliments on their 'patience under suffering' and the suggestion that 'they should either work at lower prices or . . . employ their labour in some other manner'.[18]

The weavers felt betrayed at the government's inaction. They could not believe how legislative action on their behalf could be thought improper or unnecessary when distress was so great. The less imaginative and more reactionary of the government (the majority in fact) however had always the fear that revolution was imminent. To all such there was a growing need for repression – to show too much sympathy to distress, or even admit fully its existence, was thought to be dangerous to the state.

1812 was marked by large scale disorder throughout Lancashire. Disturbances at Manchester and Middleton (strongly influenced by the 'Luddite' frame-breakers of Nottingham and the wool croppers of Yorkshire) was followed by an arson attack on a Westhoughton factory.[19]

Further repression followed during which eight men were hanged, seventeen transported to New South Wales and six men and one woman imprisoned.

The end of the Napoleonic wars changed nothing. Even though Luddism as a form of protest died out, there was still government insensibility to the sufferings of the weavers. Although petition after petition had failed another attempt was made in 1817.

There were those, however, who took no part in political agitation. Lancashire Baptists were told in a General Circular: 'We believe distress is brought about by the over-riding Providence of God – therefore it is very unbecoming to let passions rage'. Baptists were simply to help each other to bear the burdens of poverty.[20]

This did not stop John Jackson, the Accrington Baptist minister, from saying, on a day of prayer on Sunday 20th November 1816, 'multitudes crowd together with great anxiety to form petitions and offer them to a temporal prince totally destitute of humanity, desirous that their sorrow may be alleviated and they obtain more of that meat which perisheth'.[21]

Four months later, in March 1817, the resulting petition was to be taken to London to the 'temporal prince', the Prince Regent, whom the weavers naively thought was kept unaware of their condition. Shortly after the 1,000 Blanketeers (so called because each had a blanket on which to rest each night) began their march from Ardwick Green, Manchester, it was broken up by the military. The authorities were determined to suppress any form of unrest in whatever form it took.

In spite of the distress few, if any, of the weavers had any revolutionary ideas or sought to overthrow the government. Most simply wanted a freedom from poverty and to live decently by their work.

After 1817 however many weavers – and others – turned to Radicalism and reform of the House of Commons as a means of political action.

On 16th August 1819 a public meeting to consider the best means of reform and the repeal of the Corn Laws was to be held in St. Peter's Field, Manchester. Henry Hunt, the well known Radical and orator, was to address the meeting. An estimated 60,000 men, women and children from all the manufacturing towns of Lancashire attended. (A low estimate – even so it was 6% of all Lancashire's population.)

The County magistrates (amongst them John Silvester of Chorley, see Chapter Seven) were determined to arrest Hunt and disperse the assembly. Under their orders the Manchester and the Cheshire Yeomanry Cavalry swept, with drawn sabres, through the packed field to arrest Hunt and his companions. In the ensuing onslaught and panic eight people were killed and several hundred injured. The tragedy was quickly dubbed, in derision, the Battle of Peterloo. Hunt was eventually sentenced to two years imprisonment for sedition. Peterloo left a legacy of even deeper bitterness throughout Lancashire.[22]

The government was determined to suppress the waves of unrest caused by Peterloo and brought out further repressive laws. The 'Six Acts' of 1819 gave the government exceptional powers to restrict free speech and assembly. Magistrates now had power to summarily convict 'political' offenders and authority to search private houses for arms. They could stop any public meeting of which they disapproved and arrest the speakers. The Radical press, that is those with a contrary view to the government, was all but suppressed by a heavy tax on 'blasphemous and seditious' publications.

To the handloom weaver, political and non-political, it seemed the Englishman's traditional rights were fast disappearing. There was still no solution to (nor any desire by the government to solve) the causes of the distress. By the 1820s a generation of Lancashire men and women – and indeed English men and women – had grown up through the Napoleonic wars and a succession of Prime Ministers from Pitt to Lord Liverpool and known little other than hunger, poverty and government indifference.

The causes of distress were now many and varied. There was 'a web of changes whose strands cross over and over'. In addition to wage reductions, there was an unprecedented growth in population, increasing competition from abroad leading to loss of markets, the post-war slump, the Corn Laws and mounting debts, taxes and poor-rates. Also, for the handloom weaver in particular, the spectre of the powerloom was rising again.

The earlier technical problems which made powerlooms such a poor investment were now largely overcome. As early as 1814 there were purpose built factories again. Hans Casper Escher, a Swiss cotton manufacturer, on a visit to Manchester, noted in his diary for 15th August 1814, 'Today I saw a powerloom weaving factory in the course of construction. More and more factories are being built every day. This one was 130 feet long and 50 feet broad. It has six floors'.[23]

Another foreign visitor, a Prussian civil servant Johann Georg May, was also in Manchester in 1814. May visited Chadwick and Company's, Oxford Road 'weaving establishment'. Here he saw a fourteen horsepower steam engine which drove 240 looms. One weaver operated two looms. 'About half the looms were stopped at any one time. It seems to me they were not very efficient machines, yet the foreman told me the owners were satisfied and had hopes of increasing their efficiency.'[24]

The powerlooms did increase their efficiency and the main source of wealth and income began to move from the cottage/loom shop to the factory. It was at first a slow process. Manufacturers were still doubtful whether the savings in labour and production time outweighed the capital outlay. Between 1813 and 1822 therefore handloom weavers still lived fairly well although their lives were affected by the periodic trade depressions and arbitrary reductions in wages.

The way of life and the culture of the handloom weaver was however inevitably changing. The handloom was, so slowly, giving way to the powerloom. From 1,400 powerlooms in 1813 there were 12,150 in 1820.[25] As the once lucrative putting-out side of manufacture declined and the powerloom became more efficient, the richer putters-out and manufacturers transferred their monies and their energies into the factory system. It was more profitable to bring the weaver to the loom than take the yarn and cloth to and from his cottage.

As the 1820s began, putters-out such as William Turner of Helmshore, Richard Rostron of Dearden Clough, Edenfield, David Whitehead of Rossendale, Jeremiah Horsfall of Low Moor, Clitheroe, and many others, built powerloom factories at least equal in size to that seen by Hans Casper Escher in 1814.

Times were changing. The factory system was consolidating its hold on Lancashire's econony and on the lives of its free artisans. Britain had a government more determined than ever on the doctrine of laissez faire, the general principle of which was the oft-stated view that the legislature ought not to interfere with 'trade' but leave it to find its own level.

Lord Liverpool, himself a faithful disciple, in a debate in the House of Lords, gave his, and the government's, view: 'I am satisfied that government or parliament should never meddle with these affairs at all, but they do harm, more or less . . . On enquiry it would be found that by far the greater miseries of which human nature complained were at all times . . . beyond the control of human legislation'.[26] The government therefore absolved themselves from all responsibility for the distress of the labouring – and the weaving – poor.

The new breed of manufacturer exemplified by Turner, Whitehead and the others, also absolved themselves from all responsibility of the local results of their actions. All lived in a land of their own making in which there was 'plenty of law but a sad lack of justice'. Such men justified to themselves and to God their trampling over the labouring poor as they made their way to riches. In their self-interest and drive for power, they saw men, women and children only as instruments of profit. The spirit of the age was one of a universal individualism. It was a world rapidly learning the philosophy of laissez faire. Henry Scott Holland, a Baptist minister, summed it up with the apocryphal 'Wellerism', 'Every man for himself, and God for all of us, as the elephant said as he danced amongst the chickens'.[27] In the case of the handloom weavers the 'chickens' could not even get out of the way.

The early 1820s was a time of generally improving living standards and the demand for cotton and other manufactured goods continued to grow. Even the handloom weavers shared in the good fortune and regained some of their former markets. Manufacturers and weavers alike however were still in thrall to the vagaries of the trade cycles. Even in the relative boom years of 1822 to 1824 there were manufacturers concerned about the effect of the powerloom on the handloom weavers' – and their own – way of life.

As early as the time of Peterloo, 35 Lancashire calico manufacturers agreed on the principle of a regulatory minimum wage for weavers. One of the manufacturers, James Hutchinson of Elton and Bury, was a recent convert to the idea of government regulation of wages. In a letter to Lord Sidmouth in September 1819, he said, 'I have lately been of the opinion that a minimum of wages was an evil to be avoided, but the low and unequal wages that have been paid for the last three years, added to the extreme and unnecessary oppression to which the weavers have been subject, has affected a change in my sentiments'. The decline in wages he attributed to 'the number of people with little capital and less feeling who obtain credit, embark in business, and undersell their respectable competitors [such as himself] who pay higher wages'.[28] (Hutchinson before very long, along with several of his fellow manufacturers, was to be converted to the idea of his own powerloom factory in Woodhill, Elton.) Hutchinson's letter, and the proposals of his colleagues, were again ignored by the Government. All it could offer was emigration to reduce the number of handloom weavers.

The increase in the number of small manufacturers, and the ease by which they could get credit, plus the increasing numbers of powerlooms also worried the existing small manufacturers. The general feeling was that powerlooms would destroy the ratio of production and demand. They saw their own livelihoods, as well as those of the handloom weavers, at risk.

On 7th November 1822 a group of east Lancashire cotton and woollen manufacturers met at Newchurch in Rossendale and stated that: '. . . the invention of powerlooms for weaving is calculated to transfer manual labour from the cottages of the poor and leave them destitute of employment, by substituting the use of machinery; as unnecessary as it is uncalled for'. The meeting, 'deplored the evil consequences that result if some method be not speedily adopted to restrict the use of such machinery'. Whilst admitting the benefits of the machinery to some degree, they declared: '. . . We cannot contemplate the increase of unnecessary machinery without painful apprehension that it may be multiplied to a most ruinous and mischievous extent'.[29]

To help solve the problem the meeting proposed a tax on the extra profits derived from the powerloom over the handloom. The amount was to be assessed by local parish vestry committees and paid to the poor. So the small manufacturers hoped to stem the tide of the powerloom.

Weavers were also apprehensive. In a letter from the Committee of Manchester Weavers to the Government they stressed the need for '. . . a Committee of Masters, or of Masters and Workmen, chosen by both,' to fix prices periodically. They also asked for a tax on powerlooms. 'In our humble opinion, the evils of multiplying powerlooms, by first ruining half a million who depend on Manual weaving, and especially those unhappy young people they now employ, are such as no human being can think are counterbalanced by any good expected from them.' The Manchester weavers firmly believed the powerloom and the factory system to be the cause of their distress; they ended their plea: 'Sir, you have now read the real causes of the Tumult so often excited in our Districts; but Weavers too often imputed their misery to other causes and manufacturers understood their own interest too well to influence them'.[30]

Small manufacturers and weavers alike however, knew the new world of factory and powerloom had come to stay. A 'general spirit of improvement' was abroad. Powerloom installation continued apace. Factories were rising at an unprecedented rate, their owners and investors obviously having high expectations of profit.

High prosperity, in its selective and relative way, continued for the handloom weaver. There was a run of good harvests. The price of corn fell from a hundred shillings a quarter in 1817 to forty shillings in 1822. Overseas trade boomed as tariffs and excise duties fell. Between 1819 and 1824 exports increased 40%. For the handloom weaver, however, work as he may his earnings steadily went down. From an average £1 18s. 10d. a week for a family of six, including three weavers, in 1818, to £1 1s. 0d. in 1823, and 19s. 1½d. in 1824. Even in the peak boom year of 1825 the same family earned only 19s. 11¼d.[31]

In the same years the average price paid, in the Barrowford and Colne areas, for weaving a piece of calico also fell. In 1818 it was 3s. 7¼d.; 1823 2s. 4d.; 1824 2s. 11¼d. and 1825 2s. 1½d.[32] As the victims of the intense price-cutting of manufacturers competing for foreign markets the handloom weaver lost what little he gained in the price of bread.

The old vicious circle of working longer for less money persisted. William Varley a handloom weaver of Higham, not five miles from Colne, noted in his diary price cuts throughout the 1820s, for example 'November 13th 1821. This day William Hargreaves (a local manufacturer) lowers wages 3d. per cut; April 30th 1822, William Hargreaves lowers wages 3d. per cut; May 3rd 1823, John Moore lowers wages 3d. per cut; August 2nd 1824, Mr Lancaster lowers wages 3d. per cut; 16th July 1825, William Hargreaves advances 3d. per cut, which he inhumanly kept back when other masters had laid on'. Even in Britain's boom year of 1825, Varley noted on July 16th, 'The poor might hope for good days, but, alas, they do not come this year . . .'[33]

Throughout the country, however, continued high expectations of profit led to a speculative boom. At Christmas 1825 the boom burst, almost bringing down the Bank of England. Many local banks, their own paper money not backed up by gold or silver, crashed as manufacturers and tradesmen hurried to cash their banknotes. Bankruptcy followed bankruptcy as finance houses called in their loans. As the handloom weaver William Thom expressed it: 'Banks were falling like meteors but rather oftener, the world seemed hurrying to ruin'.[34]

William Varley, bitter and despairing after years of crushing work and poverty, noted without hope, the very cold, frosty, advent of 1826, 'There are many without work and what is to become of them? . . . If they would beg, I know none that will give anything; and if they would rob or plunder, they have the soldiers at Burnley to give them their last supper'.[35]

In Rossendale some ten miles away another diarist David Whitehead, a manufacturer, echoed similar forbodings for 1826: 'We have a very dark outlook as regards trade. People appear to be much dissatisfied and know not where to lay the blame'.[36] As the owner of 96 powerlooms perhaps Whitehead was a little disingenuous.

For weavers longer hours and lower wages continued into the spring of 1826. Many were in desperate straits. Manufacturers accelerated the process. Under pressure themselves because of reduced profit margins, they passed the pressure onto the weaver. The 'sixpenny down' race (sixpence less paid on each succeeding piece) which began in 1825 continued, worsening the antagonisms between weaver and manufacturer.

A letter to the *Preston Chronicle* on 18th March 1826 described how a woman weaver took in a cotton piece expecting 6s. 6d. The price had already fallen 6d. She was also 'abated' (deducted) 1s. 0d for a single fault in the cloth and 1s. 0d for 'drawing in' (trimming surplus warps from the piece), which left her 4s. 0d to buy the weft for the next piece. The writer asked rhetorically if there was any other remedy than submission in such cases. Little wonder weavers such as Varley branded the 'masters', already noted neither for kindness nor charity, as 'satanical', 'wicked' and 'inhuman'.

Depression and distress was deepening throughout east Lancashire. In Newchurch in Rossendale only twenty of a total of 110 handlooms were in use. A piece or cut of calico, thirty yards long and 64 picks (that is, lengths of weft) to an inch was woven for 1s. 3d. The parish relief for the unemployed varied from ninepence to 1s. 3d per week.[37] (A similar average price of 1s. 3¾d was paid in 1826 in Barrowford and Colne. On this price it was estimated that each member of a family of six would live on 2¼d per day.[38])

In March Blackburn and District Weavers Union Society tried to draw a wider public attention to their distress. After meeting in the Britannia Inn, Oswaldtwistle, they published the unemployment figures for the 10,686 handloom weavers in Blackburn, Rishton, Lower Darwen and part of Oswaldtwistle, an area of 32,000 in population. 2,807 (26%) handloom weavers were employed, 1,427 (14%) were 'half employed', and 6,412 (60%) unemployed. This excluded other trades dependent on weavers, such as shopkeepers.[39]

By now, no matter how hard or long they worked, or not at all, the weavers were starving and in despair. William Thom described an experience common to thousands: 'Imagine a cold spring forenoon. It is eleven o'clock. The four children are still asleep. There is a bed cover hung before the window to keep within as much night as possible: and the mother sits beside the children to lull them back to sleep whenever any shows any inclination to awake – the only food in the house is a handful of oatmeal – our fuel is exhausted. My wife and I were conversing in sunken whispers about making an attempt to cook the oatmeal when the youngest child woke up beyond his mother's powers to hush it again to sleep. He fell a-whimpering and finally broke out in a steady scream, rendering it impossible to keep the rest asleep. Face after face sprang up, each saying 'Mother!' 'Mother!' 'please give us something'. How weak a word is sorrow to apply to feelings of myself and my wife during the rest of that forenoon.'[40] There was, for Thom, no foreseeable end to the suffering. 'I look to nothing but increasing labour and decreasing strength in interminable toil and ultimate starvation – such is the fate of nine tenths of my brethren.'[41]

In late March the Blackburn Weavers Union Society tried yet another petition. The petition was directed to Robert Peel (whose grandfather was born in nearby Oswaldtwistle) as Home Secretary. It described (in the circumstances) in restrained terms, the sufferings of the weavers: '. . . Were the humane man to visit the dwellings . . . of the weavers and see the miserable pittance . . . divided between the wretched parents and their starving little ones, he would sicken at the sight and blush for the patience of humanity.' The petition blamed the Corn Laws (for enhancing the price of provisions) and the powerlooms for the distress. 'But whatever the evils of the Corn Laws, they vanish into nothing when compared with those which followed with the adoption of the powerloom . . . Our wages are 80 to 90% less than they were 20 or 25 years ago.' The weavers reminded the Home Secretary that, 'almost all the Officers of His Majesty's Government have had their salaries advanced . . . upon the plea of an advance in the price of provisions,' whilst weavers had had their wages reduced. They also reminded the Home Secretary, 'as an Englishman', that the weavers were patriots and that they considered themselves as undeserving the name of Englishmen were they to withhold their complaint.[42] (See appendix 5 for full text of petition.)

At this time, in Blackburn, the workhouse was filled beyond capacity with those completely destitute. The very name 'workhouse' carried a stigma of correction and punishment simply for being poor. For a hundred years respectable hard working men and women had had an aversion to the very word. The fear of the workhouse ever haunted those who now sank lower and lower into the wretchedness of poverty. The weak, the elderly, the fatherless, the sick and those who were beyond physical work and outrelief perforce endured confinement in the workhouse. Seventy-six people went into Blackburn workhouse in one week in April, bringing the total 'crammed together' to 678.[43]

Meanwhile several east Lancashire manufacturers again tried to set up a system of a voluntary minimum wage. The principal calico printers of the area met on 18th April in Manchester and 53 'printers and purchasers of calicoes' signed the statement to show their approval. They bound themselves to a fixed set of prices, 'provided the Poor Law authorities would pledge themselves to provide other employment or subsistence for such who are unable to obtain employment at the said list prices'.[44]

A letter to explain the policy was to go to the churchwardens and overseers of the poor in each township in east Lancashire. The manufacturers agreed to meet in Burnley on 28th April to receive the answers. It will never be known whether the 'Poor Law authorities' would have agreed to taking on the costs of paying men who refused to work below the list price. Events overtook everyone.

Those who the *Blackburn Mail* had grandly proclaimed 'had manifested a truly admirable spirit of resignation and patience' had broken.[45] The less sophisticated, less hopeful, less polite of the weavers were beyond watching their little ones starve. They saw not the complexities of trade cycles and government 'let be'; or of minimum wage rates and powerloom taxation, but the powerlooms and those installing them, as the source of their destitution.

They were not criminals or brutish louts but respectable men and women whose sense of natural justice had finally become outraged. They were resentful that their state of poverty was all but disregarded, resentful that no-one was protecting them against the introduction of the powerloom, and further resentful that no-one was protecting them against the new breed of 'master' introducing them.

Their solution was simple – destroy the powerloom. 'Somebody' would listen, and the masters would be forced to return to the 'real' loom – the handloom. Then all would be jubilee again.

On Monday 24th April 1826, the handloom weavers – and others who also starved – took matters into their own hands.

CHAPTER TWO

Monday – The Beginnings

IN 1826 Manchester had a population of over two hundred thousand. It was the second largest city in England. It was however, governed as a parish – much as any village in the country. Its government had come into the hands of the Mosley family of Rolleston Hall, Staffordshire.

The head of the family, as lord of the manor, appointed a steward who in turn appointed a jury, known as the court leet, from the freemen of the town. These in turn appointed a borough reeve and two constables.

The steward's duties were to collect rents for the lord of the manor; the court leet's to make appropriate bye-laws; the borough reeve's to call and preside over public meetings. The constables were to keep order in the town.

In 1826 St. George's Day fell on a Sunday. The Borough Reeve, Mr William Lomas, therefore decided Manchester would celebrate the official birthday of His Gracious Majesty King George the Fourth, on Monday, 24th April. It was to be a celebration in fine style.[1]

At eleven o'clock on Monday morning the civil authorities, magistrates and gentlemen of Manchester, led by the steward of the lord of the manor, assembled in the Exchange Buildings, Exchange Street. At the same time the military garrison of Manchester comprising The 2nd Dragoon Guards (the Queen's Bays), the 60th, Duke of York's Own, Rifle Corps, a detachment of the Royal Horse Artillery with two guns, and the Royal Horse Artillery Rocket Troop, formed up in St. Ann's Square. Colonel James Kearney of the Queen's Bays was in command.

Shortly before eleven-thirty the civil authorities joined the military in St. Ann's Square. At eleven-thirty precisely the whole moved off in grand procession for Ardwick Green.

At Ardwick Green over thirty thousand watched as the troops, led by an advance party of Queen's Bays mounted on magnificent bay horses, formed a hollow square.[2] The civil authorities solemnly walked to the centre, the troops saluting as they approached.

After a pause – a sharp command. The troops fired the royal salute, then the *feu de joie*. The whole party ended the tribute to His Majesty with three hearty cheers. The troops subsequently marched past the civil authorities in column and the whole procession returned via Mosley Street and King Street to St. Ann's Square where they separated.

For much of the route, and particularly in St. Ann's Square, the procession had great difficulty in passing through the huge crowds. As Major Nathaniel Eckersley of the 60th Regiment, acting as the Army's Northern District representative in Manchester, was later to assure Henry Hobhouse 'the crowd all appeared in good humour and conducted themselves in orderly fashion'.[3] (Major Eckersley clearly observed the crowd behaviour with the unrest of recent months in mind. At least today there was no disloyalty to the throne).

At six o'clock one hundred and sixty persons, including all the senior officers of the military garrison, sat down in the Large Room in the Exchange Building to a dinner in honour of His Majesty. The borough reeve presided. As the meal progressed the Regimental Band of the Queen's Bays played a 'variety of national and other airs in a superior style'.[4] Patriotic and popular songs were sung by members of the nearby Theatre Royal.

After the empty dishes and plates were removed from the tables, glasses were refilled for the Loyal Toast. This was drunk 'four times four' with great enthusiasm and prolonged applause . . . and the band played 'God Save the King'. An orgy of patriotic and self-congratulatory toasts and counter-toasts followed: 'The Duke of York and the Army'; 'The Illustrious House of Brunswick'; 'His Majesty's Ministers'; 'The British Standard', and so on. Major Eckersley, in his reply to the toast, 'Major General Harris and the Staff of the Northern District', himself proposed, 'Prosperity to the towns and trade of Manchester and Salford'.[5]

The Chairman next proposed the health of Major General Loftus and the Queen's Bays, '. . . a corps', he added, 'as distinguished for their bravery in the field as for their uniformly good conduct'. Colonel Kearney returned the thanks of the Major General and the Queen's Bays.

The Chairman again proposed a toast: 'To Lieutenant-Colonel Bunbury and the Duke of York's Own Rifle Corps. This gallant regiment,' he observed, 'was a favourite of the lamented General Wolfe at the siege of Quebec and since it has pursued for itself imperishable honours'. The toast was drunk with thunderous applause. In his reply Lieutenant-Colonel Bunbury assured the assembly 'The Corps which I have the honour to command is more than anxious to maintain its character and to acquire the esteem of its countrymen'.[6]

Captain Hardy of the Royal Horse Artillery next proposed the health of the Senior Constable. He, in his turn, ended his acknowledgement, 'May the present tranquillity prove as lasting as the veneration for the principles which have produced it'.

The Chairman next proposed a toast to Major Eckersley. Major Eckersley ended his reply in a somewhat serious vein. He told the party, 'Whatever assistance I can give the town, I will feel most proud in giving, but I trust the times will not be such as to demand my interference and that long before this time twelve months hence, trade and commerce will have resumed their wonted activity'. His toast, 'Better times and soon' was drunk 'with great cordiality'.

After many more toasts and speeches, 'Auld Lang Syne' and 'May we ne'er want a friend nor a bottle to give him', were cheerily sung by all. The Chairman formally ended the proceedings and he and his company left for home and billet, replete and pleasantly aglow. All were satisfied the King's birthday had been truly celebrated.

Only Major Eckersley had hinted anything was amiss in the harsh, real world outside the Large Room of the Exchange Building. His was the only realistic note in an orgy of complacency and self-delusion. His 'interference' was to be demanded sooner than he dreamed.

Shadsworth Hall, Blackburn, the home of William Carr, Clerk to the Blackburn County Justices. On the evening of 24 March 1826 a mob from Blackburn broke all the windows and destroyed the gardens. This was the first act of violence preceeding the riots in April. This photograph was taken in 1928.

Blackburn Library Local Studies Collection. No. 5786

There had been 'incidents' already, enough to warn anyone the present tranquillity could not last. At Shadsworth, near Blackburn, on the night of 24th March, the home of William Carr, the Clerk to the County Justices, was attacked by a mob. After breaking all his windows and destroying his garden shrubs and plants, the ring-leaders demanded fifty pounds. Someone in the house fired a gun, which however, 'flashed in the pan' (that is, the small amount of gunpowder in the firing pan 'flashed' but did not ignite the larger quantity in the barrel). Only then did the crowd disperse, pausing long enough to do more damage to the grounds.

Four days later, in Blackburn, an angry crowd awaited the Tuesday 'Market' stagecoach from Manchester. The daily service carried manufacturers to and from the Manchester Exchange. As the coach stopped outside the Old Bull Inn, in Church Street, the passengers, only four of whom were inside, with seven on the outside, were pelted with stones. Troops were needed to clear the crowd from the area.[7] In Accrington, at about seven-thirty in the evening of Tuesday 18th April, a large crowd broke the windows of Robert and Thomas Sykes' Higher Grange Lane factory.

The arrival of a troop of 1st King's Dragoon Guards from Blackburn helped disperse the mob and prevented any further damage. Hundreds of excited people

Higher Grange Lane Factory, Accrington. This was the first factory attacked on the first day of the riots, 24 April 1826. The factory was demolished in the early 20th century and Accrington Police Station, Magistrates Court and Fire Station were later built on the site.

Accrington Library Local Studies Collection.

crowded the streets but there were no further disturbances. After the cavalry had left for Blackburn, however, the mob went to the home of Christopher Lancaster, a cotton spinner and manufacturer, at Pleck House, and smashed his windows. The windows of Mr Haworth, the overseer at Edmund and Robert Peel's Church Bank calico printing works, suffered the same fate.

The following Saturday evening the Manchester coach was again met by a large crowd as it arrived at the Old Bull Inn. This time the coach was badly damaged and several manufacturers badly hurt by stones. The crowd, in a taste of things to come, showed they were not to be intimidated by military or civil authority. Thomas Bury, one of the stone throwers, was arrested by John Kay, the constable of Blackburn, and confined in a temporary 'lock-up' in the cellar of the nearby Duke of York Inn. Bury's confederates waited until the military moved on, then battered the door down and released him. In the early hours of the next morning, however, John Kay forced his way into Bury's house and rearrested him.

Over the weekend rumour abounded. There was talk of preparations for a general attack on the powerloom factories. People in the moorland villages were held to be busy making pikes and cudgels. Tales were told of hordes of strangers tramping over the moors converging on secret meeting places in remote places. Fear was in the air.

On Monday morning, 24th April, at about the same time as the steward of the Lord of the Manor of Manchester and his party assembled in Exchange Street, a mass meeting of over a thousand men and women assembled at Whinney Hill, Enfield, near Accrington.[8] Many of the men had crude pikes or sledgehammers, a few with guns or pistols. No ringleaders at this meeting were ever identified. It is highly probably there were those who knew where powerlooms were installed and told the crowd from the platform. It is also highly probable small groups of 'captains' decided a policy – 'destroy power looms only; touch no other property or machinery, no violence to persons'.[9]

The first objective was easy to decide. Two miles away stood Messrs Sykes' Higher Grange Lane Factory, its windows broken less than a week before. As the meeting ended with three hearty cheers from the crowd, a large section went directly to finish off the work previously started. Another group decided to go to Messrs Garnett and Horsfall's factory at Low Moor, Clitheroe, a market town seven miles to the north.

Somewhere in the crowd four men, George Walmsley, Robert Aspden, Lawrence Baron and Thomas Marsden, all from Blackburn, listened closely as the captains addressed the crowd. They were there as spies for the High Constable of Blackburn Hundred, Mr Christopher Hindle. Hindle, when it became obvious a week previously that tension was building up in the area, appointed at least ten special constables to act as scouts and spies. One or two were to be present at every meeting and factory and were Hindle's eyes and ears for the whole week of the riots. When the crowd split, Marsden went with them to Accrington and Walmsley to Low Moor. Aspden and Baron returned quickly to Blackburn to report to Hindle.

In Accrington meanwhile, Robert Hargreaves, of the Hargreaves family of Broad Oak, calico printers, heard that the mob, armed with pikes, cudgels and sledgehammers, was on its way. He hurried to Grange Lane Factory, a gaunt block of three storeys, its rows of ten windows unrepaired, and hid himself behind the chimney of a nearby house to watch all that passed. 'The first thing was a woman smashing a clock hanging in the passage [probably a 'clocking-in' clock for use by the employees]. The next was an onslaught on the looms with sledgehammers and crowbars. These disappeared like potterware until all was finished in the way of destruction.'[10] Sixty powerlooms were destroyed before the rioters were satisfied.

The group then on its way to Low Moor included Thomas Duckworth, a fifteen year old Haslingden handloom weaver. He had risen at dawn to help turn the grindstone on which the rioters' pikes were sharpened. With the rest he then walked six miles to Whinney Hill. 'They came to a conclusion they must break the looms at Low Moor. When we got on the road we saw the horse-soldiers coming towards us. There was a stop then. The soldiers came forward with their drawn swords glittering in the air. The people opened out to let them get through. Some threw their pikes over the dyke. Others didn't. When the soldiers got into the midst of us the officer called out 'Halt!' All expected the soldiers to then charge. The officer, however, told us what the consequences would be if we persisted in what we were doing. He said 'You will be shot down, whereas if you go home and be quiet you will see times would be better than you've ever known'.[11]

The cavalry (a troop of 1st Kings Dragoon Guards) were clearly sympathetic.

'When the officer moved on to repeat his advice to the rest of the crowd, some of the old fellows spoke to the troopers', "What are we to do, we're starving. Are we to starve to death?" The soldiers were equipped with haversacks and they all gave their sandwiches to the crowd. When the soldiers left we held a meeting and, in spite of the officer's advice we decided the looms must be broken at all costs.'[12]

The cotton factory at Low Moor was Clitheroe's oldest. The first building on the site was built in 1782. This was replaced in 1791 by a five storey spinning mill equipped with a twenty-one foot water-wheel. Garnett and Horsfall also operated as putters-out to the area's handloom weavers. In recent years they had expanded into powerloom weaving with the installation of over a hundred powerlooms.

Whilst waiting for the rioters Jeremiah Garnett took no chances. He barricaded the factory gates and ordered the removal from around the area of all stones and loose objects. Anything, in fact, which could be used as missiles. These were brought inside the factory. When Thomas Duckworth and the mob arrived at the mill: 'We saw a cannon in the middle of the road and the Yeomanry Cavalry [The Craven Legion] with drawn swords. They had taken the place of the soldiers we had seen. We turned back when we saw the cannon.'

The cannon was too much. The sight of the hated Yeomanry also very probably brought back, for the 'old fellows' at least, bitter memories of Peterloo seven years before.[13] The mob, on the road since dawn, at least fifteen miles from home, starving and ill-shod, had no heart to face cannon and drawn swords. Behind those was the determined Jeremiah Garnett. They slowly returned to Haslingden and home. As they walked, many called at farmhouses where sympathetic wives gave oat-cake and milk. 'When we got home, I don't think there was a bit of oat-cake to be got from Clitheroe to Haslingden.'[14]

In Accrington meanwhile, the mob was in a more determined mood. Leaving Grange Lane Factory a shambles they quickly moved on half a mile to a small factory on the banks of Woodnook Water. Woodnook factory was owned by the Hargreaves family. In contrast to the comparatively new Grange Lane Factory (built 1821), Woodnook factory was an old established industrial building. At least forty-five years before it was a carding and jenny mill. It had seen spinning and calico-printing in its day. Now John Marquis had leased the building from the Hargreaves' to install powerlooms. Four only were installed so the mob had no trouble destroying them.

On next for two miles across open country to the Walmsley brothers' tiny factory at Fern Gore, on the boundary of Accrington and Oswaldtwistle. The twenty-five year old, two storey, water powered factory, (known as Rough Hey from Walmsleys' farmhouse home nearby) stood on the bank of Antley Syke, a small moorland stream. In 1824 the Rough Hey site proved too small for expansion so the Walmsleys started to build the larger Moscow Mill in Oswaldtwistle. In the meantime, they used Rough Hey to experiment with powerlooms. They were unfortunate. The mob destroyed all twenty of their experimental looms.

The next obvious target was James Bury's much larger (established around 1816) three storied factory at White Ash, just over a mile away down the hill in Oswaldtwistle. As the mob advanced towards White Ash, they gathered more excited sympathizers and onlookers. James Bury watched the mob arrive. His employees advised him his life could be in danger so he hastily crossed an adjacent field to his home to await events. He did not stop to see the mob enter the factory yard.

The loom-breakers at work. The men speedily break up the cast-iron frames and gear wheels and cut the leather driving belts whilst the women slash warps and woven cloth. This was repeated in every factory.

The mob found the factory door locked and barred. Repeated blows from sledge-hammers and a large piece of flagstone eventually forced it open. Immediately the mob, men and women all, surged in, leaving men with pikes on guard outside in the yard. James Clough, a book-keeper at W. Simpson's calico print works at nearby Foxhill Bank, watched the events. It was easy for Clough, in the excitement, to follow the mob into the factory. 'A party went down the middle of the factory and broke all the spur wheels with hammers. When a few of the looms were broken others in the mob took up pieces of cast iron, wood and loom weights and helped break the remainder. Men used anything they could lay their hands on. Several of the mob broke up beams, which were in the looms, with their clogs.'

Clough watched Michael Tomlinson, an Oswaldtwistle labourer, using a heavy iron bar to break the looms. 'He stayed inside until all were destroyed. When Tomlinson came out he spoke to several of the pikemen and then went away with the mob.'[15] Ann Lonsdale, a weaver at the factory, stood with Clough. She saw from only three yards away, Tomlinson's sister Phoebe, with two younger girls, Alice Grimshaw and Johanna Oldham, tearing yarn off the beams and putting twist through the open window and into the river below.[16] The women also brought warps out of the factory and the pikemen hoisted them on their pikes in triumph. They carried the warps to a field where there was a huge crowd of onlookers. They displayed the warps to the cheering crowd. Thrilled with their success, which took just over an hour, the crowd turned and made for Blackburn four miles away.

James Bury returned to his factory. All was desolation. Ninety-four powerlooms, with their driving gear, were wrecked. Five dressing machines, one warping machine, one winding machine and one lathe were broken. A large quantity of twist, dressed and undressed, and woven cloth had suffered; in John Bury's estimation not much short of £3,000-worth.[17] Amongst the wreckage lay a severed human finger which was preserved as a grim souvenir.

The situation was already out of control. The military could not cope. As soon as Aspden and Baron brought news to Blackburn of the attack on Grange factory a troop of 1st Kings Dragoon Guards left for Oswaldtwistle and Accrington. The rioters were then on their way from White Ash to Blackburn. The cavalry met the crowd at Furthergate on the town's outskirts. The officer in command, Captain George Bray, assumed the crowd was a split-off from the main group and passed them by. (Perhaps rumour had so inflated the numbers he expected a much larger crowd). He continued to White Ash and Rough Hey. Here all was quiet, the looms wrecked; the mob gone. It was clearly useless to go on to Accrington so he turned his troop back to Blackburn. By then the mob was in Blackburn. It was three o'clock in the afternoon.

Blackburn streets and the adjacent fields filled with a noisy and belligerent crowd. A mob, now some two thousand strong, marched from the Market Place along Darwen Street. Shopkeepers hurriedly put up their shutters. Oblivious to anything but the powerlooms many told the shopkeepers, 'Ne'er mind yer shops, we shall'na meddle wi'yo'.[18] The mob went directly into Jubilee Street to Bannister Eccles' Jubilee Factory (known locally as the 'Dandy Shop', after an improved model of handloom formerly installed). Built in 1822 the four storey factory now had over two hundred powerlooms installed, the first in 1825.

Bannister Eccles, John Kay, his deputy John Morten, the Reverend Richard Noble a magistrate, and his clerk Dixon Robinson awaited the mob at the factory gates. They watched as sixty pikemen (those at White Ash) each with a pike 15"–18" long attached to a six foot pole, headed the mob to the gates. Led by an Oswaldtwistle farmer, James Chambers, the mob broke open the gates and flooded into the yard. With Chambers was Thomas Dickenson who shouted to the crowd 'Stand back! Let's come!' as they made their way into the factory. The work was becoming more organised. As the mob entered the building, half of the pikemen filed off to the right, the others to the left, either side of the door leaving a space for the crowd between them. As Bannister Eccles and his party watched helplessly, still waiting for the cavalry, several hundred men and women rampaged through the four floors of the factory as the pikemen stood guard. Inside, all the locked doors were smashed open and two hundred and twelve powerlooms destroyed. The cast iron wheels and drums of the steam engine were broken. The driving shafts of wrought iron, could not be broken so were pulled from their supports. The mob brought out into the yard several twist beams and pieces of woven cloth from the looms. The cloth was thrown about and torn up by the waiting crowd. The whole took just thirty-five minutes.

At this point (at three-thirty in the afternoon) the troop of 1st Kings Dragoon Guards arrived and the Reverend Noble as magistrate went with them, and a party of the 60th Rifles, into the factory yard to read the Riot Act. This was a formal declaration that unlawful actions or conduct must cease. If the mob did not disperse after the reading they were adjudged felons without benefit of clergy. Reading the Act also indemnified any person, authorised by the magistrate, who injured or killed any rioter who resisted arrest.[19] Mr Robinson handed the Reverend Noble the card on which the Riot Act extract was printed. Going amongst the rioters, or as directed by the Act – 'as near to them as he can safely come', the Reverend Noble, with a loud voice commanded, 'Silence!' and proclaimed: 'Our Sovereign Lord the King chargeth and commandeth all persons being assembled immediately to disperse themselves and peaceably depart to their habitations, or to their lawful business, upon the pains contained in the Act, made in the first Year of King George, for preventing Tumults and Riotous Assemblies. God Save the King!' No one took the slightest notice of the Reverend Noble. It is doubtful if he was even heard.

The cavalry immediately charged into the mob and took three pikemen prisoners. They were hustled away by riflemen. The mob, now the powerlooms were destroyed, rushed out of the factory. John Kay and John Morten courageously went inside and took hammers and clubs from men and women as they sped out. There were too many to even try to arrest. At the rear of the factory, windows were smashed as rioters escaped. John Kay, further inside, grabbed William Sutcliffe. He knew him. 'What are you doing here?' Sutcliffe made no reply and dashed outside. As the Reverend Noble stood in the yard men and women rushed past him. Simeon Wright ran up against him and hit him on the head and shoulder with a stick. Dixon Robinson immediately grabbed Wright and wrenched the stick (later described as a knobstick, a type of shillelagh) from his grasp. Wright ran off.[20]

John Kay saw Chambers again. 'How could you for shame be here? I got work for you in a warehouse in Blackburn only weeks ago.' Chambers replied 'Are we all to be clammed to dee'ath?' At this point Dixon Robinson came up and took Chambers' hammer and gave it to Kay. Chambers immediately fled the scene. Thomas Cain, an employee of Bannister Eccles, took advantage of the confusion and entered the factory with the mob. He watched Richard Entwistle break up the powerlooms. Cain, who knew Entwistle, went up to him and said 'This is queer work'. Entwistle, engrossed in his efforts, ignored him. By then however, most of the looms were destroyed and as Entwistle left, Cain pointed him out to John Morten who arrested him. (As Entwistle later committed offences at Houghton's Park Place Factory he must have somehow escaped).[21]

William Charnley, Betty Howorth, William Winder and John Howarth were up on the fourth floor when the cavalry charged. They ran down and out of the rear of the factory and waded across the River Blakewater which was shallow at this point. Shots were fired by the riflemen and John Howarth was seriously wounded by a musket ball as he climbed over a wall. (Three days later, whilst confined to his bed, Howarth sent for George Grimshaw, Bannister Eccles' foreman, and confessed his part in the riot). As the mob left the factory others pelted the soldiers with stones. The Reverend Noble was hit and after a Dragoon was seriously hurt the cavalry fired their carbines in the air. This, plus the movement of the rioters to Park Place, caused the crowd to disperse. Thirty-six pikes were later picked up in the factory yard.[22]

In the turmoil the cavalry had difficulties undreamed of in war. As they pressed their way through the milling crowds they backed their horses into a courtyard in Church Street to reform their ranks. It happened to be the home of Samuel Slater, a well known Radical in the town. Slater's wife put the whole troop 'to ignominious flight with a few well-directed blows of her broom'.[23]

Park Place factory lay four hundred yards up the hill from Jubilee Street. John Houghton and Son's factory was small in comparison. Like Bannister Eccles he had installed his powerlooms in 1825 but just twenty-five in number. When Houghton heard the rioters were at Jubilee Street he closed the factory and, leaving his son inside on watch, went to the scene. When the rioters came up the hill to his factory he could only follow. At first the mob gathered round the factory gates, its size increasing the while with onlookers. Once again the pikemen (now fewer in number) placed themselves on guard outside. When the cavalry and riflemen arrived the mob pelted them with a furious shower of stones whilst a group of men broke open the factory door.

The factory stood almost on the banks of the Leeds and Liverpool Canal with just a narrow area between factory and canal. This became so crowded neither cavalry nor riflemen could reach the factory entrance. There was room only for six or eight cavalrymen at the most. Three times the cavalry tried to disperse the mob. Three times a group of pikemen charged them. The cavalry, unable to manoeuvre in the confined space, were forced back, one trooper and his horse going into the canal. Several shots were fired, whether by riflemen or cavalrymen is unknown, but at least two in the crowd were wounded. A rioter, Edward Houghton, was seriously wounded and carried away by the crowd.[24] In the utter confusion it was impossible to distinguish between loom-breakers and on-lookers.

The crowd became angrier when rumour spread that Houghton's son was firing into the crowd from inside the mill (this was later vigorously denied). Meanwhile those of the mob inside the mill, including James Chambers, Simeon Wright, Thomas Dickenson, Isaac Hindle and Thomas Leaver, were busily destroying the twenty-five powerlooms.

As at Jubilee Street the warps and twists, with their reeds and healds, ('yelds' in dialect) were cut from the looms and thrown outside. This, and woven cloth, was thrown into the canal, to the cheers of the crowd. Leaver, in some exasperation, roared to the crowd, 'What are you standing there for? You should come in and work like us!'

One of the crowd however, had eyes only for Isaac Hindle. Thomas Breckell was the carding master at White Ash. He had seen Hindle, an Oswaldtwistle man, there with the mob. Only a week or two before they had supped ale together at the Tinker and Budget public house in Oswaldtwistle. No doubt incensed by Hindle's perfidy in breaking his master's looms, Breckell followed him to Blackburn. He watched Hindle break the powerlooms with a piece of wood. When this broke he saw him use a length of cast iron from a loom. A soon as he could Breckell pointed Hindle out to John Houghton.

The situation was still out of control, with constables and military powerless to intervene. The mob, satisfied there was nothing more at Park Place, moved on to King Street half a mile away. Rumour had spread that William Throp's factory had power-looms inside awaiting installation. As the crowd gathered outside, a group of men, armed with hammers and pikes, searched the factory. They found only spinning frames. None was touched, neither were windows broken. The crowd began to drift away.

By now it was about six o'clock (in Manchester Major Eckersley and his companions were about to dine). The exhilaration of riot and destruction had faded. The crowds started to clear and Blackburn's narrow streets quietened. The military resumed a semblance of control and patrols urged those few reluctant to go home. Six of those arrested in the afternoon were examined by magistrates at the Sessions House. The magistrates, bearing in mind the rescue of Thomas Bury, immediately sent the six, escorted by cavalry, to Lancaster Castle.

The coach from Manchester arrived, a little earlier than usual, at eight o'clock. A crowd assembled at the Old Bull Inn. As the passengers proposed to alight, a magistrate, taking no chances, prudently read the Riot Act. The crowd dispersed, leaving the passengers unmolested. At nine o'clock a troop of 1st Dragoon Guards arrived from Burnley. The streets were quiet. Rain began to fall.

There was, however, work for the new arrivals. They escorted the town's special constables – including those employed as scouts and spies – as they arrested those rioters who lived in the town. Dozens, men and women all, were taken to the Sessions House to be examined by magistrates. Soon the town dungeon, next to the Sessions House was full. An overflow of prisoners awaiting examination was placed in a room at the Old Bull Inn. The examinations took all night. It was breaking dawn before the prisoners, escorted by cavalrymen, left by chaise for Lancaster.

At about the time the coach arrived in Blackburn, Rossendale and Burnley magistrates and manufacturers held a meeting in Burnley. Alarmed by the news from Accrington and Blackburn, Burnley magistrates had already requested the military authorities in Halifax for troops, but they were not due to arrive until Tuesday evening. As all feared what the next morning may bring, it was agreed at the meeting not to wait. Two manufacturers, William Turner of Helmshore and David Whitehead of Lower Booth, Rawtenstall, were asked to go forthwith, by post-chaise, to Manchester to get a troop of cavalry for Rossendale. The two men arrived probably just as Colonel Kearney and Major Eckersley ended their meal at the Exchange Buildings.

Whilst dining at the Exchange Buildings Major Eckersley gave no hint of knowing of the riots. This is strange. A fast horse could reach Manchester from Blackburn in less than two hours. The meeting at Whinney Hill had Christopher Hindle's spies in the crowd so news could have reached Manchester by no later than two o'clock.

If Thomas Duckworth, a fifteen year old, and certainly not privy to the secrets of the captains (as the mob leaders were known), knew at dawn pikes would be in use that day, it is remarkable Colonel Kearney and Major Eckersley did not know. Even more remarkable if they knew and did nothing. Perhaps their loyalty to the Crown, and their obligations to the civil authorities of Manchester, for their troops, and themselves, to be present at the King's birthday celebrations overrode their other military duties. Whatever the reason, and whenever the news reached Manchester, it was Tuesday morning before troop reinforcements reached Blackburn and Rossendale.

CHAPTER THREE

Tuesday – 'A Disposition to Riot'

AT eight o'clock on Tuesday morning 25th April a troop of Queen's Bays arrived in Blackburn from their barracks in Hulme, Manchester. At about the same time a second troop – those requested by William Turner and David Whitehead – arrived in Haslingden. Although there was already 'a considerable ferment' in Haslingden, these troops were ordered to their quarters.[1]

They remained there until two o'clock.

Lieutenant Colonel James Kearney sent a third troop to Bury 'Where the High Constable for Bury and Bolton [Mr James Hutchinson, a local manufacturer] and a number of other manufacturers were also very anxious'.[2] This left but two troops in reserve in Manchester. Requests from manufacturers in Clitheroe (probably Messrs Garnett and Horsfall) and Heywood for troops were turned down as no more could be spared.

In Blackburn the earliness of the hour did not prevent a noisy crowd gathering to watch the Bays canter along the narrow streets. Fortunately for the troops the rain had abated. The day promised to be clear, cold and sunny. No sooner had the Bays arrived when a messenger brought news of a large crowd again assembling outside Garnett and Horsfall's factory at Low Moor, Clitheroe, six miles away. With no time either to rest their horses or have breakfast the Bays left for Low Moor.

At about the same time as the Bays arrived in Blackburn, Thomas Bolton, a handloom weaver of Ribchester, called at a cottage near Hurst Green to beg for food. He was with four others. The housewife, Ann Seed, gave the men bread and cheese. As he ate, Bolton boasted (which he must have regretted because he was later arrested as a result), 'We are going to Low Moor. We are "mischiefs" and we broke the powerlooms at Blackburn as small as the paving stones under our feet. I was at Eccles' and escaped. We'll break the powerlooms at Low Moor too before we sleep.'[3]

By the time Thomas Bolton and his men – and the Bays – arrived at Low Moor a large crowd had already gathered at the factory gates and on some open land next to the rows of cottages which comprised the village. A troop of Yeomanry Cavalry, Lord Ribblesdale's Craven Legion, backed by Garnett's cannon and armed employees, were in the factory yard. Also present, at the corner of the road near St. Paul's Church, was a troop of the 1st King's Dragoon Guards.

As on the previous day, the crowd showed no inclination to attack, only to shout insults and threats. A few stones were thrown, a few windows broken. The crowd, Thomas Bolton, and the others, knew however, that the odds were completely against them. As it was clear there was no immediate danger the Bays relieved the King's to

Top Factory Yard, Bowling Green Mill, Bolton Road, Darwen. Formerly a 'putting-out' shop, this was one of the original buildings of a later developed, much larger complex.
Darwen Library Local Studies Collection

allow them to go to Blackburn. The Bays remained, silently watching, until the crowd drifted away of its own accord and all again was quiet. So ended the second, and last, 'seige' of Low Moor.

In Blackburn, meanwhile, news of the absence of the cavalry quickly spread. By ten o'clock a crowd of some two thousand men and women had assembled at Earcroft, midway between Blackburn and the town of Over Darwen four miles to the south. The crowd, enhanced by eighty or so men and women from the hamlets of Tockholes and Lower Darwen, marched to the five storey Bowling Green factory half a mile beyond Over Darwen on the Bolton Road.[4]

Bowling Green factory was erected by William Eccles, son of Thomas Eccles of Princes, near Darwen. The Eccles family had formerly used the building as a 'putting out' shop to Darwen handloom weavers. Part of it was now leased to William Hatton Carr and his brother George as a powerloom factory. Completely unopposed by constables or military, and before a gathering crowd of onlookers, the mob quickly surrounded the building.

William Hatton Carr stood ready, with his brother, at the factory gates. Those at the front of the mob shouted at the brothers to open the gates. Although most were strangers to him William recognised three – George Haydock the son of a respected Darwen shopkeeper, John Entwistle, known as Jack O'Nancy's, a handloom weaver from Harwood Fold and Joseph Brindle a handloom weaver from Tockholes. Carr tried to reason with them at first, this failing, he then protested very strongly. None were in any mood to listen to reason or anger and the mob impatiently surged past the brothers and entered the factory.[5]

Within fifteen minutes the Carr brothers' newly installed sixteen powerlooms on the ground floor were smashed into fragments. In another part of the building were six powerlooms owned by James Garsden of Hoddlesden. These were in storage at Bowling Green whilst Garsden had premises built in nearby Astley Street. These too were destroyed. Close to Bowling Green lay Bobbin Hall, home and workshop of James Grime, a joiner and bobbin-maker. Here sixteen powerlooms, belonging to James Garsden stored in Grime's workshop, were put to the hammer in a matter of moments.

Many of the mob, satisfied all the powerlooms in Over Darwen were destroyed, quickly went home.[6] The rest, perhaps three hundred or so, exhilarated by their easy success, decided to visit James Garsden at his home in the tiny moorland village of Hoddlesden two miles away. In his deposition to the magistrates Garsden later described how three hundred men and women came to his home. 'About twenty came into my house and asked for bread. Some had sticks in their hands. I refused them bread, but they began to take it from the bread flake [a kind of wickerwork basket]. Whilst they were eating the bread my daughter Alice, aged eleven, came into the house and told me other men were in my barn breaking looms. I had fourteen powerlooms broken, seven of which were in the barn and seven in the house. None of them were fixed up because I was about to put them in a new building in Astley Street near the Bowling Green.' To his great surprise Garsden saw that one of those breaking looms was James Shorrock from nearby Pickup Bank – and a relative by marriage.[7]

The mob leaders (amongst them James Shorrock perhaps) were on the crest of a wave. Four completely unopposed, completely successful, attacks and fifty-two powerlooms destroyed. Their eyes now lay on the much larger target of Messrs William and Ralph Turner's Middle Mill in Helmshore, four miles as the crow flies, over the high moors. There was an easier way through the hamlet of Belthorn and onto the turnpike from Blackburn to Haslingden, but this was almost eight miles and the route lay dangerously near Blackburn. In their eagerness to 'finish the job' the mob decided on the most direct route – over the 'tops'. With cheers and shouts they marched out of Hoddlesden and climbed the rough moorland, passing by the isolated farms and cottages of Pickup Bank, crossed the Edgworth road and climbed the rough tracks and bridle-paths up to the flat peaty expanse of Causeway Heights. The tracks went over some of the steepest and wildest moorland in Lancashire.

The mob steadily added to its numbers as other disaffected men and women from Pickup Bank, Belthorn and Grane joined them. On the open moor the mob spread out, gathering courage from each others' shouts as they tramped towards Helmshore. The last two miles or so from the 1,200 feet high point of Causeway Heights were, although rough walking, mercifully downhill. No one knows how many, weak from starvation, fell out and rested, then returned slowly home, broken by the terrain.

As the mob quickened its pace down into Musbury Valley and past the farms of Hollin Bank to Middle Mill, other men and women from Haslingden and Helmshore joined them. Their numbers swelled the crowd to over four hundred. Witnesses later spoke of the crowd filling the width of the road for a length of two hundred yards as they marched towards Middle Mill.[8]

William Turner Clegg, William Turner's bookkeeper and cashier, saw the mob approach the mill.[9] He immediately sent Timothy Jones, William Turner's gardener, post-haste to Haslingden two miles away to warn the military. Most in Haslingden already knew. A large crowd, already excited by news of the previous day's events and added to by rumour, stood in St. James's churchyard and watched the mob as they ran over the fields towards the mill.[10] Some of the crowd, pausing only to collect staves and iron bars, ran from the town to join them.

There then began a series of events which was to lead to much confusion and delay and later recriminations between civil and military authorities. Mr Lawrence Shaw, the clerk to Haslingden's only magistrate, the Reverend William Gray, stood in the

The scene at Middle Mill, Helmshore, on Tuesday 25 April. William Turner and Reverend Gray await the arrival of the cavalry while the rioters enter the building. Meanwhile an employee of William Turner surreptitiously cuts a piece of cloth from Mary Hindle's dress

crowd. When Jones arrived, he asked Shaw to request the Reverend Gray to go to Helmshore. The Reverend Gray was attending a vestry meeting.[11] Shaw interrupted the meeting with the news. 'He [the Reverend Gray] came immediately to my office, took a copy of the Riot Act, mounted his horse and rode down the street. I followed him in about five minutes and saw him on horseback at the doorway of the New Inn, where the officers and some troops of the Queen's Bays were quartered. He was apparently waiting for the soldiers. I went into the passage. A young officer who stood there said, "The men are very dilatory." I then set off for Helmshore and arrived about the same time as the Magistrate, who had gone another way.'[12]

For reasons which never became clear the Reverend Gray left the New Inn for Helmshore without the soldiers. Colonel Kearney, the commander of the troop of Queen's Bays, was later reputed to have refused to go to Helmshore without the Reverend Gray. This conflicts with Shaw's version stating the Reverend Gray waited for the soldiers at the New Inn, who seemed, to say the least, to be unwilling to go. Shaw's version continued: 'He [the Reverend Gray] told me that the soldiers, after following him down Deardengate, [Haslingden's main thoroughfare and en-route to Helmshore] had turned back'.[13] Where the truth lies is now impossible to say, but the incident created animosity between the Reverend Gray and Colonel Kearney. From then on there was neither co-operation nor understanding between the two men most responsible for keeping the peace in the district during the riots.

At Middle Mill the mob quickly filled the mill yard. Twenty-two year old Thomas Emmett was already in the forefront. He probably joined the mob as it tumbled down the slopes of Musbury Heights onto the Holcombe Road. His home at Holden Wood was only a mile away. He was seen by several witnesses flourishing a cleaver over his head 'in a menacing manner' and calling out. 'Damn your eyes, come on', as he advanced at the head of the mob towards the mill.[14] He quickly became the leader of the attackers. Amongst the crowd behind him was Mary Hindle, Mary Marsden and Alexander Norris from Haslingden, James Shorrock, John Orrell, Betty Howorth and William Taylor from Pickup Bank, Ann Entwistle from Over Darwen, William Almond from Belthorn and Margaret Yates from Oswaldtwistle. (Some of these probably joined the mob as it marched over the moors from Over Darwen.)

Inside the mill the loyal employees of William and Ralph Turner were ready for the mob. William Turner Clegg and labourers Harry Holt, James Jarvis, James Heys and William Schofield were behind the main door. 'It was a very thick door with two locks and we placed two planks against it.'[15] For half an hour they kept the door closed. The whole of this time, to no avail, Emmett attacked the door with the cleaver.

All the time a crowd of some four hundred shouted encouragement. Inside, Clegg and the others put their shoulders to the door. They quickly moved away as the cleaver split it down the middle. A person unknown, using a hammer, helped Emmett. Finally a sledgehammer was brought from the blacksmith's smithy across the road, and the door, within moments, shattered under its impact.

Immediately, the cheering mob rushed in and ran upstairs to the loom-rooms. James Heys followed them. He went up to Emmett, and in a futile attempt to stem the tide, said, 'There are no cotton looms here'. Emmett replied, 'I'll cleave your head in if you don't go downstairs'.[16] Heys, very wisely, left the scene to the loom-breakers.

By then two hundred men and women were running free inside the building. Mary Marsden was in the van, 'Here's the looms lads, do your duty!' Ann Entwistle encouraged the fainthearted, 'Roll up, you soft devils and come forward!' Seventeen year old Margaret Yates shouted, 'Here's the fruits of your steam looms! Now, my lads, mash away!'[17]

Outside, on the fringe of the crowd William Turner stood helpless at the sight and sound of the destruction of his powerlooms. He approached Shaw and the Reverend Gray who had just arrived from Haslingden. Turner was furious. He asked Shaw where the soldiers were. 'I said, they are preparing to come. He expressed great indignation at the delay and said they might as well stay away as the mischief was done.'[18] A few minutes later the Reverend Gray decided, rather late, the 'Riot Act' must be read. He advanced on horseback closer to the mill, then gave the card containing the words of the 'Riot Act' to Shaw for him to read to the crowd. By then most of the mob were running riot inside the building. In the confusion and noise Shaw went unheeded. None of the crowd dispersed, most continued to encourage those inside. Clegg and Holt very courageously mingled with the mob inside the loom-room on the third storey. Holt watched James Shorrock attack the reeds and healds on the looms with a stick. He then got a piece of cast iron from a broken loom and continued the destruction with that.

Holt also saw Margaret Yates clapping her hands in excitement and encouraging the men. 'I did not see her break any looms, but she appeared much heated as if she had been exerting herself very much.' Clegg went up to John Orrell as he reached the loom-room and threatened to apprehend him, but Orrell shrugged him aside and carried on.

Amongst all the noise and confusion of loom breaking Ann Entwistle concentrated on shuttles. A skip (a large wickerwork box-like container) full of shuttles, was on one side of the loom-room. As Clegg watched, Entwistle 'took the shuttles one by one and struck them against the looms or on the ground and broke a great many of them'. She then spent at least ten minutes going from loom to loom breaking more shuttles with a piece of iron. When a Turner employee (name unknown) remonstrated with her, she knocked him down with the iron.[19]

Fifteen year old Thomas Duckworth, the veteran of the march to Low Moor the previous day, stood in the crowd. He watched as Harry Holt kept people in the crowd under observation. (Unknown to Duckworth he himself was under observation. One of the high constable's spies, possibly George Walmsley, who also went with the mob to Low Moor, must later have identified him. Sometime after the riot Duckworth was arrested but not charged.)[20]

Holt had previously seen Mary Hindle inside the mill breaking looms. Using a common local expression when a man addressed a married woman, he said, 'George's wife, what are you doing here?' Mary Hindle at that time ignored him.[21] Later Holt saw her again, in the crowd outside. As Mary Hindle shouted encouragement to the rioters Holt surreptitiously cut a piece from her dress, and later produced it as evidence at her examination by the Reverend Gray.

James Barker had earlier seen his blacksmith's smithy broken into and watched the mob use his own sledgehammer to break the door down. As he watched, he too noticed Mary Hindle, whom he knew, in the crowd. Mary Hindle came to Barker and asked, 'Where's John Hamer?' Barker replied, 'I saw him go into the building'. Mary Hindle was delighted. 'I've won my shilling. I bet him a shilling that the powerlooms would be broken before five weeks and I have three weeks yet to do.'[22]

Inside the building the mob, completely out of control, was milling about from room to room. One hundred looms lay in fragments. Twist beams, reeds and healds were smashed and scattered all over the floor. Six looms were discovered in storage in a garret. In a trice they were destroyed.

Suddenly a shout went up. 'Sowdgers are coming!' Some of the men began to run out but Mary Marsden shouted them back, saying, 'Damn it men, are you coming back? Sowdgers are noan coming!'[23] Accordingly the men returned. Mary was wrong. Thirty Queen's Bays, led by Colonel Kearney, had at last arrived. Too late, as William Turner had known for the past half hour. It was enough for the rioters however, and they began to flee the mill. Turner immediately organised his employees, hastily convened as special constables by the Reverend Gray, to re-enter the mill and arrest the rioters. Seventeen year old Alexander Norris of Newfield, Haslingden, was one of the first. Turner himself caught hold of him in the mill yard. Turner handed him over to James Heys. Others were held in the yard as they descended by a ladder from the loom-room. Another seventeen year old, Betty Howorth, still inside came to the top of the stairs leading out of the loom-room. She met Samuel Hamer, 'She begged me to let her out. I refused to let her go. I did not see her break any looms, nor do I know whether she broke any, but she was not employed at the mill and had no business there.' Hamer handed her over to Edward Hoyle, Mr Shaw's assistant, acting as a special constable.[24]

Ann Entwistle, Betty Marsden, Margaret Yates, Betty Howorth, (who was at Jubilee Street Mill the previous day) Mary Hindle, John Orrell and William Taylor and several others all submitted quietly to the special constables. The presence of thirty Queen's Bays with drawn sabres ensured no resistance.

The rest of the rioters ran out of the rear of the mill into the open fields beyond. Some (including James Shorrock) escaped through the 'necessary' (toilet) window at the rear and climbed over some railings to get away. (Very probably this explains why the women, hampered with long skirts, surrendered to the constables.)

William Almond was later arrested on the evidence of a child. Ten year old Joseph Woods had worked for Turner for just four months. When the rioters broke into the mill Joseph ran into the open field behind. As the riot ended he suddenly saw William Almond from his home village of Belthorn. 'The soldiers had come and had taken all that were to be held prisoners. I was in a field called Farmer Bank when I saw Will [Almond] jump over the railings. He came up to me. I said, 'Now Will, art thou come?' He said nothing. I then ran home and left him on Farmer Bank. There were several other persons who jumped over the rails but I did not know them.'[25]

The riot was over. Those who did not escape – a total of twenty-three men and women – were placed in the centre of the cavalry.[26] Prisoners and escort, led by Colonel Kearney, the Reverend Gray and Mr Shaw, then set off for Haslingden. Feelings were still running high and a large angry crowd, sympathetic to the prisoners, followed. Others stood in the fields on either side of the road throwing stones and clods of earth at the cavalry and constables.

The prospect of prison came as a relief to at least one prisoner. As Ann Entwistle walked along, surrounded by the magnificent bay horses of the cavalry, she told her escort, John Wolstenholme, a Turner employee, 'I don't give a damn about being sent to the House of Correction [at Preston]. I've been there twice before. At least I'll get skilly [a thin broth or soup] three times a day.'[27]

After a long two mile uphill journey prisoners and escort eventually passed into Deardengate, Haslingden. 'On their arrival at that place a disposition to riot was evinced by the populace and the mob which had followed the soldiers from Helmshore. In passing up Deardengate, a stone was thrown which struck a soldier who was riding near the Magistrate. The prisoners were conveyed to the New Inn – there being no proper gaol or lock-up in Haslingden. On my arrival I told Mr Neil, the landlord, there would be a riot.'[28]

When Blind Jack of Knaresborough (Jack Metcalf) completed the Accrington – Haslingden – Bury section of the turnpike road in 1789, a 'new' inn was built near its junction with Deardengate.[29]

The 'New Inn' became the main public building in the town, a centre of Haslingden social life. The Reverend Gray held his court in the 'Long Room' above the public rooms. The Reverend Gray now intended to examine, charge and hold the prisoners in the 'Long Room'.

The crowd which had followed the prisoners and escort from Helmshore gathered more numbers in the town. The Bays had to force their way along the full length of Deardengate through a jeering, howling mob. Stones and clods of earth were still being thrown at the escort. Eventually and with great difficulty the prisoners were ushered through the front door of the New Inn and up to the comparative safety of the Long Room.

The Bays immediately dismounted and, to the surprise of many, led their horses to the stables at the side of the inn. Most then went to their quarters in the 'Top o' th' Town' (an area of slums and low lodging houses behind the New Inn). Only eight or nine, including the officers, who were quartered in the New Inn, followed the prisoners inside. Just two troopers, sabres drawn, stood at the front door.

The events which followed led to a public row between the Reverend Gray and Colonel Kearney, a row resolved only by the eventual intercession of Major General Harris (the Commander of the Northern District), the Home Secretary and the Lord Lieutenant of the County of Lancaster (the twelfth Earl of Derby). The seeds of the dispute were sown in the earlier confusion and delay. Colonel Kearney had allegedly refused to go to Helmshore without a magistrate. He was clearly reluctant to go at all. Army standing orders stated troops were to be summoned to rioting, not go in anticipation of it. Even so there had been indecision. His men had been dilatory, they had started for Helmshore and turned back. There had been no clear orders or communication with or from the Reverend Gray. Once Turner's employees arrested the rioters, the Bays had the relatively easy job of escorting the quiescent prisoners to the New Inn, albeit through an angry crowd.

Once the prisoners were in the Long Room Colonel Kearney told the Reverend Gray they were no longer the responsibility of the military authority. He had delivered them to him (the Reverend Gray) for his disposal. The Reverend Gray refused to receive them, saying he could do nothing with them. The Reverend Gray was in a dilemma. He clearly did not know what to do. In truth, neither did Colonel Kearney. In the Long Room with them were twenty-three dirty, dishevelled, exhausted prisoners of both sexes, two constables, Turner's employees and two troopers. Outside stood a mob of several hundred persons getting angrier and angrier.[30]

Mr Shaw, fearful of the mob, came in and begged Colonel Kearney to recall his troops. The soldiers however, were scattered and unprepared. Some were in the stables grooming their horses, a few, in the garret above the Long Room, were washing themselves, others were two hundred yards away in their billets in the Top o' th' Town. A group of twelve or fourteen stood at the front door.

As the Reverend Gray and Colonel Kearney bickered over responsibility, a stone crashed through a front window. In seconds a volley of stones demolished every window in the front of the house. It was a concerted, spontaneous, attack by the increasingly angry and frustrated mob.

The Reverend Gray, Mr Shaw and Colonel Kearney quickly went down to the back yard of the Inn, away from the noise and crashing of stones. The prisoners and their captors were left in the room to get what cover they could.

George Heys, a navigator (navvy) by trade, and one of the mob captains, escaped at Middle Mill. He was now at the front of the crowd. Laurence Haslem, an overlooker and one of Turner's employees, stood discreetly nearby. He saw Heys turn to the crowd, point to the New Inn and say, 'Do my men stand true? I'm captain of that gang and if they are not released I'll pull the house down.'[31] The crowd roared its agreement.

It was obvious to Heys and the crowd there was dissent and indecision inside the New Inn. He, and they, knew there was nowhere else to keep the prisoners safely in custody. He, and they, knew of the fiasco at Middle Mill. This, plus the inactivity of the soldiers, convinced them the military forces were at least sympathetic to the crowd and the prisoners. Heys and the crowd had the upper hand. Colonel Kearney realised they would soon storm the building. He demanded from the Reverend Gray permission to act – to open fire on the crowd and disperse them. At the same time a delegation of local townsmen 'implored the Reverend Gray to release the prisoners as the whole town was in danger'.[32]

The Reverend Gray was decisive on one point. He would not allow Colonel Kearney, at any cost, to fire on the crowd. Time and events, though, were pressing on the Reverend Gray. To keep the prisoners where they were would mean the mob would inevitably storm the building. To allow the troops to fire was morally unthinkable. To free the prisoners would appear to condone their behaviour. As a humanitarian, however, and for the immediate sake of those inside the building – and those outside – he had no choice. The Reverend Gray returned to the Long Room and ordered the prisoners free.

Within seconds the prisoners surged downstairs, the front door flew open and the prisoners, to the wild cheers of the crowd, ran off in all directions. Almost as quickly, the crowd, cheering in triumph, broke up and paraded away from the scene. Left behind was a furious Colonel Kearney, a much relieved Reverend Gray, and Mr Neil,

After the angry mob had shattered every window and threatened to storm the building, the prisoners are allowed to leave. The scene at the New Inn, Haslingden (now, 1992, the New Thorn) on Tuesday 25 April.

who could only survey his shattered windows and the debris in his house, twenty pounds' worth of damage in all.

The time was about six o'clock. Haslingden became relatively quiet except for street corner groups and the curious watching the cleaning up at the New Inn. The military showed no concern about the escapees. There was no need. Turner's men had earlier given their names to the Reverend Gray.

The Bays indeed rested in their quarters after a day which began for them in Manchester before dawn. Colonel Kearney was on his way to Manchester to write his report to Major General Harris. The Reverend Gray, a genial and kind-hearted man, for his part could only await the morrow. Unfortunately for him, and Colonel Kearney, it brought even more riot, dissension and controversy.

Sometime later in the evening, somewhere in the area, the 'captains' met. Amongst them were Thomas Emmett and Laurence Rostron and George Heys, from Haslingden. The mob had had, beyond all dreams, a successful day. Fifty-two looms in Over Darwen and all one hundred and six looms of the detested William Turner – one hundred and fifty-eight in all – were now reduced to fragments. Plus, as an unexpected bonus, twenty-three prisoners rescued from the military. Utterly convinced the troopers of the Bays – and most of the populace – were on their side, the 'captains' made plans for the next day.

George Heys, who later was to deny being the leader of the mob in front of the New Inn, had already reconnoitred the field. In the early evening he had walked the two miles to Rawtenstall, a village at the head of the Rossendale Valley. On his way home to Haslingden, Heys met Laurence Haslem and his brother John, a warp dresser at Whitehead's factory in Rawtenstall. Not realising Laurence Haslem had already shadowed him at the New Inn and that their meeting now could hardly be coincidental, Heys boasted to the Haslems, 'I've been having a look round to see what we should do tomorrow. We'll begin at Whiteheads.'[33]

CHAPTER FOUR

Wednesday – Watch and Ward

APART from the Haslems' report of their meeting with George Heys, David Whitehead's own commonsense told him they were next. The Whitehead brothers' factory, with ninety-six powerlooms, was barely two miles from Haslingden.[1]

David Whitehead knew the mighty William Turner was defeated inside half an hour; the law and the military had proved no protection, the Whiteheads had many enemies amongst the displaced handloom weavers and the mob's 'blood was up'. What chance, David reasoned, had the Whitehead brothers?

Well before seven o'clock on Wednesday morning on 26th April, David Whitehead went by chaise to Burnley Barracks to get the help of a troop of the lst King's Dragoon Guards. (He evidently believed the Queen's Bays were not reliable.) At the same time he sent his brother Benjamin to the Reverend Gray's house in Haslingden with a signed affidavit concerning his knowledge of the impending attack and requesting civil and military assistance. Benjamin confirmed, on oath, the truth of the affidavit and the Haslems' report.

The Reverend Gray, with Benjamin Whitehead, immediately went to the New Inn and presented the affidavit to Colonel Kearney, who had just arrived, on horseback, from Manchester. Present also in the room was Lawrence Shaw and Mr Townsend, the parish constable. With Colonel Kearney was Major Eckersley.[2]

To the Reverend Gray's great surprise Colonel Kearney was sceptical. He dismissed the Whiteheads' fears as something based on rumour. Even when Mr Townsend, as parish constable, offered to swear on oath that he had already seen the mob collecting and moving in the direction of Rawtenstall, Colonel Kearney would not take the threat seriously. The Reverend Gray urged him to act, but Colonel Kearney was in no hurry. He merely shrugged aside all pleas. His troops would not go to Rawtenstall. The Reverend Gray and his group waited, with a rising sense of panic, for half an hour outside the New Inn. Colonel Kearney did not appear. Benjamin Whitehead was becoming very agitated about his brothers at the factory. Now desperate, the Reverend Gray ordered two horses saddled, for himself and Lawrence Shaw, with the intention of riding to Whiteheads' factory.

After waiting a short time the Reverend Gray, inexplicably decided to go on foot.[3] More than half an hour elapsed before the Reverend Gray and his group (Lawrence Shaw, Mr Townsend and Benjamin Whitehead) arrived at Oakenhead Wood, the point on the highway where the half mile descent to Rawtenstall began. Whiteheads' factory was easily seen in the valley below.

By then of course, the mob 'to the number of almost three thousand' had arrived at the factory by another route.[4] At this time the mob was restrained and orderly. 'As they entered Rawtenstall they were courteous to the villagers. Some four or five knocked at the door of a handloom weaver and asked him for meat. He told them he was, as they were, a poor man with a family. He had only bread, which he offered them. They politely refused and left the house quietly.'[5]

The long procession marching along was soon added to by men and women coming down the Rossendale Valley – from Newchurch and Waterfoot. Even some of Whiteheads' own employees at the factory joined. The crowd, waving sticks and clubs soon surrounded the factory.

At the main door the mob captains, Emmett, Heys and Rostron, asked the Whiteheads' employees inside to open the locked door. John Haslem, who had been in the factory all night was one of those inside. With others he had secured a large piece of timber behind the door. The captains were civil and patient. Heys promised those inside to 'injure nothing but the powerlooms'. He added, 'We have broken all so far and we'll break these as well'. Heys declared dramatically, 'I am captain of this gang. If any man breaks anything other than the powerlooms that man will be put to death'.[6] (Unknown to Heys he was again being watched by Lawrence Haslem, his 'shadow' from the previous day at the New Inn.)

The door remained locked. Whiteheads' men made no reply. Emmett, Heys and Rostron then attacked the door. Emmett used an axe, Heys a maul (a type of sledgehammer), and Rostron a large stone. 'Strike harder!' ordered Heys. The assault lasted fifteen minutes. The door burst open and a crowd of men and women tried to rush inside. As Heys and Emmett led the way, Rostron stood by the door and told the women to make way for the men with hammers and bludgeons. He pushed aside the women who tried to enter.[7] Once inside, Heys again gave orders that nothing but the powerlooms were to be broken. In the doorway Rostron himself was quickly pushed aside by the women, desperate to join in, as they swarmed inside the building. The women immediately slashed the warps with anything to hand. Reeds and healds were dashed to the ground and trampled on. Shuttles were smashed and woven cloth scattered about. The men concentrated on smashing the cast iron framework of the looms. The whole operation was carried out quickly but methodically. There was no opposition within the factory or without. The absence of the military confirmed the rioters' belief that 'The soldiers are on our side'.[8]

The Reverend Gray and his companions at Oakenhead Wood could only watch and listen to the cheers of the crowd as they encouraged those inside. Benjamin Whitehead continued down to the factory to be with his brothers, watching at the edge of the crowd. David was there also, his visit to Burnley unsuccessful. For the Reverend Gray his cavalry were not yet in sight – they were for all he knew still at the New Inn.

The Reverend Gray did not feel the need to be at the factory. There was an administrative complication. Rawtenstall was not within his jurisdiction as a magistrate. The local magistrate was James Whittaker of Broadclough, Bacup. Where he was no one knew. The Reverend Gray's experience at Middle Mill the day before convinced him that reading the Riot Act would not prevent the looms being destroyed. He preferred this time to await the military. At least twenty-three of the leading rioters were known so at least they could be kept under observation. Under the 1812 'Watch and Ward' Act magistrates had the power to require persons to perform the duties, in circumstances such as this, of 'watching by day and warding by night'. Before Benjamin Whitehead left Oakenhead Wood the Reverend Gray gave him and his brothers the authority to select loyal employees to 'watch and ward' the rioters.

At the factory, Whiteheads' loyal employees, under David and Benjamin's instructions, began following and noting the mob leaders. (Haslem was already doing this on Heys.) So the 'watch and ward' policy began. It was done with great patience, with the knowledge that retribution would surely come for the rioters. Individual observers mingled freely with the mob and kept a close eye on those already known and others who were most active.

Inside the factory ninety-six powerlooms were destroyed in thirty minutes. Emboldened by their easy success the captains decided on the next target. They and the mob moved on to Thomas Kay's relatively small cotton mill at Longholme, half a mile away on the other side of the village.

The Reverend Gray at Oakenhead Wood still awaited the military. Eventually, an hour after his request to Colonel Kearney, the Reverend Gray watched with 'indignation' as Colonel Kearney and a detachment of Queen's Bays could be seen 'advancing, or rather creeping, along the road, as if attending a funeral'.[9]

Immediately the two men met there was a bitter row. Each accused the other of indecision and indifference to his duties. It was, however, all too late. It did not matter. The mob were well on their way to Longholme Mill. It was now past nine o'clock.

The Reverend Gray returned to Haslingden. Any civil action in Rawtenstall was James Whittaker's responsibility. Colonel Kearney, in the absence of James Whittaker's authority, decided to play safe. He led his troop down into Rawtenstall but kept himself and his men at a distance from the rioters. He simply kept them under discreet observation.

Colonel Kearney's non-intervention was misinterpreted. Some in the mob, quick to take psychological advantage, called out to the Bays and loudly thanked them for their 'services and assistance'. The Reverend Gray's supporters were later to describe Colonel Kearney's decision more bitterly as 'the disgraceful conduct of the troops'.[10] Already, and the day had hardly begun, Colonel Kearney was misunderstood and reviled.

Longholme Mill was a small building on the banks of the River Irwell. It was built in 1810 by Thomas Kay of Burnley who used it for a variety of purposes before deciding to install powerlooms. Kay had twenty brand new powerlooms inside, not yet ready for use. Entering Longholme Mill posed no problem for the mob. With the Bays a distance away and the parish constable powerless to act, about forty men and women went inside. Under the direction of the three captains the gang industriously and methodically destroyed all twenty powerlooms.

Whiteheads' observers were there. They saw James Rostron from Rawtenstall and John Ingham from Haslingden go into the mill. The observers, however, did not at the time appreciate a fine legal point. One must actually witness a felony to be sure of conviction. At their later trial Rostron and Ingham were acquitted for lack of evidence.

Three hundred yards along the river bank, beyond the bridge crossing the Burnley – Manchester road, lay Messrs Hoyle and Ashworth's New Hall Hey factory. For many years up to 1825 it was a fulling mill. By the time of the riot a steam engine was installed to drive their new powerlooms for weaving woollen cloth. The mob marched along from Longholme and in no time at all destroyed the only three powerlooms in the building. Again Ingham and Rostron were seen going inside. They were not seen breaking looms. Again both were acquitted.[11]

In less than an hour one hundred and nineteen powerlooms in three factories had been destroyed, ninety-six of them Whiteheads', the biggest and most hated employers in Rawtenstall and Rossendale. The Whitehead family were hated, like so many others, for their 'betrayal' of the handloom weavers they had employed, and been 'putters-out' for, over many years.

Their success put the captains in a buoyant mood, their dream of wiping all powerlooms off the face of the earth now so near to fulfilment. To the south of Rawtenstall lay Ramsbottom, Bury then Manchester. The captains decided they must go south. They were confident their fellows in those towns would rise up in support.

Ramsbottom was five miles from Rawtenstall. Between them, on the Manchester road, lay Edenfield. At the far side of that village just on the Rochdale road was 'Pinch Dick's' newly erected factory at Dearden Clough.[12] Lawrence and John Rostron there had fifty-eight powerlooms. In the Irwell river valley below, only half a mile away, Messrs Aitken and Lord's Chatterton factory had forty-six powerlooms. The captains decided – first Dearden Clough, then the hamlet and factory of Chatterton.

As soon as Colonel Kearney knew the mob's intentions he at once led his troop of Bays by a more direct route along the banks of the Irwell to 'Springside', the Ramsbottom home of William Grant, a local manufacturer and magistrate.

Colonel Kearney knew he could not save Rostron's mill at Dearden Clough. He was determined however, the mob must be stopped from marching on towards Bury and Manchester. Colonel Kearney had already seen, even in the sparsely populated rural areas, how quickly onlookers and supporters joined the mob as it moved from one factory to another. If this happened in the densely populated urban areas of Bury, Manchester, Rochdale, Oldham, Bolton and Stockport – all but a few miles apart – the simple vengeful powerloom breaking could erupt into a general insurrection. If this happened not only property and lives but the rule of law itself would be at risk.

The village of Edenfield stands on the high ground which marks the edge of the Rossendale hills as they meet the Lancashire Plain which stretches to the sea. The road from Rawtenstall climbs steadily for three miles to some eight hundred feet. It was a wearisome climb for those in the mob. The morning's success, their determination and the leadership of the captains helped sustain them in their march.

As always, some drifted away to their homes. Some were afraid of what they had done, others simply reluctant to be away too long from wives and children living in desperate straits. Others, however, replaced them. Some who were exhilarated at the destruction of the hated powerlooms and now anxious to join in, others, often of trades not connected with handloom weaving, but simply opportunists and trouble makers joining in riot and violence for its own sake. There were yet others, curious onlookers anxious to keep just on the fringe of events.

At Dearden Clough the Rostron brothers, in common with Colonel Kearney, knew they could not stop the attack. They knew they could not save their looms. They decided, however, to minimise the damage. Whilst the mob was on its way, the brothers, with their loyal employees, amongst them James Whatacre, a warp dresser, and Richard Leech, a weaver, worked against time to remove as many warps from

The scene on Chatterton Lane as William Grant JP reads the Riot Act to the mob captains shortly before the attack on Thomas Aitken's factory in Chatterton on Wednesday 26 April.

the looms as they could. These they stored away out of sight. They stopped work only when the mob arrived.

The captains now had an established procedure. First, they asked for admittance to the building. If refused they broke the door down. (At Dearden Clough there was no need – the door was open.) Second, a guard was placed outside. Third, the women dealt with the warps, wefts, reeds and healds. (At Dearden Clough of course the women were partly denied this satisfaction.) Finally the men did the heavier task of breaking the looms. At Dearden Clough all fifty-eight were systematically destroyed.

The Rostron brothers, their employees and Edenfield's parish constable could only look on. Whiteheads' watchers were, however, still in the crowd. Ann Ingham from Haslingden and Anthony Harrison and Aaron Gregson, both only seventeen, were under surveillance as they took part. Again mere presence at the scene of a riot was not enough and all three were later acquitted.[13]

In William Grant's home Colonel Kearney outlined his decision to stand at Chatterton. William Grant gave him his full support. A detachment of the 60th (Duke of York's Own) Rifle Corps led by Lieutenant David Fitzgerald, twenty men in all, was at the time guarding Messrs Ashton's factory in Ramsbottom, a mile from Chatterton.[14] Colonel Kearney ordered the detachment be brought to Chatterton at once. He had with him a half troop of fifteen Queen's Bays (the other half – fifteen – he earlier transferred from Rawtenstall to Bury.) All under his command were already fatigued. The Riflemen had, only hours before, force-marched from Manchester, sixteen miles away. His Bays had been on continuous duty for over six hours. He himself and Major Eckersley, had ridden the twenty miles from Manchester to Haslingden well before dawn. It was now almost mid-day. Colonel Kearney had thirty-five tired and weary officers and men with which to confront a mob four thousand strong.

Colonel Kearney ordered his troops to Chatterton. All there, however, was quiet. The mob had not arrived. At about the same time, the triumphant mob, finished with Dearden Clough, turned towards Chatterton. Their route lay across the Manchester road then down the steep, narrow Chatterton Lane. Immediately Colonel Kearney was alerted, the troops, with Colonel Kearney and William Grant riding at their head, advanced up Chatterton Lane towards Dearden Clough. Half way up the hill a quarter of a mile from Chatterton the troops formed across the lane to stop the mob.

It was a good place to stop. The lane was no more than ten feet wide. On Colonel Kearney's and William Grant's right was a high hedge then rising ground, from which troopers could look down on the mob. On their left a stone wall, behind which was a drop of some ten feet on to rough sloping ground.

The mob halted. 'The rioters were armed with bludgeons and clubs, some with fragments of the machinery which they had destroyed. They did not look able to fight or fly, they could scarcely bear their weapons. One wretch shifted his club every moment, it was too heavy for him. Address more than force was required. It would be cruel to use force against these people.'[15]

No doubt with similar thoughts in his mind William Grant decided to use his good reputation as a local employer and businessman, and his authority as a magistrate, to appeal to the mob. Still seated on his horse, he called in a loud voice for the mob captains to listen to him. He expressed his deep personal sympathy to them in their distress. 'I assure you, if you would exercise a little patience, I will exert myself to get your condition represented to His Majesty. I have no doubt this would be the means of something effectual for your relief.'[16]

The appeal was fruitless. It was far too late for promises. Beyond the murmurings and shouts of the impatient crowd he got no answer, except, from an individual leader, 'our object is the destruction of the powerlooms, which we will do our utmost to do before we return to our homes'.[17]

Grant entreated them to go home. The mob made no move. Grant told the captains he had no alternative but to read the 'Riot Act', ignoring which was deemed a felony punishable by death. He read the 'Riot Act'. Again no move. Grant again pleaded with them to return home. It was no use. The mob responded by suddenly breaking out of the lane over the wall and down onto the rough slopes. With wild cheers they made their way down the field towards Chatterton and the factory.

Colonel Kearney and his troops could only follow. As they turned Colonel Kearney and Grant could see across the valley, several groups of men and women running across the fields towards the factory from the direction of Helmshore and Holcombe. Other were coming from the direction of Bury. Still others were running up the lane from Ramsbottom. The scene was set for tragedy.

CHAPTER FIVE

Wednesday – The Chatterton 'Fight'

AITKEN and Lord's Chatterton factory stood on a bend of the River Irwell. The river here was broad and shallow so a 'lodge' (a small reservoir to provide the mill with a controllable supply of water) had been constructed between the factory and the river bend. A row of cottages faced the factory gates, the cottage gardens fronting onto a narrow lane. Beyond the cottages, nearer the river, stood two short 'streets' of cottages, at right angles to the lane. On rising ground, at the junction of Chatterton Lane with the equally narrow road to Ramsbottom, stood the detached house of Mr Aitken, the factory owner. Chatterton was a small factory community, in a remote cul-de-sac and – apart from the hustle-bustle of factory work – normally very peaceful. That is, until now – eleven o'clock, 26th April 1826.

The mob arrived at the factory only moments before William Grant and the military. Three thousand men and women raced round the cottages and gardens and gathered round the factory gates. Colonel Kearney positioned his Bays and the 60th Rifle Corps in readiness on the road outside Aitken's house.[1]

The 60th Regiment were smart and businesslike in dark green jackets and pantaloons and black leather belts and ammunition pouches. They wore flat-topped shakos fitted with a short green feather. Each man carried a nine and a half pound Baker rifle – a muzzle loading flintlock. As a firearm the Baker rifle was far superior, both in accuracy and range, to the normal infantry musket. Its 0.625 calibre, thirty-inch barrel with seven rifling grooves making a quarter turn in its length, gave the Baker an effective range of over two hundred yards against the seventy-five yards or so of the smooth bored infantry musket.

The 'Light Bobs', as the riflemen were disrespectfully called, were a different type of soldier from the scarlet 'Lobsters' as the ordinary infantry of the line were known. The riflemen were less regimented and better treated by their officers. They were highly trained as skirmishers and sharpshooters and worked more on their own initiative in the field. They were truly professional soldiers.

The riflemen contrasted sharply with the Queen's Bays at their side. The Bays, on their now tired horses, were resplendent in scarlet jackets with gold epaulettes, dark blue trousers, black leather boots and gold plumed helmets. Each Bays trooper was armed with a sabre and a pistol. The Bays represented the traditions and attitudes of the old just as much as the riflemen those of the new.[2]

At Chatterton the captains' somewhat restrained procedure for entering the factory and methodically destroying only powerlooms collapsed. The mood of the mob changed – now a strong sullen determination was evident. Everyone and everything

– masters, military and property – was the target. For the first time lives were threatened.

As the military awaited orders Thomas Aitken went to the factory gates with Colonel Kearney and Major Eckersley. Several of Aitken's employees were inside and he gave them instructions to protect the factory if they could but without endangering their lives. The factory gates were then closed and barred. Aitken knew the significance of Grant's reading the 'Riot Act'. He implored Colonel Kearney to send his troops away – he could see their presence made the mob more determined than ever. Like the Reverend Gray the day before, Aitken had a clash of loyalties. He wanted law and order and the protection of property yet he did not want bloodshed, but Aitken was already helpless to influence events. Colonel Kearney ignored his pleas.

As the two officers returned to their men they left Aitken momentarily on his own at the factory gate. He was immediately surrounded by some of the mob. One, William Barnes, of Laneside, Haslingden demanded of Aitken, 'Give me some money!' Aitken replied, 'I have none to spare'. Barnes persisted, 'Swap coats wi' mi' or give mi' thy coat – come on, or give us some cheese and bread'. After several similar demands with no reply from Aitken, Barnes shouted 'Damn thi' then, thi' mun tek care of thi'sel 'afore two hours end! We'll finish thee before we leave.' Very frightened by these and more threats from those surrounding him Aitken at once fled to his house. He collected his family and left the scene, not to return for two days.[3]

At this time some of the mob broke the windows at the rear of the factory, climbed inside and began to destroy the powerlooms on the ground floor. The mob at the front of the factory began to smash those windows with stones whilst others pelted the troops with stones, sticks and clods of earth. Several men – amongst them Major Eckersley – and horses were hit and injured. The troops held their ground while the mob kept up an incessant volley of stones. Much of their ammunition, unfortunately for the troops, came from two cart loads of paving stones intended to be laid near the mill.

Colonel Kearney now had a more sympathetic ear than the Reverend Gray's the day before. He told Grant he had, for the safety of his troops, no alternative but to order them to fire on the mob. Grant saw the situation was out of hand and quickly agreed. Colonel Kearney then ordered his Bays to withdraw to the higher ground behind the cottages. He ordered Lieutenant Fitzgerald to position his riflemen in the road in readiness to fire and await further orders. They stood at ease in two ranks.

Lieutenant Fitzgerald enlisted in the Rifle Corps in 1825. Now nineteen, he had been a Lieutenant barely four months. Of all the places in the world a young officer could serve his King it was Lieutenant Fitzgerald's misfortune to be in the United Kingdom when he was in action for the first time. Worse still, in action against his own countrymen. The danger of injury or even death was hardly less, however, as he calmly awaited events.

The mob saw the riflemen moving into position. Completely undeterred, some taunted the soldiers and showered them with stones, injuring three riflemen. Lieutenant Fitzgerald still awaited Colonel Kearney's order. Colonel Kearney had by now seen enough. The mob was going to overwhelm him and the riflemen. He ordered Lieutenant Fitzgerald to fire.

The Baker rifle could fire two types of bullet. The first, for accuracy, was a tight fitting lead ball of twenty to the pound enclosed in a greased cloth patch. This was forced down upon the powder, with a great deal of pressure, by an iron ramrod. This tight fitting ball was accurate to three hundred yards. The second type used a lead ball of twenty-two to the pound enclosed in a paper cartridge. This was easier and quicker to load but because of its smaller size was accurate only to about a hundred and fifty yards. Trained riflemen could fire these at a rate of more than two to the minute. In the circumstances where the mob was almost surrounding the riflemen and certainly within thirty or forty yards, the second, less accurate but quicker loading, was the obvious type to use.

Lieutenant Fitzgerald, in what Colonel Kearney later described as 'exemplary fashion,' gave his orders.[4] Shouting above the uproar of shouts and screams and ignoring the hail of stones falling on him and his men, he ordered: 'Detachment will prime and load!' A pause, then, 'Prepare to load!' 'Load!' As one the riflemen turned half right and brought their rifles to a horizontal position forward of and just above the right hip. Each man primed and loaded his rifle in a sequence, which in training had been in nine separate commands but now for skilled riflemen, was one almost continuous motion. 'Pan' – push open with right thumb; 'Cartridge' – out of case, bring to the mouth, twist off and bring to pan; 'Prime' – shake a little powder into pan; 'Shut pan' – with fourth and fifth fingers, 'About' – turn to front, knees bend, barrel between, shake powder in barrel, insert ball, still wrapped in its cartridge paper, in barrel, grasp ramrod; 'Rod' – lift from its carrying pipes beneath the barrel; 'Home' – force ball home with ramrod; 'Return' – ramrod to pipes; 'Shoulder' – rifle to right shoulder. All in less than thirty seconds. Firing on the spot, in closed ranks, was a drill seldom carried out by riflemen in action. They were used to sharp shooting and skirmishing on their own initiative. This situation, however, was different from any on a foreign battlefield.

The riflemen awaited Lieutenant Fitzgerald. 'The detachment will fire!' He paused, then: 'Detachment!' At this word the right hand file took three quick paces to the front whilst the rear rank men stepped to the right of his file leader. More were hit by stones. 'Ready!' Quickly, yet not appearing to hurry, each man brought his rifle to the centre of his body and cocked his rifle, 'ever so gently'. The roar of the mob was deafening.

'Present!' The butt of each rifle came up to, and nestled in, the hollow of the right shoulder, the right foot stepped back behind the left, left knee bent, body forward, head bent, cheek on rifle. With the left eye shut, the right took aim. As soon as each rifleman fixed upon his target he fired without waiting for any command.

How many riflemen fired over the rioters' heads and how many fired directly into them will never be known. At thirty to forty yards it was impossible to miss. To the amazement of Colonel Kearney and Major Eckersley the volley of shots seemed only to encourage the mob. Even more missiles flew. Major Eckersley was again struck by a stone. Men at the front of the mob jeered at the riflemen. Some waved their hats or handkerchiefs as if to defy them to do their worst. The pandemonium increased as more stones crashed through the factory windows.

The riflemen continued their fire. As the file leaders (those at the front) fired, the rear rank men primed and loaded, stepped to their right, aimed and fired. Each rank loaded as the other fired. The result was an almost continuous series of shots.

The determination of the rioters was undiminished. They held their ground and threw a shower of stones in return. Major Eckersley could hardly believe his eyes. 'The obstinacy and determination of the rioters was most extraordinary and such as I could not have credited had I not witnessed it myself.'[5] One rioter, completely unafraid, approached the riflemen and shouted, 'I'd rather be killed on this spot than go home to starve. I'm not leaving this place until every loom is destroyed.' A rifleman immediately shot him. He fell, wounded in the neck.[6]

Those inside the factory ignored the firing and continued to demolish the power-looms. One man was hit in the arm by a stray shot. Notwithstanding this, he went on cutting the warps from the looms. 'Never mind, lads, we met' as we'el bi' shot bi't sowdgers as clammed to de'eath bi't maisters.'[7]

Men were indeed beginning to die. At such short range the 0.595 diameter, three quarter ounce, rifle balls were devastating. James Lord, a fulling miller from New-church, threw a stone which hit Colonel Kearney. He was shot dead at the same moment by two balls, one passing through his body, the other blowing off the back of his head.[8] John Ashworth, a weaver from Haslingden, died shot through the abdomen. James Rothwell, another weaver from Haslingden, died instantly, shot through the heart. Richard Lund, a Haslingden blacksmith, received a fatal wound in the stomach. Bleeding profusely he struggled across the river, reached the bank and died, unattended, in agony. Many men and women were wounded, at least four seriously. Exactly how many is unknown – most were carried away and hidden by friends.

The sight of dead and wounded did not deter most of the mob. Only a few took flight when the firing started. (John Hoyle, a fourteen year old handloom weaver from Haslingden, ran home and so took the news to Haslingden.) William Barnes, who earlier threatened Thomas Aitken, was as truculent and unafraid as ever. An onlooker, John Ratcliffe, the licensee of the Ewood Bridge Inn (two miles away) was looking at the dead men and at the wounded crying in agony. By his side stood William Barnes. John Grant, William Grant's brother, came up to them and observed tersely, 'It is a pity the poor had not more conduct'. Barnes went towards Grant and retorted, 'Idd'l nod be above a month before thee'll lay like these'. Grant, 'greatly afraid', quickly left the scene. As Ratcliffe watched, Barnes then joined the mob and broke several factory windows. Another onlooker, Haslingden weaver John Rothwell and a neighbour of Barnes, also saw Barnes defy ten riflemen. 'Shoot me, go on, shoot me! You can't hit me!' Rothwell knew Barnes as a normally quiet man. Barnes' behaviour at Chatterton convinced Rothwell that Barnes was not in his right mind.[9]

Rothwell was probably right. By now many of the rioters, in the extreme of starvation, exhaustion, rage and exhilaration, were light-headed – beyond fear. As the shooting continued, those inside the factory had time to destroy forty-six power-looms. More of those on the fringe however, were beginning to break away. Some waded across the river and ran across the fields towards Edenfield and the Rawtenstall road. Those inside the factory, their work complete, climbed out of the rear windows, waded across the river and followed.

Colonel Kearney saw the mob was dispersing. He ordered Lieutenant Fitzgerald to cease firing. (Ironically the mob was moving off because the looms were broken, not because of the firing. There was now no reason for them to stay.) Lieutenant Fitzgerald's riflemen were trained to fight, not in the conventional close order ranks they had been in up to this moment, but as skirmishers in dispersed order, working alone. The emphasis was on individual effort and self-reliance. The riflemen now came into their own.

Lieutenant Fitzgerald ordered one section onto the high ground behind the cottages to harry the mob from behind. A second section went through the cottage gardens to the factory and the river beyond. The Bays' role as observers now came to an end. Colonel Kearney ordered one section to assist the riflemen on the high ground. Another section covered the lane to Ramsbottom to disperse those going in that direction.

The Bays drew their sabres and moved off quickly. In spite of stones and clods continuously falling on men and horses they behaved with admirable temper. The troopers, 'veterans' now of Middle Mill, the New Inn and Rawtenstall, were very clearly not unsympathetic towards these brave, much enduring, men and women. As they overtook the running mob the troopers used the flat of their sabres across their backs. 'Move on! Move on!' They quieted their horses to avoid them trampling on those who stumbled and fell.

It was however a running battle. Stones and clods of earth were still flying. Riflemen, now in 'dispersed order', were firing at will into the crowd. The Bays, anxious to save lives, told those they overtook to get out of sight amongst the bushes. 'Get away! Get away!' The riot by now was as good as over.

The captains' original plan to destroy only powerlooms with no damage to other property had gone tragically wrong. The presence and determination of the military had provoked those disposed to violence for its own sake to overwhelm the captains' authority. The attack turned into an affray – a contest with the military. None had won, in fact, even as the mob was fleeing the captains regained control. Men were seen going from one running group to another. Those to whom they spoke turned on to a particular path through the fields – a path which lay to the Rawtenstall road.

The scenes on the high ground were repeated at the factory. As riflemen pursued the mob through the streets and around the factory, troopers told men to hide in the goyt (an artificial water course leading from the factory lodge to the river). The riflemen, however, did not have everything their own way. One chased seven or eight men along the banks of the lodge. The men saw the rifleman pause to re-load, but as he seemed to have no ammunition left, they immediately turned on him and threw him in the lodge.[10] Incredibly, when the troops had got past the factory a few determined men re-entered the building and destroyed some dressing machines on the second floor before escaping again.

The riot was almost over when two more deaths occurred. A married woman, Mary Simpson of Haslingden, was shot in the left thigh and her femoral artery severed. She bled to death on the spot. The military were later to claim Mary Simpson was a rioter and extremely violent and abusive towards them. Others, however, insisted she had come to Edenfield from Haslingden to catch the Manchester coach. She missed the coach and so watched the riot from the high ground near the Manchester road. This was confirmed by a verdict of Accidental Death at the inquest on 2nd May. It is possible Mary Simpson was hit by a stray ball or perhaps a ricochet fired from the higher ground.

There were no doubts about the second death, although the circumstances were to lead to great controversy. Earlier in the day James Whatacre and Richard Leech had removed the warps from the looms in Dearden Clough mill. Afterwards for some reason, possibly curiosity, they followed the rioters down to Chatterton and watched the events there. When the riot seemed over they turned to go home. They were passing the cottages next to Aitken's house when they suddenly saw riflemen running towards them. They hurried to get out of the way. They went through an archway connecting Aitken's house and the cottages. On the right was Aitken's back garden and back door. Leech stayed there but inexplicably Whatacre ran to the left across the archway towards the cottage door of a Mrs Upton. As he laid his hand on the door-latch Whatacre was shot. Leech ran off, past Whatacre's body, as fast as he could.[11]

A Mr Hollis, a schoolmaster, saw Whatacre going under the archway. He then saw a rifleman go towards the archway 'as if for the purposes of making water'. He saw him under the archway, then heard a shot. 'I've popped one off!' he heard. The soldier fired from twenty yards range.[12]

John Coupe, a weaver from Laneside, Haslingden had been with John Dewhurst to Summerseat for weft and was returning home. Each had a sack of weft on his back. They got to Chatterton just as the riot was over. They saw riflemen firing at people running away so they passed by the front of the factory to avoid the soldiers who were then on the higher ground. As they came by the cottages they saw a rifleman shoot Whatacre. They were barely six yards away. Three riflemen were at a cottage

The murder of James Whatacre at Chatterton, Wednesday 26 April. Whatacre is at the door of Mrs Upton's cottage as the rifleman (left of picture) opens fire. The witnesses are only yards away.

door (which they knew later to be Mrs Upton's) trying to get inside. The door was barred so, as Coupe and Dewhurst watched, the riflemen smashed the windows with their rifle butts.

Inside Mrs Upton had heard the shot.[13] During the riot, she, her father, two sisters and a little boy had hidden upstairs. She looked out of the window and said to her father, 'Whatacre is shot'. She heard a rifleman say, 'Damn your eyes you are foxing!' Another rifleman said, 'Damn him! Run him through!'[14] She and her father went downstairs and the second rifleman said, 'Damn her! Shoot her!' They demanded she open the door. She refused. Then, with their rifle butts, they smashed the windows. After failing to get in, they returned to the door and broke it open with their shoulders.

The riflemen were sure rioters were in the house. One seized Mrs Upton's father. 'Who are you?' He explained who he was – that he lived there. Another rifleman threatened to blow Mrs Upton's brains out. She begged him, in terror, 'For mercy's sake, don't hurt me. Spare my life!' The two riflemen went upstairs, there they roughly handled the two girls and the little boy as they searched the room. The boy said piteously 'Don't touch me, I'm a good lad'. Notwithstanding this, they kicked him and sent him downstairs.[15] They then pulled a rioter out from under a bed. As the riflemen left the cottage a distraught Mrs Upton pleaded with them to help Whatacre who lay at the door in agony dying from a stomach wound. The riflemen refused and turned away, taking the rioter with them.[16]

Whilst this was going on the rifleman who shot Whatacre came up to Coupe and Dewhurst. Coupe later related, 'I took courage, thinking his ammunition had expended, and grappled with him. I threatened to throw him and his rifle into the river if I were molested.'[17] Three or four other riflemen came up and demanded Coupe's sack. He refused to give it to them. Two riflemen on the far side of the river saw the melee and threatened Coupe and Dewhurst with death if they did not instantly wade across to them. After one fired a shot which entered Coupe's sack, they did so and were taken prisoner.[18]

The cold-blooded murder of an innocent man was later to have repercussions far beyond Chatterton but for the moment the riflemen were concerned solely with driving the rioters from the field. They ceased firing only when all had gone. The rioters, though gone from the field maybe, were not in complete disarray. They were gone simply to continue the destruction of the powerlooms. Several hundred turned towards Rawtenstall and the Rossendale Valley. Another smaller group went south along the river Irwell towards Ramsbottom, Summerseat and Bury. Chatterton, and its dead, was left to the military.[19]

CHAPTER SIX

Wednesday – On Two Fronts

THE smaller group of rioters, about two hundred strong, swarmed across the river and ran down the lane, through the hamlet of Stubbins, towards Ramsbottom and Summerseat. Neither Bays nor riflemen moved to stop them.

The most direct route for the mob lay along the banks of the River Irwell. The river skirted the village of Ramsbottom and ran through woods and fields by the hamlet of Nuttall, through Summerseat to Bury, Manchester, the River Mersey and the sea. The vale of Summerseat, just over two miles from Ramsbottom, was a remote, idyllic place. The Irwell slowly meandered by deep cloughs and steep ravines with an abundance of trees and flowers, yet its broad flat valley had been the scene of industry for many years. Terraces of tiny back to back houses clustered round small factories.

Richard Hamer and his son Daniel had run four such small factories in Summerseat since 1812 when Richard bought all four from Peel, Yates and Company for £5,514. Only one, on the river bank in Higher Summerseat, had powerlooms. The others were fulling mills or spinning mills. Richard and Daniel Hamer, with several employees, were waiting outside their locked factory gates when the mob arrived in Higher Summerseat. Daniel noticed it was four o'clock. The mob's captain was quite matter of fact. He said to Richard, 'We have come to destroy the powerlooms. Where are they?' Richard (a man fifty-four years old) refused to tell him. The spokesman replied, 'You'd better, we'll destroy them before we leave this place!'[1] Daniel joined the conversation and offered money for them to go away. They all refused. Richard was glad to see most of the mob were empty-handed.

The mob became impatient with the delay. They pushed the Hamers and their employees aside and rushed the factory gate. They got into the factory yard by simply lifting the locked gate off its hinges. In an instant the mob flooded across the yard (about twenty yards long) and into the factory. Only then did Daniel see men taking hammers out from under their 'brats' (aprons).[2]

Forty or fifty men entered the building as the rest of the mob filled the yard. Someone, possibly the captain, cried, 'Break nothing but the powerlooms!' Ten long minutes passed as the Hamers listened to the sounds of cast-iron loom frames being smashed to fragments. After a time some of those inside reappeared. James Crawshaw, a nineteen year old from Darwen was one. A voice inside the factory shouted, 'They're not all broken yet!' Crawshaw turned and went back inside.[3]

After several minutes the men walked out of the building. The captain came up to Richard and Daniel Hamer. 'We have finished them.' The crowd gave three cheers and turned towards James Hutchinson's factory at Woodhill, down the river in Elton, on the outskirts of Bury. The Hamers went inside their silent factory. Thirty-eight powerlooms were in pieces. Richard estimated it as three hundred pounds worth. He was relieved to see there was no other damage. Not a window was broken. He, his son, and his men, started to clear the debris.

At Summerseat the captain (name unknown) was clearly in control. The attack, if an attack can be so, was carried out in a well conducted, almost civil, manner. There was an air of determination not to be thwarted, but no personal violence, nor any unnecessary damage. The rule 'Break nothing but the powerlooms' was observed. Daniel Hamer did notice one of the mob leave with a length of leather driving belt in his hand. This, however, was of small moment compared to what could have been.

As the Hamers contemplated the remains of their powerlooms, the townspeople of Bury, three miles away, were understandably anxious. There were several factories equipped with powerlooms in the town. All were guarded as well as could be by loyal employees but the thought of this mob, a mob undeterred by volleys of shots at Chatterton, its determination confirmed at Summerseat, alarmed civil authority and manufacturers alike.

Much earlier in the day, before Dearden Clough or Chatterton, Bury magistrates appointed scores of special constables and ordered them to keep a watch in the direction the mob were expected. Edmund Grundy, a woollen manufacturer, had a house in the Wylde, near the Market Place. This commanded a view to the north so men were placed on the roof to give any alarm. James Hutchinson also placed men on the roof of his house at Woodbank, near Woodhill, and almost a mile from the Market Place.[4] One detachment of twenty men of the 60th Rifle Corps, under Captain Goldfrap, stood by in the Market Place. A second detachment, that previously at Chatterton, was brought into the town. Under the command of Major Schoedde, its orders were to stay in Bury, to defend, if necessary, the town centre.

The mob meanwhile, neither knowing nor caring about these preparations, came to Summerseat and then took but little time to march down the highway, through the hamlet of Brandlesholme, to the roadside factory of James Hutchinson at Woodhill. In spite of all the sentinels on rooftops the mob came down Brandlesholme Road and was in the factory yard before the alarm was raised in Bury Market Place. Captain Goldfrap's detachment found it necessary to run at full speed from the Market Place to Woodhill.

Even so they arrived too late. James Hutchinson's book-keeper, Thomas Pilkington, was inside the factory as two hundred or so men, armed with hammers and staves, came into the yard. Pilkington asked what they wanted. This time there were no discussions. 'We have come to destroy the looms.' They immediately broke down the door and went inside. As at Summerseat a large section of the mob stayed outside and completely surrounded the factory.

Hutchinson's factory was much larger – and newer – than the Hamers'. Two hundred new powerlooms had just been installed. The men inside were busy breaking these looms when the riflemen arrived. The detachment was greeted with jeers and shouts of derision from the crowd outside. Stones began to fly. The riflemen, led by Captain Goldfrap on his horse, pressed through the crowd and pushed most of them away from the factory entrance. Feelings at once ran high. Many in the crowd had probably been fired on at Chatterton only hours before, so were in no mood to tolerate lightly any action by the military. More insults and stones were hurled.

For the first (and as it turned out, the only time) in a riotous week the powerloom-breakers did not complete their work. After about ten minutes, in which they destroyed a number of powerlooms (later counted as forty-nine) and cut and tore a quantity of cloth, they came out of the factory and joined the mob attacking the riflemen. On their way out they fought with several riflemen coming into the building. As at Chatterton, the presence of the military had provoked stone throwing and violence.

Harry Melling, Edward Yates and sixteen year old James Buskey were amongst those who came out of the factory. As Melling got to the factory gate he picked up a large stone and threw it at Captain Goldfrap. Sergeant William Hamilton saw the stone knock his captain off his horse.[5] Hamilton ran through the hail of stones to help him and saw he was badly injured in the head. He ordered two riflemen to take Captain Goldfrap inside the factory to safety.

Thomas Pilkington and another employee, John Livesey, had earlier seen Melling, Yates and Buskey enter the building. Both saw James Buskey, amongst all the uproar, slowly walk outside with his hands in his pockets. They went over and held Buskey and handed him over to the riflemen. (Later Buskey was seen running away so he must have escaped.) After Melling threw the stone he and Yates also ran away but Pilkington, after a quarter of a mile chase, caught them both and brought them, unresisting, into custody.

Melling's stone was almost the final act of defiance at Woodhill. Hutchinson's employees and the riflemen took fourteen prisoners. Some had hidden inside the factory, others such as Melling and Yates were taken whilst running away. The prisoners, bound together with rope from the factory, were marched into Bury and placed in the dungeon in the Market Place. The riot was over.[6]

Many of the mob were a long way from home. Even by the most direct route through Edgworth, Darwen (where some are known to have come from) was almost eleven miles away. Haslingden, through Holcombe to avoid Chatterton and the turnpike, was seven miles away. Either journey meant a hard climb over moorland roads.

Two days of continuous mental exhilaration, plus the physical effort of walking long distances, breaking powerlooms and indeed running away from the military meant all were totally spent, burnt out. With little food except bread and cheese begged from a sympathiser if lucky, no food at all if not, many had been on the road since dawn, at least fourteen hours ago (it was now sometime after six o'clock).

The long walk home would be made with a satisfaction that many powerlooms were destroyed, but this was tempered by the failure at Hutchinson's factory. Only a quarter of his powerlooms were destroyed. Powerlooms remained intact in at least three other factories in Bury alone.

At Woodhill the drive south to destroy the hated powerlooms lost its momentum through sheer exhaustion. The riflemen, in their determination to confront the rioters, proved the last straw.

Those at Chatterton who ran north, in the direction of Rawtenstall, were larger in number, perhaps four to five hundred. Many of the exhausted, the hurt and those simply frightened for their lives, went home, of course. Some of these were temporarily harboured in nearby cottages and farmhouses until it was safe to continue.[7]

The rest – the more determined, of tougher breed – formed up on the Rawtenstall road under the control of the captains. The captains were jubilant. The 'sowdgers' were nowhere to be seen, the constables were too few and too afraid – there was nothing to stop them now. The captains and most of the mob knew of several factories containing powerlooms up in the Rossendale Valley. These were on the banks of the River Irwell as it flowed along the steep sided valley linking Rawtenstall and Bacup. It was resolved to go 'up the Valley' to continue the destruction.

The mob retraced its steps towards Rawtenstall. It passed again over New Hall Hey Bridge and passed New Hall Hey and Longholme factories and onto the Haslingden to Todmorden turnpike towards the hamlet of Waterfoot. The road closely paralleled the winding river for a mile then crossed two sharp bends in quick succession. At the second of these, a mile and a half from Rawtenstall, just outside Waterfoot, was Holt Mill Bridge. Nearby, on the river bend stood Holt Mill.

There had been an industrial building of some sort at Holt Mill since the mid-eighteenth century. In recent years, from 1818 to 1822, David Ashworth, a woollen manufacturer, used it as a fulling mill. In common with several others in Rossendale at the time, he and his brother James then converted the mill into a powerloom factory to weave baizes and bockings.[8]

Nothing is known of the attack on Holt Mill. It is likely it took place about 2 o'clock in the afternoon. There was no opposition, no special constables on 'watch and ward', no captains singled out for special attention. Twenty powerlooms, however, are known to have been destroyed. They were very likely all the powerlooms the Ashworth brothers possessed.

The mob of men, women and even children, gathering supporters and onlookers as it went along, then marched through Waterfoot and up the valley towards Waterbarn and Bacup. They passed through the narrow pass known as Thrutch Gorge, through which the turnpike road was still under construction. After one and a half miles the mob came to George Ormerod and Sons' woollen factory on the far bank of the Irwell at Waterbarn. The time was three o'clock.

Ormerod's factory was only two years old and already stonemasons were at work on an extension. A new bridge connected the factory with the road. The mob, estimated at over five hundred strong, crossed the bridge and stopped outside the front of the building.

There is no evidence Thomas Emmett, Lawrence Rostron or George Heys were at Chatterton or Holt Mill. Perhaps those appointed at Whiteheads' to watch them, considered their duty done when the rioters left their employers' premises. Perhaps, understandably, the watchers did not want to march many miles with a potentially hostile mob. Although very possible, there is no conclusive evidence Emmett, Rostron and Heys were at Chatterton.[9] What is sure, however, is Thomas Emmett took the leading role, starting at Waterbarn, in the rioters' 'second front' in Rossendale on this fine, sunny Wednesday afternoon.

Samuel Haworth, George Ormerod's book-keeper, saw the mob approach. He immediately locked the door, with himself and fifty employees inside. Thomas Emmett, armed with an axe on his shoulder, led the mob to the door. Haworth noticed one man had a pike, others had sticks or hammers.

In a conversation uncanny in its similarity to the one between the unknown captain and the Hamers at Summerseat, Emmett asked Haworth, 'Have you any powerlooms inside?' Haworth was terrified. He saw one man had a pistol. He replied, 'I'm not the master, we do have powerlooms but none are working'. Josiah Baldwin stood with

Emmett. He asked Haworth to show them where the looms were. In spite of his fear, Haworth refused. 'We'll break them whether you do or not!', came the reply. Emmett asked again. 'Give us the key!' Haworth knew resistance was in vain but he stubbornly refused. For answer Emmett attacked the door with his axe, helped by Baldwin with a cleaver. A few blows with a large stone then forced the lock open.[10]

The mob went inside and spread throughout the ground floor and smashed thirty-four brand new powerlooms. The women in the mob, by now an organised group in their own right led by Betty Cunliffe, followed the men inside to destroy the reed, healds and woven cloth. They were disappointed. The powerlooms were so new, many had not been fitted ready for weaving so there were neither reeds nor healds to break. Perhaps because of this, the destruction at Waterbarn was more extensive than most. In all, three dressing frames, ten main and ten cross shafts, twenty gear wheels, ten pedestals, and ten galleries (shaft brackets) were broken. Even the steam engine was damaged.[11]

As always at a riot, a large crowd gathered to watch. Lawrence Hardman, a stone-getter (quarryman) lived near the factory and had recently worked on its construction. He stood with a neighbour, Mary Crabtree, and a number of stone-masons, including a John Moden, who had stopped work to watch.

After the destruction Emmett, Baldwin and the rest came out of the factory to the cheers of the waiting crowd. As Emmett and Baldwin passed Hardman's group, Hardman shouted, 'Tha's not brokken 'em all yet!', and pointed to the second storey. Emmett and his men re-entered the building, went upstairs and dispatched sixteen (eight pairs) of powerlooms.[12]

When they re-appeared the mob greeted them with a tremendous cheer. They rushed forward and hoisted Emmett and Baldwin onto their shoulders. The rioter (name unknown) whom Samuel Haworth had noticed had a pistol, came over to Hardman's group. In an obvious case of mistaken identity he singled out John Moden. He handed his pistol to the surprised Moden and asked, 'Why did you tell us? Ar you with us?' Moden was terrified and said, 'Not me, I'm a stranger to the mill', and gave him back the pistol. At that moment someone blew a hunting horn as a signal for the mob to move on, and the man turned away.[13]

As Emmett led the exultant men and women over the bridge and onto the road Samuel Lord, a Bacup weaver, watched Emmett closely. Lord, a newly appointed special constable, had already watched Emmett at the factory door, had followed him into the building and watched him hewing the wooden crossbeam of a powerloom with his axe. Lord was to follow Emmett the rest of the afternoon.[14] (It is noteworthy that the official 'Petty Constables of the Forest of Rossendale', their status so lowly they were known by most by their nicknames, such as 'Long George', Bill i'th Loyne' and 'Jim Blacksmith',were conspicuous by their absence during the riots.)[15]

The mob moved on about four hundred yards up the road towards George Ormerod and Sons' other woollen factory at Tunstead. This factory, managed by George Ormerod's brother John, was older and smaller than Waterbarn. It stood a hundred yards up a narrow steep lane which joined the turnpike at the Hare and Hounds Inn. George Ormerod rode down from his home at Fern Hill nearby and met the mob at the bottom of the lane. He tried to reason with Emmett and Baldwin. He told them their conduct was stupid and could not possibly succeed. Ormerod was not threatened but his arguments were totally in vain. The captains and their followers were in no mood to listen as they continued past Ormerod up the lane to the factory.[16]

Samuel Lord mingled with the crowd as it went up the lane. This time the doors were not locked and Emmett and his men went straight inside. Once again Lord watched from the doorway as Emmett, Baldwin and the others destroyed twenty-eight powerlooms. It was a quick and easy job. Their success made Emmett and his men even more determined to complete the destruction of all the powerlooms in Rossendale.

In the small town of Bacup, two miles away, James Hargreaves and John Hardman operated their small, new (1825) factory on the banks of the Irwell near the town centre. Inside Irwell Mill, as it was known, were twenty-eight powerlooms for weaving cotton. The mob, to the tooting of the hunting horn, now set out for Irwell Mill.

Samuel Lord went 'a little way before the mob' to warn those at Irwell Mill. It was about four o'clock. The hunting horn could be heard in Bacup as the noisy triumphant mob came along the road. John Sutcliffe, the engineer at Irwell Mill, heard the horn and went to a point where he could see the mob approaching. He ran to the factory and he, Richard Haworth and John Clegg, both labourers, locked and barred the door. Shopkeepers in the town centre nearby hurriedly locked their doors. They did not know it, but they had no cause for alarm. The mob, tired and hungry as they were, were more interested in the powerlooms in Irwell Mill.

By now the pattern of events was set. Emmett, as captain and spokesman, politely asked Sutcliffe to open the mill door. Sutcliffe refused. Emmett and Baldwin together picked up two large stones from a nearby stack of building materials and threw them at the door. Baldwin threw a second stone which burst it open.[17]

Emmett directed his forty or fifty followers into the loom room. He himself made use of his axe amongst the powerlooms. Baldwin seized a piece of cast-iron from a broken loom and helped smash the rest with it. Betty Cunliffe applauded and cheered from the doorway. Lord, like a shadow, ever present, watched them all.[18]

Such was the methodical approach to the loom breaking, plus the number of men and women involved, it took only fifteen minutes to smash twenty-eight powerlooms, their ancillary shafts and gearing and the reeds and healds. When all had departed the whole floor of the loom room was a mass of iron fragments.

Just one factory was left and the day's work for the mob would be complete. Robert Munn's Old Clough factory was two and a half miles away, in the high open country off the road to Burnley. Robert Munn was born at Holt Mill in 1800. At the age of seventeen he had his own spinning mill near Bacup and 'put-out' from there to handloom weavers. In 1824 he and his brother John decided to invest in the new steam powerlooms. They bought Old Clough factory and installed a steam engine and fifty-two powerlooms to weave cotton. The mob left Bacup to deal with these looms. It was about four thirty in the afternoon.

At about five o'clock the mob could be seen from Old Clough factory roof. On the factory roof a belfry gave the work-people the starting, finishing and meal break times. This time the bell rang out to warn the work-people of the mob. Amidst the constant clamour Robert Munn put John Pickup, his book-keeper, in charge and instructed him and Nelson Hoyle, his young engineer, to lock and bar the door. Munn himself then rode to Burnley, five miles away over the moors, to get the help of the military.

Once again the captains went through the formality of requesting entry. Once again entry was refused. Once again the factory door was hammered open. Pickup, Hoyle and the rest of Munn's employees, under orders not to resist, were swept aside as forty or fifty men and women burst into the loom room.

John Pickup and Nelson Hoyle followed the mob inside. Pickup passed Betty Cunliffe standing a few yards past the shattered window. She shouted to Pickup, 'Damn you if you go in!' Notwithstanding the threat Pickup went with Hoyle into the loom room with the mob.[19]

Inside the men quite calmly took off their coats and hung them on the wall before starting work on the powerlooms. Nelson Hoyle took particular notice of one John Hoyle – known as 'Red John' from his fiery hair. For ten minutes Nelson watched from ten yards away as John, at the far end of the loom room, used a piece of broken loom to smash the others. Nelson then heard a voice say, 'Look at Red John! Watch out!' He saw him swinging a swagger weight (a cast-iron weight used to keep tension on the warp in the loom) left and right in such a violent manner he was a danger to the others.[20]

Pickup, perhaps because of her threat, kept his eye on Betty Cunliffe. As she watched the men break up the powerlooms he watched her. 'Damn them lads, smash them!' she cried. Within thirty-five minutes all fifty-two of Munn's powerlooms were indeed smashed. Wrecked pipes, shafts and three dressing frames completed the damage.[21]

The large crowd outside gave three cheers as the wreckers came out of the factory. They gave three loud cheers again when several men went up onto the roof and, as a symbol of their victory, rang the bell used only shortly before as a warning of their approach. It was six o'clock and the mob were finished. As the crowd celebrated the shout went up 'Sowdgers are coming!'

No soldiers, or indeed any opposition, had been seen since Chatterton at mid-day. Those of the mob present at Rawtenstall ten hours before, had seen only the Bays, silently watching. The soldiers now thundering down the hill from Burnley were a different kettle of fish indeed. They were a troop of Royal Horse Artillery, complete with a nine pounder cannon and limber. The mob were not to know the artillery troop was simply a show of force, with no serious intention to use the nine pounder. Taking no chances, they immediately fled back into Bacup, into the Rossendale Valley and beyond, and dispersed to their homes.[22]

The artillery, however, only half achieved its purpose of impressing and subduing the mob. The mob disappeared, because, as at Chatterton, their work was done. There were no more powerlooms to destroy. Some had talked of going to Todmorden to join up with men there. Todmorden was five miles away over the steepest and roughest of roads. At this time of day, however, to continue was simply a physical impossibility.

In truth the riots were over, artillery or no artillery. As was happening at Woodhill at about the same time, the rioters were exhausted and ready to go home. They had lived through a long day of constant physical effort and nervous tension with little or no food. Some had endured the experience of Chatterton. Only their determination and commitment had sustained them until now. They had now nowhere else to go but home – to await whatever vengeance the 'masters' and the law would wreak.

CHAPTER SEVEN

Thursday – 'Along by Botany Bay'

THE town of Chorley is nine miles from Preston and eleven from Bolton. In 1795 John Aikin described Chorley as 'a small neat market town with mills, engines and machines for carding and spinning of cotton'. In the neighbourhood were 'many bleaching and calico printing grounds with cotton factories intermixed. There were also quarries and coal-mines'.[1]

Some twenty-five years later Chorley had a population of seven thousand, and although the town lay outside the manufacturing regions of the east Lancashire moorlands (it is ten miles south west of Blackburn) it was a respectable manufacturing town in its own right. In addition to its spinning mills, bleach works and print works, hundreds of handloom weavers, living either in Chorley or in the surrounding villages, wove muslin or fustian. The handloom weavers were employed by Blackburn or Bolton putters-out and manufacturers.

By the mid 1820s however, the larger manufacturers were investing in much bigger spinning mills in Chorley. Several of these were financed by the prominent Blackburn manufacturer, Henry Sudell.[2] One of the largest of these was in Water Street, on the north eastern approaches to the town. Water Street was a half mile long, winding street in the shallow valley of the River Chor. It was a street of contrasts – a street of small workshops and large factories, of mean cottages and 'residences of the gentry'.

In 1826 the Water Street factory was primarily a cotton spinning concern employing about four hundred hands. In addition to its 26,000 spindles (for spinning), over eighty powerlooms had operated since at least 1824. Although Messrs Thomas Lightoller and William Harrison of Chorley had leased the premises and spinning machinery from Messrs George and Robert Hilton of Blackburn since January 1824, the eighty powerlooms belonged to Henry Sudell.

Lightoller and Harrison very quickly became known as hard and unscrupulous employers. In 1824 they were convicted of employing at least one boy at the age of eight years (nine was the legal minimum age), and employing children under sixteen for over twelve hours a day (the normal working week was six days at twelve hours a day, that is seventy-two hours per week). Neither was Lightoller above using violence towards his employees: 'He [Lightoller] violently struck me, and in the Lancashire fashion, purred me, [kicked him on the shins with clogs] and thrust me downstairs . . .'[3] It could be said that Lightoller had few friends amongst the Chorley 'lower-classes'. The presence of powerlooms in his factory did nothing to allay their hatred of him.

Although the handloom weavers of Chorley and the surrounding villages lived in a relatively fertile agricultural area, they were no less affected by the current distress

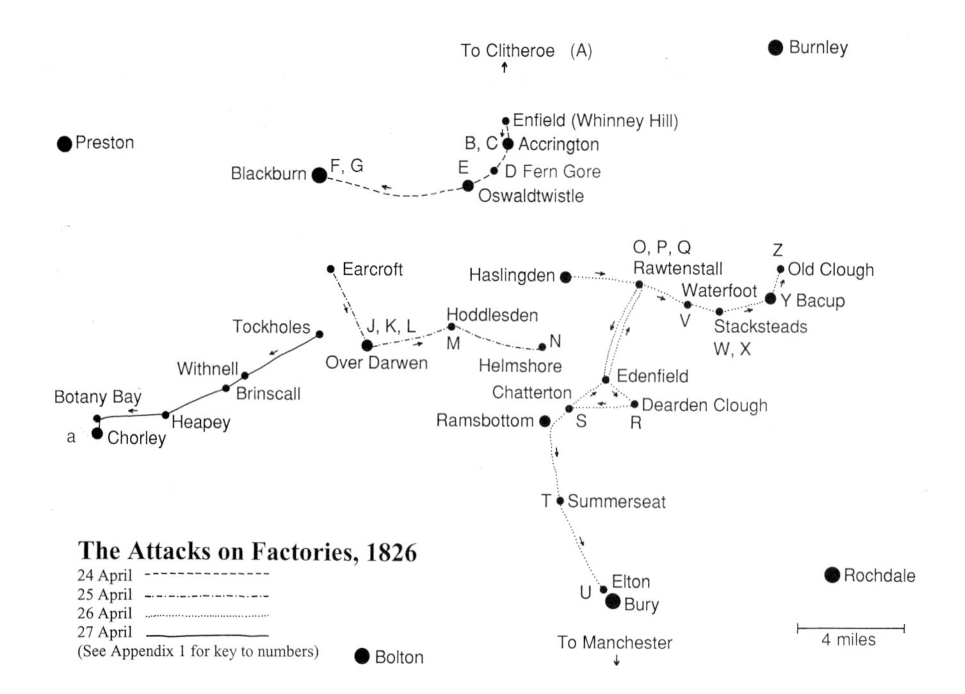

than their fellow-weavers of the east Lancashire moorlands. They also shared their wretchedness and poverty. They watched their children, weakened by starvation, die from the common childhood diseases. They were, also, almost totally dependent on the charity of those better off than themselves.

In Chorley, as elsewhere, money was raised by subscription to purchase oatmeal, potatoes, meat and barley. In Chorley, however, this was not simply distributed free to those in want. The practical citizens of Chorley sold the food, at reduced prices, to those who applied for relief. By this, the subscription fund received back some of the original outlay with which to buy more food. In one instance £170 9s. 6d. was raised and £122 11s. 11d. received back from sales to the poor.[4]

Notwithstanding the efforts at charitable relief some handloom weavers were reduced to begging. Many local people were alarmed and shocked when a doctor, riding home to Chorley from Brindle (a nearby village) one evening was accosted by a man who siezed the reins of his horse. The man asked for a shilling as he, his wife and five children were starving. Two other men stood in the shadows. The doctor nervously asked who they were. The man replied they were in the same situation as he. Deeply moved that men were driven to this, the doctor gave each a shilling and they quietly went away.[5] Despite their obvious sufferings, and despite the upheaval and disorder in nearby Blackburn and Darwen on Monday and Tuesday, the handloom weavers of Chorley and district remained peaceful. By Wednesday the townspeople had hopes the violence throughout east Lancashire and Bury would leave Chorley untouched. On that day, however, somewhere in the area of Tockholes, a scattered moorland hamlet near Over Darwen, a group of rioters, some veterans of Monday's events at Jubilee Street and Park Place, met secretly to decide how best to destroy the powerlooms in Chorley's Water Street factory.

The captains of the group were James Chambers, a handloom weaver and farmer from Oswaldtwistle and veteran also of the White Ash destruction, James Aspden of Blackburn, and Thomas Sharples, a Tockholes handloom weaver.

Since Monday all three had lived in hiding from the law, sheltered by friends in farmhouses or cottages on the moors around Over Darwen. It is clear they were determined – and desperate enough – to make one final effort to rid the whole area of powerlooms. There was also a need for urgency. Already, on Wednesday morning, five men involved in the Blackburn riots, including one from Livesey, only a mile from Tockholes, were arrested and taken to Lancaster.

Early Thursday morning therefore, the captains and their supporters gathered on the high moors by Tockholes. Most were armed with the now usual cudgels and hammers. It promised a fine sunny day. Led by Sharples, who as a local man would be familiar with the network of almost secret lanes and tracks in the sparsely populated area, the mob set out for Chorley, some eight miles distant. They easily avoided the Blackburn to Chorley turnpike, along which the 1st King's Dragoon Guards would surely approach from Blackburn.

The mob's route soon took them past the bleach works at Withnell, then through the hamlet of Brinscall. As they passed the small Brinscall Hall calico print works, thirty year old Thomas Butterworth was sitting in his cottage in nearby Harbour Lane eating his dinner. When Butterworth saw and heard the mob he decided, for no real reason – perhaps curiosity, perhaps sympathy – to go with them. Butterworth however, was not all that curious, was not all that sympathetic perhaps, to join the mob immediately. He decided to finish his dinner first.[6]

The mob meanwhile grew in size and momentum as it marched along, passing by Heapey village with its delph (quarry) and sandpits. Men and women in dozens hurried from their homes to follow. Many of these, although perhaps fearful themselves of joining the mob, were not unduly unhappy at the prospect of seeing powerlooms destroyed.

A detour across some rough broken country took them away from Gorse Hall, the home of one of the local gentry and then – no soldiers visible – across the Blackburn to Chorley turnpike. Keeping to the fields, they reached the narrow wooden Knowley footbridge spanning the Leeds and Liverpool Canal. They hurried past Cabbage Hall, another large residence, and continued in the fields to the banks of the River Chor, and soon reached the bottom of Water Street at its junction with the turnpike in Harpers Lane. They were within sight of the 'big chimney', the distinctive feature of Water Street factory.

Because of the contours of the land along their chosen route at no time could the mob – now numbering about sixty persons – be seen from Chorley. Anyone waiting for a mob to arrive would probably expect it to advance on the direct route of the turnpike as it approached Chorley through Botany Bay, a canalside settlement of wharves and cottages. By avoiding Botany Bay the mob leaders achieved almost complete surprise. They came up almost out of the ground.[7]

Within minutes the mob reached the factory itself. By this time, about half past one, Thomas Butterworth caught up with the mob and prepared to join in the proceedings.

The arrival of the mob did indeed take the town by surprise. William Blades, the brother of James Blades the landlord, was standing in the doorway of the Gillibrand Arms in Market Street about three hundred yards from the factory. Suddenly the overseer of the poor came running from the workhouse in Eaves Lane (near the rioters' route into the town) and asked for Thomas Ellison, the parish constable: 'I wish you would go and tell him – the mob are coming!'[8]

Blades ran to Ellison's grocery and provision shop in nearby St. Thomas's Square and took him to the home of Colonel Silvester, a Chorley land and property owner and magistrate, in Hollinshead Street, next to Water Street. Colonel Silvester hastily appointed several special constables (including William Blades) and, with Ellison and Henry Leaver, the clerk to William Fox, a Chorley solicitor with offices in Water Street, hastened to the factory.

Scores of townspeople came from every direction. Some, anxious about law and order, were hostile to the mob. Many others, of course, were sympathetic and prepared to help if necessary. In no time a 'great multitude' of onlookers filled the street.

William Farmer, book-keeper to Messrs Lightoller and Harrison, and Thomas Swift, book-keeper to Messrs Hilton (who had another factory next door) were already inside the factory. When the mob arrived they filled the factory yard and stopped. Farmer, very bravely, went to speak to them. He told them, 'The powerlooms have not been used for some time. If you refrain from damaging them, I promise you they'll never be used again'. James Chambers, as captain and spokesman, was not to be baulked so easily. With unanswerable logic he replied, 'If you don't intend to work them any more, they can be of no further use to you, so let us have them out of the place and break them'.[9]

Farmer and his colleagues quickly got out of the way as Chambers, Aspden and Sharples put words into action and attacked the locked factory door. Using cudgels and a large iron weight they soon smashed the door. When they ran inside they came to a second locked door leading to the loom room. This door was easy. A few kicks with a clogged foot knocked out a panel. A young boy was brought from the crowd of onlookers and pushed through the hole. He simply unlocked the door from the inside and the mob surged into the loom room.

Colonel Silvester, Ellison, Blades and Leaver followed the mob inside. Another who went in was the Chorley correspondent of the *Preston Advertiser*. He could hardly believe his eyes. 'I saw the rioters at work and the coolness and determination with which they destroyed the machinery was surprising. There was no appearance of haste, but on the contrary, the greatest serenity.'[10]

Colonel Silvester and his entourage discussed the situation. 'It was wished to close the mill door and so take them prisoner but people [the special constables] were unwilling to take them on at close quarters. Perhaps it is as well no attempts were made, for a great multitude of the townspeople outside were their friends.'[11]

Colonel Silvester was in the presence of felonious activity so as a magistrate he was obliged, legally and morally, to read the Riot Act to acquaint the rioters of the consequences of their actions. Colonel Silvester, thereupon, quite courageously, walked alone amongst the loom-breakers. He first called for silence – as he was required by law to do. Not surprisingly, his call was totally ignored. Colonel Silvester, however, formally read the words of the Riot Act. As he ended his reading with 'God Save the King!', the loom-breakers paused long enough to give a mocking three hearty cheers for His Majesty. By this time they had been at their task for over half an hour.

Ellison and his special constables were not inclined to otherwise interfere. They were content to watch from the doorway. Blades was satisfied to observe Butterworth busily cutting cloth with a piece of wood broken from a loom. There then began a period of high farce. Colonel Silvester, in a ludicrous attempt at restoring order, ordered the special constables to take the names of the loom-breakers.

'They began to ask the names of the most prominent actors, but received, not unexpectedly, only a number of aliases. Amongst which was one given by a little fellow, who being asked his name, replied, 'Hammering Jack'. It was a very appropriate one, for he was at the time using a large hammer to some purpose amongst the looms.'[12] One employee of the factory did, however, have a small success. As one man attempted to destroy a gas-bracket, the employee 'remonstrated with him and he left it alone'.[13]

When the captains were satisfied the destruction was complete they ordered another three hearty cheers and all turned to leave the building. At this point the mood of the whole affair changed. Up to now the frame of mind of the mob was one of simple, quiet determination to destroy the powerlooms. Up to now only the eighty powerlooms and two factory doors had suffered. No threats, no violence to any person had been offered.

As the mob came outside, Ellison and Leaver, inexplicably, in spite of the previous decision not to, tried to close the outer door and trap the loom-breakers inside. Chambers and the rest quickly broke them open again and a fierce fight began. Ellison grabbed one man by the collar and tried to pull him aside to arrest him. Chambers and some others, however, punched and kicked Ellison on the head and body until he let the man go. Leaver went to help Ellison but he was no match and he was immediately felled by a punch in the face. Special constables tried to arrest others. In the melee one rioter had his jaw broken.

Ellison and Leaver's action enraged the crowd of onlookers and stones began to fly. Colonel Silvester and his group retreated inside the factory as scores of onlookers threw stones at the special constables gathered round the factory gate. The whole street was in uproar. As more joined in, women gathered stones from the roadside, filled their aprons and ran to supply the stonethrowers with fresh ammunition. During the uproar, Chambers, Aspden, Sharples, Butterworth and the rest of the 'outsiders' ran off, back towards Tockholes and home.

A cry rang out that the cavalry, on their way from Blackburn, were at Botany Bay, so once again the fleeing mob kept to the fields. Again passing Cabbage Hall and Gorse Hall they disappeared into the network of secluded lanes as quickly as they came. By the time a troop of 1st King's Dragoon Guards made their belated arrival in Water Street (it was now mid-afternoon), the crowd there had also disappeared. All that was left were eighty shattered powerlooms, the smashed doors and windows and a few constables with bruises and broken heads.[14]

The destruction of the Water Street powerlooms was the final shot of the loom-breakers' campaign in east Lancashire. It was all over bar the retribution of the law. Time had run out. Even as they plotted at Tockholes the captains knew their early arrest was certain. Even as they fought the special constables at Water Street they knew it was the end. It is a measure of their determination and belief in their 'cause', however illogical to others, that they continued to that end.

This came to Chambers, Aspden and Sharples two days later when they were arrested, examined by the magistrates and despatched to Lancaster Castle. The luckless Butterworth stayed at home, awaiting the inevitable, until 13th May. Chambers, at the age of fifty-five, in time faced the rigours of transportation. Aspden, Sharples and Butterworth were lucky to be only gaoled in Lancaster Castle.

Although Chorley and east Lancashire were now quiet, later in the evening of Thursday there was an outbreak of disorder in Manchester, hitherto quiet all week. At six o'clock a crowd estimated at five to six thousand gathered in St. George's Field. Archibald Prentice, a Manchester printer and proprietor of the *Manchester Gazette*, stood on the fringe of the crowd.

The meeting was addressed by two men – strangers to Prentice – who clearly took their cue from the events in east Lancashire. 'We urge the necessity of standing firmly to each other to destroy the powerlooms which are the cause of your unemployment. No military force can withstand you if you assert your rights like men!'[15] As a large group in the crowd roared its approval, Prentice saw a local man, Jonathon Hodgkins, 'whose name was pretty well known by his plain and untutored eloquence', succeed in getting a hearing from the noisy crowd. Hodgkins expressed his sympathy with their distress and appealed for patience. 'No one can relieve distress by attacking provision shops and destroying looms. You would only suffer the swords of the military and not the slightest alteration would be made to the system of which you complain. The parish is bound to support you. If not you can appeal to the magistrates who would order your relief. Until all the legal resources are tried, every attempt by other means is illegal.'[16]

Prentice could see many were unconvinced – no one had faith in parish officers or magistrates. As Hodgkins urged the crowd to refrain from violence, Prentice decided to speak to the crowd himself. He pushed his way to the front. 'I got on a high pile of bricks and what with the insecurity of my footing and my apprehension, I did not feel I was standing firmly on my legs. Some threatening cries were uttered, but were met by cries of 'Hear him'.[17]

Prentice told the meeting of the money being subscribed for the relief of distress – that £8,000 had already been expended; that a new subscription fund had just raised £1,000; that the King had sent a £1,000 each to Blackburn, Manchester and Macclesfield; that there was ready for distribution 20,000 lbs of bacon and more than 100,000 lbs of meal.

'The announcement of this liberality was favourably received and I begged and prayed that as working men of Manchester they would respect the reputation they had for exemplary patience and would continue to manifest the same disposition. I asked them to disperse peaceably.'[18]

Perhaps half the crowd were convinced and made their way home. The remainder, however, unswayed by argument or pleas, went by different routes to Ancoats, first to J. Kennedy's cotton factory in Great Ancoats Street. For a time the mob shouted and jeered at those inside but made no attempt to attack the building. They moved to Clarke and Harbottle's factory in nearby Pollard Street. A volley of stones broke all their windows. The mob, on seeing men inside with firearms, decided to leave for Mr Hugh Beaver's factory in Jersey Street.

Here the mob was bolder and the factory was entered. Two thousand pieces of woven calico, some dressing machines and possibly some powerlooms were destroyed by half a dozen small fires which quickly got out of control.

Whilst this was happening, another part of the mob broke all the windows of Mottershead's cotton factory in Miller Street near the town centre.[19] At Messrs Clegg, Norris and Company's factory nearby in Long Millgate, however, loyal employees inside fired warning shots over the heads of the crowd. The mob left after breaking many of the windows.

The main riot was at Beaver's in Jersey Street. The town's regular constables, helped by hastily recruited special constables, arrived at Long Millgate too late but went on to Jersey Street. Here the mob was so big, the fire so advanced, they could do nothing. A troop of Queen's Bays and a company of Riflemen arrived at ten o'clock, by which time the factory was burnt out. The mob, after a rampage lasting two and a half hours, quickly dispersed. Street patrols by Bays and Riflemen all night and the following day finally repressed the disturbances and Manchester remained quiet.

The final, far ranging, ripples of the Thursday disturbances reached the tiny Yorkshire village of Gargrave in Craven, near Skipton. There a mob of handloom weavers from Addingham, some eight miles away, destroyed twenty newly installed powerlooms at Mr Joseph Mason's Middle Green Mill in the centre of the village. The cavalry, based at Skipton, 'compassionately' kept their distance.[20]

Friday and Saturday were quiet throughout the county. On Sunday morning, 30th April, however, a mob from Rochdale entered J. Clegg's cotton factory at Higher Crompton, near the village of Shaw. They also visited Messrs Milne and Travis's factory at Luzley Brook, Royton. This time the military were ready. On that day William Rowbottom, an Oldham handloom weaver, noted in his diary; 'The Oldham cavalry [Yeomanry] was called and the Cheshire Yeomanry arrived from Manchester with some flying artillery who eventually dispersed the mobbers'.[21] No damage was done at Luzley Brook but twenty-eight powerlooms were destroyed at Higher Crompton.[22]

The following day, May Day, the mob was out in Oldham. William Rowbottom recorded; 'They assembled in very large numbers at Greenacres Moor and attended several Oldham factories, particularly Collinge and Lancashire's, but the presence of the military and the formidable appearance of the mill much intimidated the rioters that they decamped. An attack was then anticipated on a mill in Oldham but the mill was put in such a state of defence it would have been madness to attack it. The Oldham Yeomanry and the constables much exerted themselves. In the end the mob dispersed without doing any damage'.[23]

At Oldham, as in Manchester, the manufacturers were quite prepared to defend their property. The *Blackburn Mail*, in a reference to Collinge and Lancashire, said, 'The factory proprietors provided themselves with firearms and also with a large quantity of stones on the top of it [the factory]'.[24] The lessons of east Lancashire had been learned. It was also clear to the mob that the factories of Manchester and Oldham were too big, too well defended. After May Day there were no more 'riotous assemblies'. So ended the worst week of riot and civil disorder in the history of the county.

Most people now believed that loom-breaking could not solve the distress in the manufacturing districts. Only charity was left. At least the employees of Collinge and Lancashire's factory thought so. By 21st June 1826 they collected £23 for the Distress Relief Fund.[25]

CHAPTER EIGHT

Dispute and Dishonour

MEANWHILE the lack of understanding between the Reverend Gray and Colonel Kearney at Haslingden led to recriminations and acrimony. On Wednesday, 26th April, Colonel Kearney sent his report of the events at Haslingden and Chatterton by special messenger to Major General Harris at the War Office. He laid the blame for the escape of the prisoners at the New Inn squarely on the Reverend Gray. 'At Haslingden sixty [clearly an exaggerated number] prisoners had been made until liberated by Gray.' Colonel Kearney's final sentence condemned the Reverend Gray: 'I should not acquit myself to the Public did I not notice the apparent incapacity of W. Gray, the Magistrate of Haslingden, or at least indifference to the disclosure of his duties'.[1]

Colonel Kearney made the row public in letters to the *Manchester Guardian* on 29th April and the *Manchester Mercury* on 2nd May. He criticized the Reverend Gray for not responding quickly enough to requests from the military for help at Helmshore and Rawtenstall. Colonel Kearney claimed when the prisoners arrived at the New Inn he stated to the Reverend Gray it was his (Kearney's) duty to deliver them to the civil power as he had no right to detain them in custody. He continued 'Gray refused to receive them, saying he could do nothing with them. Some of the mob, hearing our dispute, immediately attacked the house [the New Inn], broke all the windows and rescued the prisoners. The soldiers were without instructions and undecided how to act. I demanded from Gray whether I was to repel the attack by firing on the people. Gray said I must not on any account, adding he would prefer to see the prisoners go and they were subsequently allowed to escape.'[2]

Colonel Kearney angrily concluded, 'The escape confirmed a belief previously impressed on the people [when Gray and the cavalry were late at Middle Mill] that the magistrate and military regarded their proceedings with a favourable eye and this encouraged them further'.[3]

A week later the Reverend Gray replied to Colonel Kearney's 'mis-statement of facts', and placed the blame back onto the military. He described how he waited for the cavalry before leaving for Middle Mill and arriving there without them. He then returned to Haslingden. 'On arrival at the New Inn with the prisoners caught by W. Turner's men the cavalry, without any sanction from me and even without my knowledge, dismounted and all (quite thirty in number) but eight or nine, including officers, went to their respective quarters in other parts of the town. It was quite impossible to retain the prisoners in custody.'[4]

Lawrence Shaw, the Magistrates' Clerk, supported the Reverend Gray. In a letter to the *Blackburn Mail* on 3rd May he claimed that if the soldiers had attacked the mob as requested by Colonel Kearney they (the soldiers) would have been sacrificed. He added, 'The soldiers exhibited throughout the whole day great forbearance and an evident disinclination to act against the populace. The conduct of the Magistrate has met with the unqualified approbation of his fellow-townsmen, some of whom implored him to release the prisoners as the whole town was in danger'.

The row simmered on through May. An anonymous letter in the *Blackburn Mail* on 10th May, brought out the second dispute between the Reverend Gray and Colonel Kearney. This claimed Colonel Kearney, on 26th April, 'treated with contempt' a request by Benjamin Whitehead for military help to prevent an expected attack on the family mill at Rawtenstall. 'Although the magistrate urged upon him the absolute necessity of despatch, still the Colonel lingered.' After waiting half an hour the Reverend Gray decided, because the road was too bad and steep, to walk to Rawtenstall, two miles away.[5]

The letter described how the Reverend Gray, accompanied by Whitehead and Shaw, stopped to await the military on high ground half a mile from the mill. Meanwhile they saw the mob at the mill. 'Three quarters of an hour later a troop of cavalry advanced along the road as if attending a funeral. On arrival Colonel Kearney addressed Mr Gray in a language and style which aroused the indignation of everyone present. 'This, I suppose', continued the writer, 'was a "ruse de guerre" by the gallant Colonel in order to anticipate Mr Gray's natural indignation. The mob had by this time destroyed the machinery and the detachment quietly followed them, as if covering their operations.'[6]

Lawrence Shaw kept up the pressure on behalf of the Reverend Gray. The same week a group describing themselves as 'some of the principal inhabitants of Haslingden' sent a memorial to the Home Secretary expressing their approbation of the Reverend Gray's conduct on 25th and 26th April. When the *Manchester Guardian* received from Lawrence Shaw a copy of the memorial for publication, the editor confessed, 'we hardly know how to reconcile this with facts communicated to us by some of the powerloom manufacturers'.[7] In spite of these allusions William Turner and Benjamin and David Whitehead had signed the memorial. Colonel Kearney evidently did not have the sympathy of even those whose looms had been destroyed.

The letters angered Colonel Kearney. He felt they imputed dishonour on himself and the Queen's Bays. His letter to the *Manchester Mercury* on 19th May strongly criticized the Reverend Gray, firstly for walking to Rawtenstall, 'after dwelling so much on the necessity for expedition'; secondly for leaving the military at Haslingden with no instructions; and thirdly for not leaving them a guide to Rawtenstall. (This last hardly valid. With Rawtenstall but two miles away any citizen could have directed them.) Colonel Kearney ended with a barb, 'I will merely add that not more than two hours after Mr Gray left the troop at Rawtenstall a detachment of Queen's Bays was called out at Chatterton, headed by a magistrate on horseback, and under my orders. That magistrate did not, I believe, find the military tardy in their duty'.[8]

The Reverend Gray replied in the same newspaper on 30th May. He made his position quite clear. 'When I set out for Rawtenstall not a soldier was visible although ample time had elapsed after my requisition for assistance for them to have mustered three times over. The only concern expressed at my going on foot was my friend's wonderment that I should have condescended to go at all.' In a pointed and unfair

William Turner of Helmshore, born 1794, died 1852. The owner of Middle Mill, Helmshore. The original painting is in the possession of the Lancashire County Museum Service, Higher Mill Museum, Helmshore.

remark, because the Queen's Bays' conduct at Chatterton was exemplary, the Reverend Gray concluded, 'If Colonel Kearney fancies he can perceive anything of a redeeming character in the transactions at Chatterton, I say all is well. I do not envy him his Bays'.[9]

The final word belonged to the Reverend Gray. On 31st May he wrote to the Earl of Derby with the news the Home Secretary had accepted the memorial in his support from the 'principal inhabitants of Haslingden'. Colonel Kearney could only yield. He withdrew his report charging the Reverend Gray with incapacity and indifference.[10] In more generous mood than formerly, the Reverend Gray confessed he had given orders to the military to go to the scene of the disturbances with all exertion but did not consider his own presence necessary. (This explains why twice he waited before, reluctantly, going to the scene.)

The Reverend Gray explained to Lord Derby that the military were called to Middle Mill only in consequence of the prisoners being taken by Turner's workpeople who were under the command of the constables of Haslingden and Musbury. (This explains the 'late' arrival of the military.) He continued, 'When they [the prisoners] were placed in the Long Room at the New Inn they were under the direction of the Constables. The military were there to prevent the prisoners being rescued by the mob'.

After everything the Reverend Gray still remained unsure of his responsibilities as a magistrate. He ended his letter by asking, 'If a Constable can charge the military to come to his aid in an emergency should a magistrate do the same?'[11] He must have known he could.

The war of words indicated two things. Firstly, both the civil and military authorities at local level at least, were guilty of indecision and lack of awareness of their duties. Secondly, it seems neither authority was anxious to be at the scene of a riot at the same time as the rioters.[12] Each also blamed the other for not doing so. The 'Chatterton Fight' resolved this problem – afterwards the rioters were left strictly alone until they had exhausted themselves.

One bright light shone in an unhappy situation. Colonel Kearney was very fortunate the Reverend Gray refused him permission to fire at the crowd at the New Inn. If the troops had fired, the 'Chatterton Fight' may well have been eclipsed by a 'Haslingden Massacre'.

In spite of the unseemly arguments the military forces performed their laborious and irksome duties extremely well. Quelling civil disorder was fraught with all sorts of political dangers unknown in foreign compaigns. (Colonel Kearney now knew this all too well.) Neither were medals to be won. The Home Office, however, was clear on one main point. There should be no employment of troops until the necessity was absolutely clear. The military was the last, not the first, line of defence. Troops were to be summoned to rioting, not in anticipation of it.

The origins and background of the troops themselves was a considerable factor. The Queen's Bays' disinclination to act against the populace', for example, was understandable. The troopers, recruited from the poor rural areas of the South West and the Midlands, themselves probably took the 'King's Shilling' to escape their own poverty. They had an innate sympathy for the poor, starving wretches they stood by and watched. To see fellow-Englishmen, no matter how strangely and roughly spoken and mannered, driven by desperation to riot could bring only pity from most private soldiers – and their officers.

Billeted as they were in public houses, and their horses kept in requisitioned stables and barns, the military lived amongst a population who were neither 'enemies' nor 'friends'. All the troops, with the single exception of one rifleman at Chatterton, did their duty with tremendous restraint. Unfortunately a bad situation was made worse because of the friction between the military and the civil authorities. This friction highlighted the invidious role of the military and the lack of a cohesive system of law enforcement in these growing industrial towns.

The Reverend Gray's inexperience as a magistrate must have contributed to his actions. Appointed only in January 1826 at thirty-four, his calling and instincts hardly qualified him to take charge in time of riot. In Lancashire, as in each county in England, the Lord Lieutenant of the County, with his Deputy, was responsible for public order. In practice individual magistrates, as Justices of the Peace, carried the burden. For many generations the 'know-everyone' system of crime detection had operated. Petty criminals were apprehended only when members of the public informed upon them. The Reverend Gray's Commission of the Peace empowered him to bring minor offenders to justice and, if they refused to be bound over to keep the peace, to imprison them. In 1826 Haslingden, in common with most small towns in Lancashire had no gaol. Convicted prisoners therefore went to the Preston House of Correction. Most of the Reverend Gray's offenders were concerned with abuses in weights and measures, and the sale of victuals, Sabbath-breaking (non-attendance at Church) and vagrancy. More serious felonies were sent to the assizes for trial. None of this would have demanded much of the Reverend Gray.

The riots overturned all this. In an unparalleled situation the Reverend Gray became solely responsible for restoring civil order. Only he could call on military forces, regular or yeomanry, for assistance. Only he could enrol special constables, issue warrants for arrest, do everything necessary to detect and detain suspects. He, as magistrate, had sole responsibility to uphold the law. Neither military, parish constables, special constables, nor private individuals such as manufacturers, could do anything except at his direction. It was a heavy burden.

In small towns such as Haslingden a magistrate's job was lonely, indeed dangerous at best. In time of riot the Reverend Gray needed to act against his own parishioners, amongst whom he had lived since 1813. He had the task of sending for trial men and women he knew personally, for offences he knew the penalty could be death. He had married Mary and George Hindle in 1818. He christened their baby daughter in 1819. He buried James Lund, son of a respected shopkeeper, killed at Chatterton. He knew the rioters and could see with his own eyes many of his parishioners were on the verge of starvation. He also knew he had to live in the town with the consequences of his actions, whereas the military would move on elsewhere. Little wonder the Reverend Gray acted indecisively at times.

The events at Helmshore, Haslingden and Rawtenstall proved the local policing system totally inadequate. Although it was the duty of every citizen to be a special constable, if called upon to do so, not everyone had the ability or the desire. Significantly, most, if not all, the special constables involved were employees of the aggrieved manufacturers. It is perfectly possible some who arrested rioters at Helmshore were not special constables, but simply acted on behalf of William Turner. There is no evidence of the Reverend Gray, as a magistrate, directing army pensioners to act as special constables as was his right under an 1820 Act of Parliament.[13] The

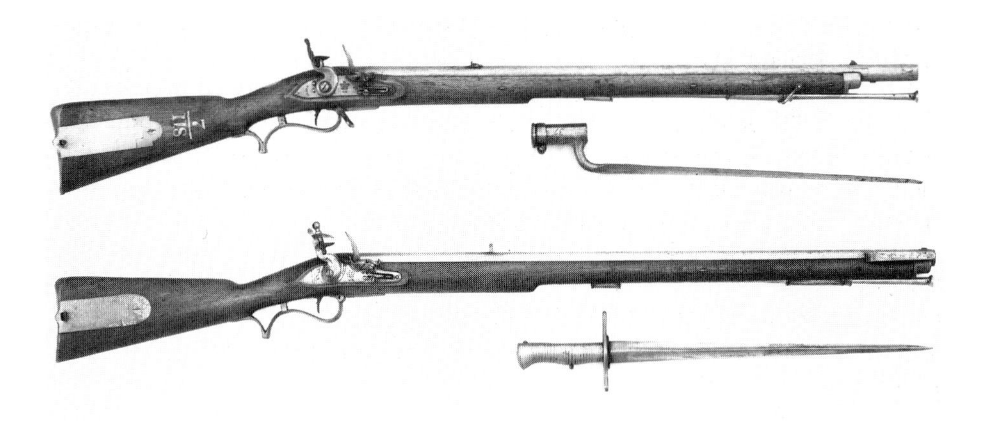

Baker rifles, with bayonets of the type used at Chatterton. Top: Baker rifle converted to take socket bayonet, 1815–23. Bottom: Baker rifle of the final pattern adapted, 1823.

local 'citizen', as such, remained a bystander in a conflict between rioters and manufacturers.

In the event, the Reverend Gray and his fellow magistrates waited fourteen years before Peel's 1830 'Constabulary Act' appointed regular, paid, uniformed police officers. For example, a permanent force of one sergeant and two constables came to Haslingden only in 1840.

Colonel Kearney and Major Eckersley however had concerns other than the Reverend Gray. The inquest on the victims of the 'Chatterton Fight' opened on Thursday 27th April at the Horse and Jockey Inn, in Edenfield. The Coroner, Mr Thomas Ferrand, a Rochdale attorney, immediately excluded the press and public. The press – the Manchester newspapers – vigorously opposed this. As the circumstances of Whatacre's death was common knowledge, they suspected a cover-up between the coroner and the military.

The newspapers had long memories. This was not the first time they and Ferrand had clashed. In September 1819, when opening the inquest at Oldham on John Lees, who died three weeks after being wounded at 'Peterloo' (St. Peter's Field, Manchester), Ferrand ordered that notes of the proceedings were not to be taken until after the inquest. The newspapers suspected he wished to prevent any adverse publicity about those in authority, particularly the magistrates and military present at Peterloo. Seven years later Ferrand again denied the press the freedom to report a matter of public concern.

Tempers were heated. Major Watkins warned Peel, 'a bad feeling prevails against the military and I regret to say this feeling is not confined to the lower orders'.[14] The 'lower orders' expressed their feelings shortly after the 'Chatterton Fight' when the crowd continually stoned the detachment of riflemen present at the loom-breaking at Hutchinson's factory at Woodhill, Bury. Their commanding officer Captain Goldfrap, was knocked from his horse by a large stone and badly hurt. Most of the riflemen were also hit by stones.

More proof of bad feeling came in an article in the *Bolton Chronicle*. This denounced the shooting at Chatterton. Lieutenant Colonel Bunbury complained indignantly of the 'unjustifiable criticism'. 'I have no hesitation in declaring the article to be totally false and a wilful misrepresentation of the facts . . . I have every reason to be satisfied with the conduct of every individual of this regiment employed on this distressing occasion.'[15] Similar letters of protest went from Colonel Kearney to Lieutenant General Byng and from Major Eckersley to the *Blackburn Mail*.

This outraged reaction to criticism of the 60th Regiment covered up an uneasiness amongst the military command about the likely consequences of Whatacre's death. Major Watkins attended the first day of the inquest. He reported to Peel. 'I viewed the evidence heard [that is, that given by Mrs Upton, Mr Hollis, Mr Leech and particularly John Coupe] as giving impressions most unfavourable as to the conduct of the military at Chatterton.' Watkins continued: '. . . to rescue the honour of His Majesty's troops, which I verily believe to be most unjustifiably assailed, I strongly urged the Coroner to adjourn the inquest until Tuesday May 2nd. This would afford time for the examination of witnesses who could speak as to the most important facts touching the melancholy catastrophe that day.' He optimistically concluded: 'I am now satisfied that on the whole of the evidence the witnesses will be satisfactory'.[16]

In the mind of Major Watkins the inquest verdicts should be 'proper' ones. The inquest was to be 'fixed' in favour of the military. Major Watkins was not, however, entirely successful. Although evidence was given of riflemen firing at people running away, in general the conduct of the military whilst dispersing the rioters was deemed proper. (Alone amongst newspapers, the *Manchester Guardian* agreed.)

Verdicts of 'justifiable homicide' were brought on James Ashworth, James Lord, Richard Lund and John Rothwell, and 'accidental death' on Mary Simpson. The verdict on John Whatacre, however, was, 'wilful murder by a soldier of the 60th Regiment, name unknown'. Three jurors, including the foreman Edmund Sagar of Edenfield, dissented. The verdict was given in spite of John Coupe telling the inquest he could identify at any time the rifleman who shot Whatacre.

The newspapers were determined to publish the story. A *Manchester Mercury* reporter even approached jurors (unsuccessfully) pretending he was a government official preparing a report. After the inquest, of course, jurors and witnesses spoke to the press. John Coupe's evidence damned the 60th Regiment. He told the *Manchester Mercury* what he told the inquest. 'He [the rifleman] had thick lips and a distinct mark on his face.' He added, 'The same soldier swore before a magistrate in Bury that I was in the mob at Chatterton at eleven o'clock, but I have proof I was in Bury at that time'.[17]

The military were determined to obstruct justice. Edmund Sagar (who generally supported the military and hinted his doubts about Coupe's evidence) nevertheless alleged that Major Schoede, of the 60th Regiment, refused a constable's request to muster the riflemen so Coupe could identify the man who shot Whatacre. Sagar asserted Major Schoede refused on the grounds he would muster them only when called upon by a 'proper authority'. Sagar added that Colonel Kearney declared at the inquest the men could be inspected 'at any time the coroner might think'.[18] This inspection never took place.

Back Pleasant Street, Haslingden, with Higher Deardengate beyond. Formerly known as Club Row, the houses were built for handloom weavers. Pleasant Street, Lonsdale Street and Hindle Street (built by and named after Mary Hindle's father-in-law) formed a sizeable handloom weavers' colony in the town. Note the raised entrances to give height to the cellar loomshop.

Mr W. Dawson

It is clear the military made no serious attempt to identify and detain the murderer of John Whatacre. The given description, plus a known appearance before a local magistrate could easily be checked in a twenty strong detachment, with or without Coupe's assistance. The military, however, chose not to, in spite of the 60th Regiment's own code of conduct and military discipline: 'The smallest inhumanity towards an enemy who in action may surrender himself, or towards an innocent peasantry will be most severely punished'.[19]

At Chatterton the 'smallest inhumanity' was balanced against murder (confirmed by a jury), using force to break into a house and abusing men, women and children. The 'innocent peasantry' were fellow-countrymen.

The 60th Regiment left Lancashire secretly within a week or so of the inquest. They went to Portsmouth, where they remained until December. They then embarked for Portugal as part of a force to assist the Portugese against the threat of invasion by Spain. The Regiment stayed out of England for at least five years.[20] (Ironically, Sergeant William Hamilton stayed behind to give evidence at the trial at Lancaster in August of Henry Melling who threw the stone which injured Captain Goldfrap.)

It is open to conclusion that the 60th Regiment was moved – at a time when military resources were thinly stretched – to mollify public opinion. The Regiment paid a heavy price for the actions of one or two riflemen. Neither the military authorities, who sought to arrange 'satisfactory' evidence and broke their own rules of conduct, nor the civil authorities who colluded with the military and did not press for positive identification, came out of the affair with any honour.

The last word came from Thomas Ferrand. On June 5th 1826 he answered some query from the Home Office. From his letter it is evident that neither he nor the Home Office knew until after the event that those of the 60th Regiment quartered in Bury had left the area. Ferrand replied, 'I can at once say the march of the Rifle Regiment alluded to [in a previous letter] need not be delayed a day for the purpose of now offering John Coop [Coupe] an opportunity to identify the soldier who shot Whatacre . . . Coop is but a poor cotton weaver and it is obvious he hath no means of going about to look for the soldier, or to any magistrate or of interfering with any proceedings . . . moreover, I am credibly informed that such part of the Regiment as attended at Aitken's Mill and all who were quartered in Bury have left the county some weeks ago.'

Ferrand left the Home Office in no doubt about one thing. He ended, 'I would however beg leave to observe that after having had considerable experience in the office of Coroner on these troublesome occasions, it is my humble opinion that soldiers of this description are the least proper choice that can be used in quelling riots and disturbances of this nature.'[21]

Least proper choice or no, the civil and military authorities succeeded in playing down the 'Chatterton Fight'. At the trial at Lancaster Assizes in August 1826 there was no mention of Chatterton. Of the twenty-eight arrested at Bury after Chatterton, only six – three arrested at Summerseat and three at Woodhill – appeared in the dock. Ann Ingham, who was kept under observation at Dearden Clough an hour before Chatterton and at Waterbarn an hour after, was also in the dock. No mention of Chatterton.

Sixty-nine men and women in all were sentenced or acquitted for their part in the riots. Only one, William Barnes (who did not appear until the March 1827 assizes), was charged with an offence at Chatterton. He was acquitted of breaking windows.

CHAPTER NINE

The Quiet Which Prevails

'THE same quiet which prevails here also happily exists at Clitheroe, Chorley, Bolton and Preston,' announced the *Blackburn Mail* on 10th May. The authorities, civil and military, finished with watching powerlooms broken and property damaged, moved in on those responsible.

Even before the 'Chatterton Fight', Blackburn constables, with the military, began to arrest alleged rioters. The method of arrest was deliberate and calculated to put fear into the population. Small detachments of cavalry or infantry, with special constables appointed by the high constable as 'spies and scouts' arrived in the dead of night at the home of an alleged or suspected rioter. If not opened quickly the door was broken down with staves or clubs, the cottage would fill with soldiers and constables and the terrified occupants – men, women, children all – pulled from their beds.

With identification confirmed and a hasty reading of the magistrate's warrant of arrest the alleged rioter was bundled outside into the care of waiting armed soldiers. If lucky, he or she rode in a chaise or open cart. If not, he or she walked to the nearest town lock-up to await examination by a magistrate.

In the early hours of Wednesday, 26th April, soldiers and special constables, fortified against the night chill by an official issue of rum and brandy, made three arrests in Blackburn, one in Livesey (James Aspden) and one in Samlesbury (Simeon Wright). The prisoners were held in the Old Bull Inn until examined by magistrates Charles Whittaker and James Hindle. The six men then went by chaise, with an escort of cavalry, to Preston House of Correction for further examination.

In Rossendale the same night, in a carefully planned move, nine persons were arrested by special constables and 1st King's Dragoon Guards specially brought over from Burnley. The nine were examined and charged by magistrates Lawrence Halstead of Burnley and James Whittaker of Rossendale. The cavalry escorted the prisoners to Burnley Barracks, from whence they were taken, in irons, in an open cart, to Lancaster later in the day.

Two nights later soldiers and constables brought James Shorrock of Pickup Bank and Thomas Sharples of Tockholes to Blackburn Sessions House for examination by the magistrates. With an escort of 1st King's Dragoon Guards the two went by chaise through Preston's curious crowds to Lancaster Castle. They were followed on Saturday by two men and one woman from Belthorn.

William Turner, David Whitehead, and magistrate James Whittaker together worked out a plan to deal with the rest of the Rossendale rioters. James Whittaker was both determined and well-organised. On Saturday 29th April, he wrote to David Whitehead: 'I understand that you are gone to Haslinden [*sic*] to arrange with Mr Turner respecting the operations that are to be taken against the Rioters. I am very anxious that prompt and decisive measures should be immediately taken – to crush the evil in the bud; Mr Richard Shaw [the Burnley Magistrates' Clerk] and I have been consulting upon another plan in the event of your not being able to provide means to put in execution the plan determin'd upon yesterday at your office . . . if your Party are of the opinion that you cannot take up all the Persons accus'd to'morrow night, I would undertake that the Bacup Constables provided with a party of Horse (which in case of need I will send to Burnley for) shall take up the Persons resident in the neighbourhood of Newchurch and Rawtenstall tomorrow evening (Sunday).'[1] (It is probable the Rossendale constables were either too well known or simply unreliable.) The offer was accepted – five more from Rossendale were arrested on Sunday.

On the same day David and Benjamin Whitehead attended a specially convened meeting of the Rossendale Society for the Prosecution of Felons at the Black Dog Inn at Newchurch. The Society was formed in 1812 by manufacturers resolved to prosecute those who committed a crime against any member of the Society. Amongst those present was Samuel Lord who named to the Committee those he had shadowed during the riots. David Whitehead also named George Heys and Thomas Ashworth. Thomas Kay named John Ingham and James Rostron. The Committee ordered that 'they be prosecuted at the expense of this Society and if afterwards any other persons should be discovered to have been implicated they also would be prosecuted'.[2] On Samuel Lord's 'lists' was, of course, Thomas Emmett.

In the early hours of May Day – by ancient tradition associated with merry-making to celebrate the beginning of summer – a detachment of Queen's Bays escorted Samuel Lord to Thomas Emmett's cottage at Holden Wood. Samuel Lord, who had kept Emmett under observation all afternoon the previous Wednesday, identified him to the officer in charge. Emmett was arrested and for the second time in five days taken under escort to the New Inn at Haslingden. Mary Hindle also was taken from her home in Club Street, Haslingden, not five hundred yards from the New Inn.

In the 'Long Room', the courthouse in the New Inn, the Reverend William Gray heard evidence from William Turner Clegg, Timothy Jones and Samuel Lord. Clegg and Jones identified Emmett, with the most damning evidence coming from Lord. Gray made out four depositions against Emmett giving details of his alleged activities at Helmshore, Waterbarn, Tunstead and Bacup. Four times Gray asked Emmett for any reason why he should not be committed. Four times Emmett denied breaking looms.

Nothing is known of Mary Hindle's examination by Gray save Harry Hey's later evidence of his role of watcher and marker for his employer William Turner. He would almost certainly tell Gray how he stood by Mary Hindle's side outside Middle Mill. He almost certainly produced the material cut from her dress as proof. Mary Hindle admitted being in the crowd but denied breaking looms.

Gray's examination took most of the morning. News of the arrests, meanwhile, had spread. A large crowd, sympathetic to Emmett and Hindle, again gathered outside the New Inn, its windows only just repaired from the attack the previous Tuesday. Emmett and Hindle, now remanded in custody, entered the open cart which was to take them, in leg irons, to Lancaster Castle. Special constables, appointed by Gray, held back the angry crowd and cleared a way for the horses of the escort of Queen's Bays. The special constables shielded both cart and escort until they moved off and left the confines of the town.

There began the six hour, thirty-five mile, journey to Lancaster. All prisoners and escorts from Haslingden, Rossendale and Burnley travelled via Whalley, Mitton, Longridge, Garstang, then Lancaster. This route, through the quiet countryside of the Ribble Valley bordering on the wild fells and bare pastures of Longridge Fell and the Forest of Bowland, avoided for security reasons most sizable towns. Towns where the mood of many was still uncertain.

In Blackburn Sessions House magistrates Charles Whittaker and John Hindle worked steadily examining and committing the accused. Four prisoners left Blackburn for Lancaster via Preston on Wednesday 3rd May.[3] The same day three men and one woman from Newchurch and three men and two women from Rawtenstall were arrested and sent to Lancaster from Bacup. Three men, Isaac Hindle of Oswaldtwistle, Richard Entwistle of Blackburn and Alexander Norris of Newfield, Haslingden, went from Blackburn on 5th May. Six more, including Betty Howorth of Pickup Bank, Margaret Yates of Oswaldtwistle and Mary Marsden of Haslingden, were examined but held in Blackburn lock-up before their journey to Lancaster on 6th May.

After the riots James Chambers fled to Manchester where he was quickly detained by the local constables. John Kay, Blackburn's constable, accompanied by an assistant, went by coach to bring him to the Sessions House to be similarly examined. On Saturday 13th May the unfortunate Edward Houghton, wounded in the neck and mouth at Houghton's factory on 24th April, was brought by sedan chair from his home to the Sessions House. On the same day Robert Butterworth was brought in from his home in Brinscall. Later both men were sent to Preston House of Correction for further examination.

By this date most of the identifiable rioters were in custody. The reign of terror had its intended effect. Many rioters – and even those on the fringe of unlawful activities, mere spectators – fled their homes. Some hid in worked-out coal pits and quarries on the moors, fed at night with what little they had, by family and friends. Some vanished for weeks, hiding first in one house, then another, harried always by the threat of betrayal. Others left the area, some never to return. Even the innocent were affected. One Harry Halstead was forced to accompany the rioters when they demanded hammers and crowbars from the Haslingden quarry where he worked. He fled from Chatterton and after living rough on the moors eventually travelled to Halifax, where, too frightened to risk returning, he settled permanently.[4]

John Fairbrother returned home to Rawtenstall on 8th September to be arrested by two special constables and taken to Lancaster. The constables were waylaid on their homeward journey and badly beaten up by 'a party of ruffians'.[5] The rioters clearly had sympathizers prepared to risk gaol. Also on 8th September Lawrence Rostron was seen in a Haslingden public house and arrested. Rostron's fellow-captain, George Heys, had fled first to Manchester, then Liverpool, and worked at his trade of navigator (navvy) at Liverpool Docks. In October, on a tip-off, John Kay went to Liverpool and arrested him.

Magistrates were busy the rest of May and during the summer. William Almond of Belthorn appeared before Charles Whittaker and John Hindle in Blackburn on 9th

May. John Hoyle and Lawrence Hardman were arrested at Bacup on 11th May. By 13th May over forty men and women were in the dungeons of Lancaster Castle. On 27th July special constable John Holden arrested Ann Entwistle at Darwen. Somehow she had eluded capture since her escape from the New Inn on 25th April. The arrests finally petered out on 13th November when William Rishton of Laneside, Haslingden was committed to Lancaster by the Reverend Gray.

Warehouse in Clayton Street, Blackburn, used by putters-out and handloom weavers. John Kay, Blackburn's constable, used the cellar as a temporary lock-up for offenders. This photograph was taken in 1953
Blackburn Library Local Studies Collection.

Not all those charged were immediately committed to Lancaster. Magistrates, at their discretion, could remand a person on bail to appear at the assizes – if someone could be found to stand surety. Magistrates could also discharge an arrested person if, in their opinion, there was no case to answer. Usually, however, in east Lancashire straight commitment was the rule. Magistrates in Bury, which suffered less from the riots perhaps, reacted differently. Of twenty-three arrested after the 'Chatterton Fight' and the attacks on Hamer's and Hutchinson's factories, only three went to Lancaster. The remainder were released on bail.

Some east Lancashire magistrates, inflamed by rumour and in fear of further outbreaks, denied natural justice to alleged and suspected rioters alike. With the honourable exception of the Reverend Gray there is no record of any magistrate formally asking an accused person if he or she had anything to say in his or her defence. Mere accusation often condemned a person to await trial in gaol. The arrests and methods used, however, worked well for the authorities. For the time being at least, it was thought, the riots were over.

The aggrieved manufacturers thoroughly approved. Their employees, as special constables, had helped deliver up the culprits. David Whitehead noted with deep satisfaction, 'The methods of arresting them in bed and taking them away at once put a terror upon the inhabitants and completely put a stop to the breaking of the powerlooms. This gave me to see the superiority of the power of the special constables to that of the military power in putting down the riots and for the conservation of the peace in the country.'[6]

Not all the inhabitants submitted easily to the inevitable injustices of a reign of terror. A Mr Grimshaw of Church awoke to a loud banging on his cottage door. An infantry subaltern demanded to see Mr Grimshaw's seventeen year old daughter,

Ellen. Mr Grimshaw asked what she had done to deserve a party of military at her door. The subaltern replied he was informed she could give information about the loom-breaking. The girl denied all knowledge but the officer insisted he was to take her to the magistrate at Blackburn immediately. The arresting party left only on Mr Grimshaw's promise to take her himself to the Sessions House at ten o'clock that morning, although he was certain she had nothing to do with the loom-breaking.

At ten o'clock Ellen Grimshaw again denied involvement in the riots. The magistrate had her placed in leg irons in the nearby house-cellar which temporarily served as a lock-up. She was released at two o'clock the following day when her distraught father returned with surety for bail until her appearance at the assizes. She never appeared – no charges were ever made.[7]

Although a surface quietness continued the military authorities were very apprehensive of trouble spreading from east Lancashire to Manchester. Military forces were stretched too thinly throughout the manufacturing districts for their peace of mind. It was impossible to ensure a garrison in every affected town and village. Magistrates in Clitheroe and Heywood were refused troops because none could be spared.[8]

Manufacturers were also anxious about protecting their property. To help overcome the problem Major Eckersley met during May several groups of manufacturers, firstly with David Whitehead and other Rossendale men, later with Bannister Eccles, William Fielden, William Throp and Mr Townley of Blackburn, then with Mr Ashton representing Ramsbottom manufacturers. The Blackburn group offered Major Eckersley money for arms and ammunition for the defence of their mills – an immediate sum on deposit, the remainder on delivery. Major Eckersley thought the manufacturers very nervous: 'Mr Throp seems very uneasy, Mr Ashton likewise'.[9]

Arrangements were made for manufacturers who wished to have arms to apply to their local magistrate who would requisition the military authorities. Notwithstanding Major Eckersley's worries about transporting arms and ammunition in open carts, with only a small military escort through villages likely to be 'hostile', the war *materiel* reached the manufacturers. Trusted employees were hurriedly instructed in musket and bayonet. Factories became armed camps.

At Rawtenstall David Whitehead had other problems. In early May, together with the Reverend Gray, he had a meeting with Major Watkins of the Bolton Yeomanry. 'Major Watkins told me, "There are nightly meetings in which they are laying a plot to burn your mill down and take your life. I shall know the exact time they have determined to do it, of which I will give you timely notice. I shall have plenty of disguised soldiers in the mill – arms and ammunition I will send up on the night. I will send you two true men, whom you may allow to come and go in the night as they wish. They will take care of you. It is not necessary to know their names. I shall have information of every meeting and everything said or done in them".'[10]

David Whitehead later recorded, 'The two were very civil men who remained at my home near a fortnight. They were out a great deal – night and day. They would not answer my questions but gave me to understand we bore a good character generally with the workpeople.'[11] He did receive an anonymous letter threatening his life but nothing came of it. Neither did he lose his mill by fire. David Whitehead had no more cause for concern.

It is difficult to assess how successful Major Watkins' spies had been. No further arrests were made. It is probable the mere suspicion spies were attending meetings caused any plotters to drop their plans. Whoever the spies were, it is difficult to see how they could infiltrate into the close and unique Rossendale communities. Accent alone would mark a man a stranger.[12]

It is equally difficult to see what prompted Major Watkins' actions in Rawtenstall. All the mob ringleaders were supposedly in Lancaster Castle. Many others had fled their homes. Even in the worst incidents the rioters had been careful to destroy only powerlooms – there was never any real threat to other property or human life. So why now when the riots were over? The use of soldiers disguised as civilians would never have been countenanced by the military authorities. There was precedent however in the use of civilian spies. Colonel Fletcher J.P. of the Bolton Yeomanry used them as spies and *agents provocateurs* in the 1811 disturbances in Bolton. It is highly probable, therefore, the Rossendale events owed much to Major Watkins' and, to some extent, David Whitehead's, overwrought imagination.

Spies and informers were, however, at large throughout Lancashire all summer. Major Eckersley reported to Lieutenant General Byng a nocturnal meeting of a thousand people on the moors near Padiham. 'The speakers said "Prepare yourselves! Lose no time in getting ready!" ' Major Eckersely enclosed with his report a 'favour'. 'The Colours are those of Cobbett at the Preston Election, although he was not spoken of, Sir Thomas Beevor was mentioned as a 'good gentleman'. No person could approach the meeting without such a distinguishing mark.'[13] It is perfectly possible Major Watkins' 'two true' men attended this meeting. Padiham is not five miles over the moors from Rawtenstall.

Similar reports from spies and informers attending meetings throughout the manufacturing districts alarmed the military authorities. Confirmation of a county-wide system of 'delegates' added to their fears. In July two mass meetings were held in St. George's Field in Manchester. 'If these assemblies are not stopped they may yet lead to great disorder. The system of delegates is carrying on actively. Some went today to Stockport, Macclesfield, Ashton, Hyde, Blackburn, Bolton and Bury – and no doubt to other places.'[14] In a note to Henry Hobhouse, two days later, Eckersley referred to a Blackburn delegate speaking of having 'plenty of arms and two cart-loads of ammunition in the town.'

Rhetoric this may have been, it alarmed the authorities. None of the meetings was interrupted by the watching constables or troops. Both were content to observe for the time being.

Colonel Fletcher of the Bolton Light Horse Yeomanry and a local magistrate, using his own long-established network of spies and informers, reported to Major Eckersley of delegate meetings at Haslingden and other places and that they had a central committee at Manchester. He added the improbable information of 'two Frenchmen and persons from Ireland whom they communicate with'.[15] This seemed unconvincing even to Major Eckersley as he commented to Lieutenant General Byng five days later: 'The two Frenchmen are neither seen nor heard'.[16] Colonel Fletcher also perhaps had an over-wrought imagination. Most of the rioters lived with poverty and semi-starvation all their lives. Outbreaks of unrest were part of their folk-memory. After two decades of suffering Lancashire people did not need any outsiders or radical leadership to protest their plight.

Not all magistrates were as keen on intrigue and plot as Colonel Fletcher. The timidity and caution of some magistrates annoyed and frustrated Major Eckersley.

He complained to Lieutenant General Byng of their general reluctance to interrupt meetings and apprehend the instigators, adding 'But in truth, I have seen neither a magistrate nor any kind of civil authority on business. If wanted they must be sought for – such I have always found to be the case.'[17]

This lack of common ground is perhaps understandable. As Colonel Fletcher and the military searched for intrigues and organisations bound on treason, most magistrates, with their close local knowledge, firmly believed there were none such. Only the military and the Government saw plots afoot.

As early as 16th April the Weavers Union Society of Blackburn sent a petition to the Home Secretary (see Appendix 5). Hobhouse immediately asked Major Eckersley to investigate the Society. Major Eckersley in turn asked the Reverend Whittaker, Vicar of Blackburn. The Reverend Whittaker, although never a friend of radicals or rioters replied, 'The Society has been in existence two years. I'm quite convinced their object is neither political nor connected with any combination system respecting the raising of wages. They levy certain sums amongst themselves to cover committee meetings. They have subscriptions amongst themselves for the relief of the fraternity who labour under any particular affliction. There are such benefit associations and sick clubs without end in this neighbourhood. They are entirely lawful.'[18]

As late as 19th August the Reverend Gray told Major Eckersley 'There is great distress in Haslingden but we receive great assistance from the London Committee. I do not perceive the smallest political feeling amongst the people and as to arming themselves, there is no such idea.'[19] Only then, and after the Lancaster Assizes, did the military authorities and the Government stop looking for revolutionaries, although rumours of moorland meetings and caches of pikes found here and there, abounded all the year.

From May onwards, though, troop reinforcements poured into Lancashire. The 58th Regiment (Rutlandshire) left Dublin on 4th May in two steam packets for Liverpool (the first time the regiment used steam packets as troop transports). The regiment force-marched to Wigan, then Bolton and Bury. A detachment of seven officers and one hundred and thirty-seven men arrived in Blackburn on 8th May.

Only two and a half days after receiving the signalled instruction from the War Office four hundred officers and men of the 73rd Regiment (Highlanders) disembarked at Liverpool from Dublin. They arrived in Blackburn on 9th May. After a few days however, they moved to Halifax, leaving a detachment at Todmorden.

A troop of Royal Horse Artillery, under Major Wynyates, transferred from Sheffield, where all was quiet, to Manchester. A second troop, under Major Chester, came from Woolwich to Manchester in the record time of forty-six hours, the men riding on the guns which were drawn by post-horses. The 10th Royal Hussars came from Nottingham. The 2nd Battalion, Coldstream Guards, and the 1st Battalion, Third Guards (later known as the Scots Guards) came from London by canal barge to Manchester.

The 36th Regiment (Herefordshire), fresh from service in the Ionian Islands, marched from Chatham, then Colchester to Manchester, leaving detachments at Stockport and Oldham. A second troop of nine pounder cannon of the Royal Horse Artillery transferred from Manchester to Burnley. Even the twenty-seven man Rocket Troop, with its seven pounder and twelve pounder rockets, stood on full alert at Manchester.

As speed was the essence, stagecoaches were hired 'Three coaches full of soldiers have been sent off to Wigan'.[20] By 6th May troops were in Wigan, Warrington, Chorley, Preston, Blackburn, Bury, Bolton, Burnley, Haslingden, Rochdale, Oldham, Ashton under Lyne, Hyde, Stockport and Macclesfield. The manufacturing districts of Lancashire and north Cheshire were under military occupation.

At Manchester the barracks was full to capacity with 943 officers and men. These included 232 Queen's Bays and 530 Duke of York's Own Riflemen. (Twenty-five Queen's Bays and forty Riflemen were in hospital – probably the result of the Chatterton and Bury stone-throwing.)[21]

The numbers were still not enough. Two months later Major Eckersley was still concerned about the strength of the military forces: 'To credit all one hears the county [Lancashire] is in a lamentable state. I believe it is worse than it has been what with want of work and the high price of provisions. If a sufficient and efficient military force be not kept in the manufacturing districts the most serious consequences may ensue'. He continued, 'In riding on horseback in Manchester from St. Ann's Square to Piccadilly today (being the commercial market day) I was accosted by fifty different manufacturers each wanting to tell me his tale of woe. There seems to be more alarm in the town and in the neighbourhood of Blackburn and Bury than I have witnessed since the breaking-out of the late disturbances. Expectations are entertained of immediate attacks on private property. The Riot Act was read at Blackburn last evening to a considerable assemblage of people.'[22]

At that time, in Middleton, lived Samuel Bamford. He was a prominent Radical and agitator for parliamentary reform. A veteran of Peterloo, he later spent twelve months in prison for conspiracy and convening an illegal meeting. His name was familiar to all in Lancashire, rich and poor alike. Early in July Bamford received a visitor who told him of fanatics living in Middleton who were in contact with a group of east Lancashire loom-breakers. There had been secret delegate meetings at which the Middleton men were seeking to persuade the east Lancashire men to join them in a march of revolt in Manchester. Bamford was appalled. It was suicidal: 'I could not fully believe that any parties in the neighbourhood could be so wicked or were so mad as to encourage such a thing'.[23] He also knew that the Middleton handloom weavers at that time were relatively well-off. They were earning eight or ten shillings a week. He knew they would not leave their homes or their work to join any uprising.

Bamford was determined to prevent the attempt from taking place. He decided to meet the east Lancashire men. On a hot Sunday morning in early July he walked alone from Middleton to Haslingden. Here he met a friend who took him to a 'lonely place' to meet the captains. (According to Bamford's description it was probably Moleside Moor, Accrington.) Bamford's sympathies went out to the men: 'They were all decent thoughtful looking men and the ghastliness of want was on their features and though their clothing was poor indeed there was no filth or squalor about them – their garments were neatly darned or patched and their calico shirts were clean. Such were a group of Englishmen, of English Saxons in truth, fathers of families, living on two pence halfpenny a day.'[24]

They discussed the plot and Bamford urged upon them by every argument he knew to abandon the project and give up their connection with the Middleton delegates. Bamford knew these would desert the east Lancashire men if they did march on Manchester. The men, at length, agreed to put Bamford's arguments to a meeting to be held on nearby Hambledon Hill the next day. At this meeting those who believed and supported Bamford won the day. There was to be no march on Manchester.

Before Bamford left home on Sunday he took the precaution of informing several of his friends, and the editor of the *Manchester Guardian*, about what he was doing. Major Eckersley already knew of the possible uprising. He had to hand an alarming deposition by a Blackburn man, Thomas Howson, signed before magistrates Charles Whittaker and James Hindle. Howson was a delegate, a captain. Howson was also an informer. With sixteen other local men he met delegates from Chadderton (contiguous with Middleton) in a lane near Shadsworth, Blackburn. For one and a half hours they discussed loom-breaking. A general attack was to take place fifteen days hence. Howson stated to the magistrates 'The Lower Darwen factory is the principal point of attack here, but they intend to go to Bury, Manchester, Ashton and Stalybridge where there are a great deal of powerlooms'. Howson attended other meetings on Rishton Moor and at Cobwall, Blackburn. 'The plan to break the powerlooms is to use mechanics who are out of employ to break looms and do nothing else. They have a great many arms and ammunition. They are determined to take the cannon if they are passing through the county. They have taken over, or can take over, Ralph Railton's foundry [in Blackburn] to cast balls . . . If the soldiers oppose them they will give no quarter.' For reasons of his own Howson added improbably, 'I believe the Catholics are at the bottom of all this'.[25]

The plan, such as it was, was indeed suicidal. Anyone, even in the despairing rage of starvation, must have known it so. In the event common-sense – and Bamford's strong influence – prevailed. Major Eckersley, of course, had to take it seriously. Discussing the deployment of a troop of Queen's Bays to Bury, he wrote to Lieutenant General Byng on 9th July, 'There are five thousand souls in Blackburn. If they commence the work of pillage they may come down to Bolton and Rochdale en route to Manchester. A force at Bury would stop it, in all probability.' In addition, in the heat and drought of this long hot summer, the prospect of winter already worried Major Eckersley. He continued, 'I meet with no one who does not despond – Major Bailey's [1st King's Dragoon Guards] man of business [another informer] writes from Blackburn about firearms and pikes being in preparation. Sinclair [Major, Royal Horse Artillery] hears something of the same at Burnley, yet one can hardly believe they have gone so far. But they are a desperate people in that part of the county.[26]

Major Eckersley's pessimism proved unfounded. The area remained quiet. The military authorities, however, were in serious need of permanent or at least semi-permanent barracks in the smaller towns. From May to September, in fortunately a long dry summer, Major Eckersley spent much of his time negotiating for, and arranging, accommodation for the occupying forces. Unluckily perhaps, he needed to deal with the magistrates, including the Reverend Gray, of whom he held no high opinion. He complained to Lieutenant General Byng on 6th July, 'as is usual the magistrates are aloof and seem not to know nor care about what goes forward'.[27]

Progress was slow at first. Magistrates did not hurry to reply to letters. Permanent forces of troops would add to their responsibilities and they were not anxious to take this on. Manufacturers were keener. Adam Dugdale, a partner of Thomas Hargreaves at Broad Oak Print Works, Accrington, untouched by the rioters, several times visited Major Eckersley in Manchester. 'He is offering a barracks at Accrington saying it is more important than one at Haslingden. I told him straight you were only arranging for a barracks at the latter place.'[28]

By the end of July Major Eckersley made some progress. A temporary barracks for a hundred cavalry and two hundred infantry was completed at Burnley. The Reverend Gray finally replied to his letters, offering a 'large building' in Haslingden. This turned out to be suitable for fifty infantrymen, but still not quite enough to please Major Eckersley. Another fifty men were placed in nearby houses in High Street.[29] There were stables for twenty-seven horses in a nearby yard. The Queen's Bays remained quartered over their horses in a room over the yard. There was a 'cooking-house' adjoining. Major Eckersley thought the accommodation 'might be made rather good'. Additional emergency places were needed however and later Major Eckersley with the Reverend Gray, 'went in every house, cellar and attic in Haslingden searching for billets'.[30]

Adam Dugdale's persistence for barracks in Accrington changed minds. Eighty infantrymen were billeted in a building in the workhouse, their N.C.O.s in nearby cottages and the officers in lodgings elsewhere. A nearby 'club-room' provided emergency accommodation for fifty men. For a rent of thirty pounds *per annum* the military, and no doubt Adam Dugdale, considered it a bargain. Better than Haslingden's, this barracks was enclosed by a high wall.

By the time Lancaster Assizes was over, other and similar barracks and billets were arranged in most towns in Lancashire. The absolute necessity for military accommodation became less urgent however as summer came to a close. Almost as Major Eckersley completed the arrangements, the military authorities, confident the area would remain peaceable, reduced the garrison strength. As early as 5th July the 58th Regiment returned to Dublin. In early October the Queen's Bays and the 73rd Regiment left for garrison duties in Ireland. In mid-October the 53rd Regiment moved its detachments from Bolton, Chorley, Blackburn, Accrington and Haslingden to Liverpool en route to Ireland. The 36th Regiment detachments came from Manchester to take their place. The 36th Regiment remained in east Lancashire until April 1827.

As the detachments of the 36th Regiment settled in their accommodation Lieutenant General Sir John Byng made a tour of inspection. He pronounced the barracks at Blackburn, Accrington, Haslingden, Oldham and Bury 'satisfactory' – no doubt much to the relief of Major Eckersley.

The distress continued. The *Manchester courier* spoke of 'the roads around Padiham . . . crowded with famished wretches soliciting the charity of those who pass along. Unless relief be offered to them – they must surely perish from extreme want.'[31]

Local clergymen were also alarmed that lives were at risk. The Reverend Sandford Adamson of Padiham (population 3,000) in a letter of thanks to the London Relief Committee, wrote: 'The state of the district every day assumes calamitous appearances – had it not been for your unexampled generosity [a £250 grant], more misery would have existed than I have power to depict'.[32]

From Chorley, the Rector, John Whalley Master, wrote '. . . we found in our visits to the poor that amongst 200 families we found only four entire blankets'. From Darwen: 'we find about 700 families in want of the most necessary articles of clothing'. From Bacup: '. . . painful scenes of raggedness and wretchedness meet the eye – whole families covered partially with tattered garments destitute of blankets

A detail from the family gravestone of Richard Lund of Haslingden, killed at Chatterton. The burial register of St. James' Parish Church, Haslingden, has 'shot in a mob' annotated in the margin by his name. The extent of the family tragedy can be gauged from the death of his baby daughter less than two weeks after he was shot.

and coverlets for their beds – their wants innumerable'. The Reverend William Wood of Altham near Accrington, thanking the Committee for fifty pounds for the townships of Altham, Clayton-le-Moors and Huncoat, said it was barely sufficient 'to provide the wretched sufferers each with a pair of clogs upon an average of 1s. 6d. each – whole families are lingering on in a state of wretchedness for want of clothing and bedding'.[33]

Between 3rd May and 21st December 1826, the London Relief Committee distributed almost £27,000 in cash and goods throughout east Lancashire. A total of £1,000 went to Padiham, £2,700 to Chorley, £450 to Darwen, £700 to Bacup and £325 to Altham. Amongst others, Haslingden received £1,380, Accrington £500, Blackburn £5,400, with the tiny hamlet of Rishton, near Blackburn, a mere £15.[34]

The relief was not meant, however, to extend to all in distress. On 6th May 1826 Henry Hobhouse wrote on behalf of the Home Secretary [Robert Peel], to the Reverend Adamson. Whilst agreeing in principle to Adamson's request for help for 'the distressed artizans of Padiham', Hobhouse added, 'He [Peel] trusts that in the distribution care will be taken that no person is relieved who has been implicated in the Disturbances'.[35] It is extremely doubtful if much notice was taken of this. The distress was too deep and too crushing for any decent person to discriminate one famished wretch and his children against another.

The London Relief Committee did, however, keep a close watch on how its money was spent. On 9th September 1826, they wrote to all local clergymen responsible for distributing money and goods. 'We have learned with much pain – that some have administered relief gratuitously, without demanding any labour in return. It is needless to point out the injurious effect invariably produced in supporting the labouring classes without employment – therefore, the Committee has engaged Mr John MacAdam to survey all the roads in the suffering districts, with the intention of effecting such improvements as may confer a permanent benefit to the public'.[36]

The Committee was equally concerned about domestic matters. They complained to the Reverend Adamson that blankets issued by him to the poor had been 'pawned or seized for rent'. They suggested blankets be stamped with some 'cognisable mark in the middle to prevent abuses in future'.[37] The distressed womenfolk also were encouraged to work. The Committee granted £200 to Blackburn Ladies' Charity Committee to open a sewing room in which women and girls were employed to sew calico and flannel garments.[38]

In November 1826 the Haslingden Ladies' Committee distributed shirts, stockings and four hundred pairs of clogs to the poor. The newspaper report of this ended with the terrible, familiar words: '. . . otherwise, the great majority must literally perish from extreme want'.[39] To add urgency to all charitable works many more children were dying, particularly those under four years old. These were the weakest and most vulnerable to such childhood diseases as scarlet fever and whooping cough; a virulent epidemic of measles was, however, the main killer.

In Haslingden, with a population of just over six thousand, during the dry summer months of May to September, thirty-five children under four died – an average of seven per month. In the cold wet winter months from December 1826 to March 1827 one hundred and two children under four died – an average of twenty-five a month. During December the Reverend Gray conducted no fewer than forty-seven funerals. Thirty-five were of children, the oldest but nine years old. On Christmas Eve the Reverend Gray buried five baby girls, the oldest four years old. On New Years Eve he buried a baby boy five months old, and three girls, aged two and a half, three and four – and a man forty-nine years old.[40]

As 1826 came to an end, 1827 offered no more, either in Haslingden or the rest of east Lancashire. William Varley, a handloom weaver of Higham near Padiham, noted in his diary, 'This year [1827] commences with very cold rough weather, sickness and disease prevails very much, and well it may, the clamming and the starving and hard working which the poor are now undergoing, it is no wonder if it should bring death itself – for there is no aid, no succour to be had – hunger and cold are our true companions.'[41]

The quietness prevailing was born of necessity. The defeated poor of east Lancashire were preoccupied solely with survival.

Chapter 10

'A Melancholy Catalogue'

FOR over two thousand years a defensive position has crowned the crest of the hill overlooking the town of Lancaster and the River Lune. Pagans, Romans and Saxons built fortresses on the site. When the Normans took over large parts of the country after the Conquest Roger de Poictou was granted the lands of Lancaster and the surrounding district.

Roger de Poictou built a keep on the site of the ancient fortifications. The Great Keep, or Lungess Tower, became the heart of further extensions. Two round towers plus the Well (or later Witches) Tower and the Dungeon Tower were later built. In the early fifteenth century was completed the massive gateway, so symbolic of the castle's strength and dominance, now known as John O'Gaunt's Gateway, 'from whence there is a prospect of great extent, comprehending the hills of Cumberland and Westmorland, the Plain of South Lancashire and the whole extent of the River Lune terminated by the expanse of the Irish Sea'.[1]

John Howard, the prison reformer, visited Lancaster Castle in his tour of the Northern Circuit in 1776. After commenting adversely on the 'close, dark and unwholesome' Low and High Dungeons, Howard albeit concluded 'Lancaster Castle would, after slight improvements, be a good Gaol'.[2] Somewhat more extensive enlargements and improvements were started in 1788. Male and female felons' prisons (completed 1793) the Crown Court and Grand Jury Room (1796) and the Shire Hall (1798) were built. In 1818 the Dungeon Tower was demolished to make way for the female penitentiary, completed in 1821.

Although the male and female felons' prisons were, at the time, hailed as a great advance, they were unsatisfactory in many ways. The male felons' prison consisted of two massive towers each containing eight sleeping cells on each of ten floors. The cells were built back to back on the inside of the tower with a corridor between them and the outer wall. 'Since they were on the inside of the tower – the cells – had no windows at all, only a small ventilation hole over the door to the corridor outside. Since the ten floors were surrounded by extremely thick stone walls it was difficult to provide moving air, even for ventilation or heat.'[3] Consequently, even in winter the cells were close and airless.

Nevertheless, by the standards of prisons in London and elsewhere in the country, Lancaster was a 'good gaol'. There was a large inner courtyard containing almost an acre of ground, a clean water supply and many large rooms. Jailed debtors lived in small groups in the various 'rooms'. They were almost a law unto themselves. They made their own 'house' rules, were frequently drunk and were free to gamble. Their daily allowance of a quart of beer was sold by some for spirits smuggled in by visitors. Their rooms were permanently unkempt and dirty. Some debtors being kept at the County's expense were not anxious to leave. One prisoner, entering the castle in 1822 on an order for contempt of the Court of Pleas at Lancaster, for not signing certain deeds, was destined to remain over twenty years. 'Every attempt has been made to induce him to comply with the order of the Court, but in vain.'[4]

There was, of course, punishment for unruly prisoners. Anyone quarrelling, fighting or refusing to work could be punished by solitary confinement, on a pound of bread with water a day, for three days. Those imprisoned with 'hard labour' worked on a treadmill. This treadmill, introduced in the early 1820s, provided the power for twenty-three looms for weaving calico – a system used nowhere else in England.

Although Lancaster was the first prison in the country to have fixed, written rules and a code of practice for prisoners (since 1785) overall discipline was of a fairly relaxed nature. Robert Hindle (although writing sometime after 1826, the same regime of head gaoler Thomas Higgin, and his son John, was in power), commented tartly, 'Discipline is not of a deterring or reformatory nature. This is evidenced by the number of times the same prisoners are found here. Enforcement of discipline would clear Lancaster Castle from the moral obloquy of being preferred by the criminal population to the other prisons on the Country.'[5] Indeed Lancashire vagrants knew very well prison was more comfortable than the workhouse. Every autumn the prison filled with men and women who deliberately offended to come inside for the winter. In the hard desperate years of the mid-1820s, it is certain many were a great deal worse off outside prison than within.

Thomas Emmett, and those of his fellow-rioters remanded in custody, spent the long hot summer of 1826 awaiting trial. As male felons they were held in one of the two massive towers of the male felons' prison. Lancaster Castle held an 'absolute' capacity of 495 prisoners. In 1826 it reached a maximum of 578.[6] (This peak was reached just prior to the assizes.) This over-capacity meant several prisoners shared a cell designed for one. Each cell in the tower was just 8' 6" long, 6' 8" breadth and 8' 5" high.

Seven years before, in August 1819, a number of leading radicals were arrested in the aftermath of Peterloo and lodged in Lancaster Castle to await trial. One such was Samuel Bamford. Bamford's description of his cell in the male felons' prison indicates the conditions to be endured. He was placed in his cell. At first Bamford was impressed by the cleanliness of the nearby day-room and the exercise yard. Somewhat to his surprise, his cell was 'as white and sweet as constant application of quicklime could make it.' His bed was a perforated iron slab resting on projections from the wall. His bedding – which was also clean – was a straw-filled sack, a couple of blankets and a 'good horse-rug'. 'A capital prison thought I – we turned in – and I began to feel as if I were being smothered. I now began to feel as if I were closed up in a coffin and not a breath of air above and around me. My chest heaved for air – I leaned on my bed, pumping and gasping, in the close suffocating den.'[7]

In such cells and conditions, and with up to five persons in a cell (Bamford was alone in his), Emmett and his associates spent the summer. In these circumstances the cells were obviously hot, noisome, crowded and claustrophobic – as Bamford had discovered. The fear and tension of awaiting trial added to the ordeal. When prisoners arrived at Lancaster they were washed, the men's heads shaved and the women's cropped short. If a prisoner's own clothing was deemed to be insufficient, dirty or improper in any way, he or she was provided with new prison clothing. For the men a jacket, waistcoat and a pair of trousers of plain brown woollen cloth, two shirts, a pair of clogs, two night-caps and a pair of drawers. For the women, a woollen petticoat, an under-petticoat, two shifts (chemises), a pair of clogs, a bedgown, two night-caps, two plain caps, one apron and two pairs of woollen stockings.[8]

The women rioters (some twelve in number including Mary Hindle) were more fortunate in their accommodation. The female felons' prison was a detached building of four storeys, each containing eight wedge-shaped sleeping rooms. Each was fitted at one end with open railings to enable the occupants to be seen at all times by a matron from her room in the centre of the semi-circle. Each sleeping room was 17' long and 4' wide at the entrance widening to 8' 9" at the far end. The females took their meals together in one large room. (The males took theirs in their 'dayrooms' adjoining the cells.)

Daily routine was the same for all Lancashire prisons. At six o'clock a bell rang. The cell doors were opened by the turnkeys and prisoners went down to wash. Those who had jobs, for example, gardening, whitewashing, weaving, tailoring or clogmaking, worked until half past eight, then had breakfast of a quart of oatmeal pottage (porridge). After breakfast all attended chapel for thirty minutes (men and women were strictly segregated), then worked until noon. A period of exercise followed a lunch of stew or boiled beef or potatoes and cheese. For example Sunday lunch was quite specific: 'One quart of stew, made from Cow shins in the proportion of one shin to every fourteen prisoners'.[9] Work continued until supper – again a quart of oatmeal pottage.

For those, such as Emmett and Mary Hindle, awaiting trial there was no prison requirement to work. Prisoners sentenced to hard labour worked the treadwheel to enable other prisoners to weave calico on the looms. Emmett and the others, however, who most likely had not the means to maintain themselves (for example, debtors had to pay up to a guinea a week towards their food) were required to work to earn a little money. One third of their earnings was for their own use.

There was, however, time to relax and privileges were available. A schoolmaster taught reading and writing to any who wished. Prisoners were allowed free use of pen, ink and paper, but any letter containing anything 'improper' was held back by the gaoler. The chaplain kept a small library of religious books which were not entirely popular. 'The Matron states that the females refuse to avail themselves of the books, saying they want some of a livelier sort . . . they are instructed but not regularly; they are not anxious for it; if there is any work by which they can make a little money, they prefer it to the school.'[10]

So it was in this strange mixture of laxity and confinement, adequacy and discomfort, Thomas Emmett, Mary Hindle and the rest of the rioters awaited the August assizes. Prison life, in spite of a natural apprehension of the trial, was at least, as Ann Entwistle had already said (see Chapter 3), 'Better than being clammed'.

During the first week in August Lancaster's hotels and lodging houses filled with visitors to the assize – witnesses, officials and the simply curious. There was the usual air of expectancy in the town, but with many more visitors than usual. Much public interest centred, not so much on the rioters, but on the expected trial of a thirty year old fortune-hunter, Edward Gibbon Wakefield. Six months before, Wakefield abducted and married fourteen years old Ellen Turner, the heiress daughter of William Turner, a wealthy Cheshire manufacturer. (Ellen was a great niece of William Turner of Helmshore.) The story of the couple's Gretna Green marriage and their subsequent flight to Calais pursued by Ellen's relatives was the newspaper sensation of 1826. The bride's outraged parents had the marriage annulled and Wakefield prosecuted – hence his appearance at Lancaster.

Sir James Alan Park, Judge of the Common Pleas, His Majesty's Justice on the Northern Circuit, although Scottish by birth, was brought up, the son of a surgeon, in England. In 1791, at twenty-eight years of age, he married Lucy Appleton, of Preston. In the same year, he was appointed Vice-Chancellor of the Duchy of Lancaster. In 1811 he became Attorney General of Lancaster. Mr Justice Park, therefore, had strong personal and public ties with the County Palatine of Lancaster.

On the morning of Tuesday 8th August, 1826 the High Sheriff of Lancaster, Mr James Penny Machell, as was his duty, met Mr Justice Park and his fellow Justices of the Assize at the county boundary with Westmorland. (The judges had previously sat at the Westmorland County Assizes at Appleby.) The High Sheriff, with his retainers armed with halberds, escorted His Majesty's judges into Lancaster. With the High Sheriff were large numbers of the local gentry who deemed it a privilege to escort the judges – the King's representatives – into their town and castle. A troop of Yeomanry followed in the rear.[11]

Once all were inside the castle and the Crown Court the court proceedings were formally opened by the reading of the Commission of Assize. The representatives of state, law, church, army, civil government and landed gentry of the county spent much of the remainder of the day at a civic banquet in honour of the judges. Legal matters did not start until the next day.

On Wednesday morning the judges, accompanied by the High Sheriff and all those who had supped and dined with them the previous evening, went in stately procession for divine service at St. Mary's Priory, the parish church of Lancaster, situated by the castle. The Reverend Mr Perry, chaplain to the High Sheriff and now chaplain to the assize, preached 'a most appropriate sermon' to his congregation, taking for his text, Ezekiel, chapter eighteen, verse five: 'But if a man be just, and do that which is lawful and right . . .'

As the chaplain and his eminent congregation intoned their prayers, those prisoners in the castle due to be dealt with in the afternoon were transferred to the dungeons immediately below the Crown Court. These cells, in common with the others, were completely windowless with the only ventilation a small aperture over the solid wood door. When aperture and door were both closed the cell was in complete, claustrophobic, darkness. The only furnishing was a wooden board for a bed and a solid block of wood for a seat. Even on this bright hot August day the stone walls ran with damp. Lighted candles were needed to illuminate the outside corridor, at the end of which sat the turnkey escort. Into these confines were packed as many wretched prisoners as were necessary to be dealt with that day. If one were lucky, the wait was only an hour or so.[12]

The Crown Court above stood in complete contrast. The courtroom was a high spacious hall with a magnificent painted ceiling. The hall was furnished completely with oak panelling. Doors, benches and the bar were of polished solid oak. Behind the judge's seat was a magnificent oak panelling in the Gothic style. On the wall behind the judge and overlooking all was a life-sized equestrian painting of George the Third mounted on the white horse symbolic of the ruling House of Hanover. On the judge's left was the Grand Jury bench, well elevated above the well of the court. From the well of the court the stone floor raised in tiers up to the rear standing area reserved for the public.

The dock, or bar, stood on the first of the tiers. The dock was entered by the prisoners coming from below through a trap-door in the floor. Lancaster Crown Court was one of the finest in the country. 'Every attention has been paid to the convenience of light and air . . . to render it worthy of the great commercial and opulent county to which it belongs.'[13] The whole made up a resplendent and awesome setting for the dispensation of the King's justice.

Once the church service was over the judges walked, again in procession, to the castle and entered their respective courts. At about mid-day Mr Justice Park, gowned in red and be-wigged in grey, sat down in the Crown Court. The traditional reading of His Majesty's most gracious proclamation against vice and immorality took place and the names of the Grand Jury were called. The Right Honourable Edward Smith Stanley (commonly called Lord Stanley) was elected foreman and the twenty gentlemen of the Grand Jury were sworn in.[14]

It was the duty of the Grand Jury to decide whether the Bill of Indictment against a prisoner or prisoners was valid – if there was a case to answer. Only then could the case or cases go to trial before a Petty Jury of twelve 'good men and true'. (The twelve were not necessarily impartial – they were usually small farmers or tradesmen perhaps living in property rented from, or were otherwise dependent on, those in the Grand Jury.)

Before a packed court, with several hundred spectators fighting and jostling for a place in the public section of the hall, Mr Justice Park addressed the Grand Jury. He prefaced his remarks by his personal sorrow in seeing such a distressing picture of crime in what he considered his own county. 'The Calendar contains an immense number of cases (223 to be exact) of almost every crime which human depravity can commit [in contrast the Westmorland Assizes was a 'Maiden' – no criminal or civil cases at all, the only one ever known]. One class of cases gives me, and must have given you, infinite concern. No fewer than sixty-six prisoners are charged – with rioting and the destruction of property. The annals of the county provide there has been much distress – it might be charitably hoped that much of the crime which crowds the present Calendar arises out of it. I need not say to you, gentlemen, that men must not take the remedy into their own hands .. . . However misguided they might be or however pitiable their situation – it is necessary they be taught, sometimes by fatal examples, that they must not attempt to remedy their distress by acts of violence. In criminal matters, if our nature prompts us to pity, we ought always to recollect that there is a duty owing to the country in which we live. Many of the present cases will probably turn on the Statute commonly called the 'Black Act'.[15] However painful it might be for you to return these Bills, I fear it will be your duty, in some cases, to return Bills for the capital offence. Temper your justice with mercy: but, I fear I may be going too far in saying this, for it is your business to examine if there are probable grounds for presuming guilt, leave mercy to me, to whom the administration of justice is here confided, subject to his Majesty's human considerations.'[16]

Mr Justice Park concluded his address by referring to the 'extraordinary number and atrocity' of the highway robberies in the Calendar, the legal complications of the Wakefield case and the charge of murder, 'most heinous', against Alexander and Michael McKeand which remained to be dealt with. Finally, he directed the Grand Jury to retire to their own room to consider the Bills of Indictment. Thus Mr Justice Park set the scene for the trial of the rioters, with allusions already to the sympathy he felt for the wretchedness of their condition.

The rest of Wednesday the judge dealt with the gangs of highway robbers. Firstly Peter Walsh and John Ketland were found guilty of violently robbing a jeweller of a watch and sentenced to death. Then Michael Donnell and Thomas Fitzgerald were sentenced to death for robbing a traveller of five sovereigns and ten half-sovereigns. Thursday and Friday were taken up with the usual court business of felonies and misdemeanours. In the meantime the Grand Jury examined the Bills of Indictments of the rioters.

The Bills were written on parchment and listed the counts, or charges, each person or persons faced. Those for the rioters were so lengthy and detailed they were presented on lengths of parchment sewn together. Each separate indictment listed a group of persons, with their offences, concerned with a particular factory. The Bill of Indictment, for example, against Ann Entwistle, Mary Marsden, Margaret Yates, William Almond and William Taylor for their part at William Turner's Helmshore factory needed to be fifteen inches wide and over ten feet long. The detailed charges on each Bill running to thousands of words, were couched in such repetitious legal phrases as to be almost incomprehensible to the layman.

If the Grand Jury requested, witnesses for the prosecution, and the prisoners themselves, could be examined on details of evidence but the only other person allowed in the Grand Jury Room was the solicitor for the prosecution. The Grand Jury's deliberations probably took the best part of two days. When complete, the Grand Jury entered the court and, with much ceremony the foreman was asked by the Clerk to the Assize if a True Bill was found or not. Needless to say, considering Mr Justice Park's address to them, with its implications, they had. The Bills of Indictment, bound in their judicial red tape, were thereupon handed down from the Grand Jury bench into the well of the court. A Petty Jury would now be selected to sit on the trial and render a verdict to the court.[17]

On Monday morning 14th August, a mass of men and women jostled and pushed into the Crown Court until almost a thousand packed the public area. Many had waited outside since the early hours. Some with relatives on trial, had walked the long miles from Blackburn, Rossendale and Bury, sleeping in the hedgerows on the way. Others, fresh from their lodgings in the town were simply curious, anxious to witness people on trial for their lives amidst the pomp and ceremony of the assizes. The pressure of the crowd spilled those in front almost into the well of the court and almost into the dock itself. In the intense heat, it was not long before the sour, pungent, smell of unwashed human bodies filled the court.

Amidst the hubbub the prosecuting counsel opened the trial of the rioters by stating the statutes on which their case was founded. They were formidable: the Riot Act of 1714, the Malicious Injury Act of 1768, the Malicious Damage Act of 1812 (see note 15) and the Malicious Injuries to Property Act of 1823 – which made it a felony to destroy cloth in the loom.

The first group of six rioters was brought into the dock. James Riding, William Sutcliffe, James Lathom, James Ormerod, James Howarth and Thomas Bolton, in clean prison clothes and with hair freshly cropped, listened uncomprehendingly for at least twenty minutes as the Clerk to the Assize read out the long list of charges against them arising out of the attack on Bannister Eccles' factory at Blackburn.

The prosecution witnesses, Bannister Eccles himself, John Kay and the Reverend Richard Noble, as the law required, simply repeated their previous statements to the magistrates – no more, no less. At the same time the written statements, now depositions, were handed to the judge. The defendants, again as the law required, had no knowledge of the evidence against them until the prosecution witnesses spoke. The depositions were prepared solely for the trial judge. The prosecution had access to them, but not the accused.

Neither was any defendant indicted of a felony allowed to have a defence lawyer to cross-examine witnesses. Neither could he give evidence on his own behalf, nor make a speech to the jury. By the judicial standards of the day these things were seen as an advantage to the defendant as no questions could be put to him which might lead to proof of his guilt. Neither could a defendant's previous convictions or bad character be put in evidence by the prosecution.

Because the rioters' crimes were capital, Mr Justice Park, again as the law required, acted as their defence counsel in his capacity of trial judge. This was in spite of their numbers and in spite of seeing the depositions only on the same day as the trial.[18] This principle was defended as a safeguard against any improper influencing of the defendant by the prosecution.[19] However well-meaning and sincere a judge may be, a poor, simple, inarticulate labourer on trial for his life was entirely at the mercy, whim, and prejudice of the court and its judge. The only redeeming feature of the proceedings was that they were held in public.

After Bannister Eccles and the rest of the prosecution witnesses gave their evidence, Riding, Sutcliffe, Latham, Ormerod, Howarth and Bolton were in turn asked by the judge if they had anything to say. All simply denied breaking machinery. 'Character' witnesses were then asked to make their statements on behalf of individual defendants.[20]

The judge summed up briefly for the jury. They retired for only a few minutes before finding all, except Bolton, guilty, but recommended them for mercy. Sentence on the five guilty, as on all the defendants, was to be pronounced at the end of the trial.

So the trial continued for four days. On Tuesday morning there was a stir of interest in the crowd as two of the captains, James Chambers and Simeon Wright, entered the dock. With them was Thomas Dickenson and Richard Entwistle. All were charged with riot at Bannister Eccles' factory. The witnesses, now including Dixon Robinson and John Morten, repeated their evidence. The hammer Robinson took from Chambers was produced in court, as was the 'knobstick' Wright used in his assault on the Reverend Noble.

When asked to speak Chambers said he had been without any work for thirteen weeks and did not intend to break any machinery. Wright denied being at the factory and did not know how he came to assault the Reverend Noble. Dickenson said he was forced along by the crowd. Entwistle simply said he was at work when the riot took place.

The scene in the courtroom in Lancaster Castle as a witness gives evidence of Mary Hindle's presence at the riot at Middle Mill, Helmshore. The prosecution barrister is holding up the piece of cloth cut from her dress.

Even at this early stage of the trial it is clear the rioters were thoroughly cowed. There were not to be any defiant statements, nor pleadings for a cause – simply inarticulate denials.

Character witnesses were called. Henry Harwood said he had been a neighbour of Chambers' for many years and believed him to be an honest man. Dickenson was a 'sober, steady and honest lad'. Entwistle's employer John Houghton (even though his own factory was attacked in the riot) said Entwistle behaved exceedingly well in the three years he had worked for him. Wright had no character witness.[21]

Mr Justice Park summed up by quarter to twelve and the jury retired. At half past one they returned with a verdict of Chambers being guilty only of being at the riot. The judge found this unacceptable and directed them to give a distinct verdict. The jury returned at quarter to two and declared Chambers, Wright and Entwistle guilty and Dickenson not guilty.

Throughout the rest of Tuesday and all day Wednesday similar groups, several charged with offences at Oswaldtwistle, Edenfield, Summerseat, Woodhill, Darwen and Chorley were dealt with. The jury, knowing now what was expected of them, in each case retired usually for just 'a few moments' before returning a verdict.

Thursday, the final day for the rioters, concerned the events at Helmshore and Rossendale. Six separate groups appeared. The first group included Thomas Emmett,

Mary Hindle, Betty Howarth, James Shorrock, Alexander Norris and John Orrell. A total of ten witnesses repeated their statements. Thomas Emmett, as he did when examined by the Reverend Gray four months before, denied breaking looms. Mary Hindle, whose piece of dress material, cut out by Harry Holt, was produced in court, admitted being in the crowd but denied being in the factory. The jury quickly found all six guilty but recommended Norris and Orrell for mercy. None had character witnesses. Mary Hindle was doubly unfortunate – her character witness (not identified) did not turn up at court.

Of the second group the three women, Ann Entwistle, Mary Marsden and Margaret Yates were found guilty of breaking machinery at William Turner's. William Taylor and William Almond were acquitted. (There is no reference to ten year old Joseph Woods being in court. It is likely his evidence was read out by the prosecution counsel.)

Thomas Emmett appeared again in the Rossendale cases together with Josiah Baldwin and Lawrence Hardman, and found guilty, in spite of his denial, of destroying machinery at Messrs Ormerods. There was no recommendation for mercy for any of the three. Josiah Baldwin appeared again in the next group with Joseph Clayton and John Hoyle. They were quickly found guilty and not recommended for mercy. The main prosecution witness in the Rossendale cases was the Bacup weaver, Samuel Lord, who shadowed not only Emmett but at least eleven others.[22]

After the final group (which again included Baldwin and Clayton) appeared, Mr Justice Park gave his closing speech. His final words brought little comfort to the rioters. 'I fear some dreadful example must be made as a warning and put to an end these enormous offences . . . and to teach others in future that if they so offended they would have to undergo some most serious punishment and perhaps suffer death.'[23] The court rose at half past six. The trial, at least, was ended.

The correspondent of the *Leeds Mercury* was moved to comment, 'The convicted prisoners form a melancholy catalogue, but it is gratifying to know that they have had the fairest trial possible, that the prosecutors have not manifested the smallest degree of vindictiveness and that the judge appears fully convinced the riots were the effects of distress and of an erroneous judgement and did not proceed from wicked and malicious motives.'[24]

In other words there was no evidence of a plot. There was no evidence of an organised uprising. There was no evidence even of a leader, apart from one or two self-styled 'captains'. The appearance and demeanour of the prisoners, the sympathy almost of at least one of the manufacturers and the humane treatment of the prisoners in court by the prosecution, decided the judge. There was no other conclusion than that the prisoners had committed the crime of taking a grievance into their own hands. They had not waited for their 'betters' – Parliament, the manufacturers, the magistrates, the landed gentry – to apply their remedy of the charitable works. That the problem of the handloom weavers was too large for charitable works seemed to escape all except those in the dock. They tried to solve the problem in the only way they knew how. Now the price was to be paid.

The prisoners were sent down to their cells to await sentence. Mr Justice Park considered it would probably be on Monday. For the prisoners there was no right of appeal against either the verdict of the jury or the sentence of the court.

Meanwhile Mr Justice Park had other things on his mind. An application by defence counsel to postpone the trial of Wakefield took up three hours of legal discussion. Mr Justice Park decided the trial would go on, to start on Monday, 21st August. On Friday (the 18th) a new Petty Jury found Alexander and Michael McKeand guilty of the murder of Elizabeth Bates in a drunken quarrel. The law required murderers to be sentenced immediately after conviction. Mr Justice Park accordingly sentenced both to death by hanging – to take place on Monday the 21st.

At half past seven on Monday morning, whilst the sentenced rioters still waited to know whether or not they would receive the death sentence, the McKeand brothers were brought out of their cells to the multiple scaffold erected outside the castle wall facing St. Mary's churchyard. Also with the McKeands was Patrick Rafferty convicted of highway robbery, Patrick Mullen, of murder, and John Wainwright of 'malicious cutting and stabbing with intent to disable'.

Five coffins were stacked by the scaffold. A huge crowd, using the churchyard as a grandstand, watched as the five were led out of the large window (in reality a door) of the Castle Drop Room directly on to the gallows at Hanging Corner, a recess in the castle wall. None of the five were given the opportunity to speak to the crowd. The noose was immediately put in place and a black hood put over their face. The five were allowed three or four minutes 'for a brief address to their Maker'. Then, whilst the chaplain murmured a prayer, 'their mortal thread was cut and they were launched into his immediate presence'.[25] The bodies were brought back into the Drop Room, from whence they were taken, as directed by the judge, to the surgeons for dissection.

It can be safely assumed that news of the hangings went through every recess of Lancaster Castle gaol. The news would certainly have a direful effect on the apprehensive minds of the waiting convicted rioters. They were to know their own fate sooner than they thought.

At half past nine the same morning the trial of Edward Gibbon Wakefield was set to begin. It was common knowledge, however, that Wakefield left the town on Friday and had not been seen since. After the legal formality of the Court Usher calling Wakefield's name three times, a warrant for his arrest was issued.[26] Because of the premature ending of the Wakefield trial Mr Justice Park ordered the convicted rioters to be brought up for sentence.

It was an irony that the hundreds of onlookers who packed the public area to see Wakefield, the child bride abductor, were now to witness the sentencing of those, who in the eyes of some at least, were much more mundane. So many, in fact, filled the hall that spectators spilled over into the witness box and the dock itself. The confusion was such Mr Justice Park was forced to ask some ladies who had seated themselves in the dock 'I'm very sorry to disturb you, but you must make way for those more guilty than yourselves'.[27]

After this undignified delay and confusion, Mr Justice Park ordered as many of the prisoners as could be placed at once in the dock to be brought up from below. Eventually eleven, one of them James Chambers, were packed into the tiny dock to be addressed by the judge.

Mr Justice Park, in common with his fellow-judges, firmly believed it was the duty of every person to submit without question to the law. He also believed that a man committing a felony such as rioting was guilty of a sin; against himself by endangering his life and liberty; against his family by exposing them to misery and disgrace;

against society by violating the security of property and against God and King by disobeying the King's God given law.

Above all a man sinned by neglecting the sacred precepts so conducive to a well-ordered society – be subject to those in authority and submit yourself to every ordinance of man 'for the Lord's sake fear God and honour the King'. Mr Justice Park's attitude to those who knew nothing only hunger and poverty was that distress was a natural part of life, to be alleviated, not by economic theory, but by charity. Obedience to the law was the condition of security and a social order which was beneficial to the poor.

Some years after the rioters' trial, Mr Justice Park summed up his view in an address to a Grand Jury at Reading Assizes: 'Never was there a country [England] which showed such concern for the young, old, deaf, blind, widows and every child of wretchedness and woe. There is not a calamity or distress . . . that is not endeavoured to be mitigated or relieved by the powerful and the affluent . . . in this, our happy land, which for its charity, benevolence and boundless humanity is the admiration of the world.'[28]

Mr Justice Park was a bold defender of the status quo, the rights of capital and its economic system of 'laissez faire'. It was this mind that now addressed itself to the rioters before him. 'You are most deluded persons, for you have been destroying the means by which you were to live . . . The law has affixed the crime of which you are guilty the punishment of death. It is not my intention to carry out the law to its fullest extent and I shall be pleased to recommend to His Majesty to be pleased to pardon you so far as your lives are concerned.' He went on to single out James Chambers, 'the oldest amongst you and the most grievous offender. It was my intention to have made you an example by taking your life, but I shall not select you singly on this occasion. However,' he added to the rest, 'do not flatter yourselves . . . that you will escape without very severe punishment. I earnestly trust you will be convinced that no happiness can result from a life of turbulence and riot but that peace and good order are conducive to the interest and happiness of men.'[29]

Mr Justice Park then formally pronounced sentence. A crowded, yet silent, court heard him sentence a total of forty-one, including six women, to death. Four other women, and one man, whose charges were not capital, were given immediate sentences of imprisonment (see appendix 2).

There were few, if any, cases in which the Crown turned down a judge's recommendation for a reprieve. The effect of a death sentence, was therefore undermined. Hardened criminals treated the death sentence lightly . . . secure in the knowledge of a reprieve. People such as Emmett, Mary Hindle and most of the rioters were relatively innocent in criminal matters. Overwhelmed as it was by the dignity and gravity of the judge and his words, the prisoners would be crushed by the sentence. In spite of being told otherwise it is sure they would now live in dread until the reprieve arrived.

Throughout the trial there was no mention of Chatterton. No rioters were convicted of offences at Chatterton. No one connected with Chatterton gave evidence – no depositions, no witnesses. Prisoners were sentenced for offences committed at factories before the mob arrived at Chatterton – and after it left Chatterton. The military took the trouble to send Sergeant Hamilton of the 60th Foot to give evidence against Henry Melling for throwing a stone at Captain Goldfrap at Woodhill (Melling received three months imprisonment), yet not one stone-thrower or loom-breaker at Chatterton appeared in court.

It was as if Chatterton had never been. It was almost as if the Military and the Law – the bastions of Mr Justice Park's society – did not want their role at Chatterton to come too much to the public notice in a court of law.[30]

At the end of each Lancaster Assizes, as indeed at all assizes, a Circuit Letter signed by the judge was addressed to the King. The Letter contained the names and offences of all the capital prisoners recommended for His Majesty's mercy on condition of their being transported or imprisoned for such terms as the judge thought adequate for each individual. In practice the Circuit Letter went to the Home Office from whence it went to the Palace for the King's pardon and signature. The Home Office returned the signed pardon to the judge. A separate Order of Court signed by the Home Secretary, for the transportation of each pardoned prisoner went from the Home Office to the High Sheriff of Lancaster.

The prisoners waited three weeks for the King's decision. Three long weeks for them, but considering the distances, personages and bureaucrats involved three weeks was a reasonable time.

The sentences of transportation for the prisoners – 'for the terms of their natural lives' – was to come into effect on September 8th. On that day the High Sheriff notified the head gaoler, Thomas Higgin. Higgin, accompanied by the chaplain, in turn notified each prisoner.

Those fortunates with their sentence of death remitted to a term of imprisonment thanked God and the King for his mercy and continued the relatively comfortable routine prison life. The remaining male prisoners, or transportees as they were now known, whilst also being extremely grateful to the King for their lives, were immediately secured in six-pound leg irons and separated again from their friends, never to see them again.

For Thomas Ashworth, a Rawtenstall carter and Emmett's fellow-captain at Whiteheads' factory, the strain of imprisonment, the trial and waiting for his reprieve was too much. On 26th September he collapsed and died. The Coroner's verdict of 'Death by Visitation of God' (possibly a heart attack) could only have put more fear and melancholy into the hearts and minds of his fellows.[31]

On 8th October the High Sheriff received a further order from the Home Office. He was to remove 'with all convenient speed' the male prisoners under sentence of transportation and deliver them to the Superintendent of Convicts, Mr J. H. Capper, or his overseer, on the hulk *Dolphin* at Chatham, Kent.

The hands of Capper were to be very different from those of Higgin.

CHAPTER ELEVEN

'Like a Wicked Noah's Ark'

AT six o'clock on the morning of Wednesday 18th October Thomas Emmett, with the rest of the prisoners of Lancaster Castle, arose, cleaned his cell, washed, and breakfasted on a quart of oatmeal porridge. Afterwards Emmett, and the six others warned for transfer to the hulks,were examined by the castle surgeon, Dr John Smith, to check they were fit to leave the castle.

The surgeon attended the castle daily. Although those in the prison, in general, had a better diet than the poor 'free' beyond the walls, a large proportion of prisoners were affected by pulmonary, or chest complaints. Lack of food and warmth over the years before imprisonment undoubtedly gave prisoners a predispositon to these complaints, which were made worse in the exposed, cold, damp buildings of the castle. Dr Smith also worried about a puzzling 'laxity of the bowels' amongst the prisoners, of which again the damp cells and poor ventilation were assumed the cause.

This almost permanent condition occasionally led to epidemics of dysentery and cholera. From the middle of August to the end of September most prisoners had been affected to a degree. There was one death from *cholera morbus* and four from dysentery. Although the epidemic was in decline, even yet in mid-October upwards of a hundred persons were still sick.[1] Naturally, because of the fear of epidemics in this and other prisons in England and Wales (and Lancaster was considered a clean and healthy prison normally) the hulks insisted on taking only 'healthy' prisoners.

Once pronounced fit, Emmett and the others were given a clean yellow woollen jacket and waistcoat and blue trousers – the colours of a transportee. They were also given a clean shirt, a cap and clogs. The prison barber close-cropped their hair. As 'transportees' they kept on their six-pound leg irons. Now, in addition they were fitted with hand irons, a long light chain connecting the two. (An essential item was a piece of string tied to the chain and round the waist, to keep the chain off the ground.)

In 1826 the county of Lancashire bore the cost of sending to the hulks or prison ships her convicts sentenced to transportation.[2] From Lancaster a castle turnkey (warder) escorted them on the regular stagecoach to Manchester, then on a fast stagecoach to London's Newgate Prison. Beyond, for the male convicts, lay the ultimate destination of the hulks in Woolwich, Deptford, Sheerness, Chatham or Portsmouth. (Women went direct to the prison ships at Woolwich.)

Now on this October morning as Charles Wilkes, the turnkey responsible for delivering the seven men to the hulks, completed the transfer documents, his assistant (who was to travel with them) issued the prisoners with top-coats and cloaks – their only cover from the October weather.

Leg irons and chains of various weights and sizes displayed in Hadrian's Tower, Lancaster Castle. These were secured to prisoners both within the prison and whilst travelling to convict hulks or ships en route to Australia. They were almost certainly used on those imprisoned and transported in 1826–7. These artefacts can still be seen at Lancaster Castle

Reproduced by permission of Lancashire County Property Services, Lancaster Castle Project Team

Thomas Emmett was in rough company with his travelling companions. Peter Walsh, aged twenty-six, Michael Bonnell, aged twenty-nine, and John Kelly, aged twenty-two, had all been members of gangs convicted of violent highway robbery. Oliver Collins, aged twenty-two, was a thief convicted of larceny of goods worth over forty shillings. Of the rioters, even Josiah Baldwin at twenty-two years old had two previous convictions. Only Emmett and the fifty-five year old yeoman farmer James Chambers were therefore not experienced criminals. For these two a long hard journey would be made worse in such company.

At length the seven, now chained together and with their armed escorts alongside, walked out of the castle gateway and through the streets of Lancaster to the King's Arms in Market Street. Although the town was filling up for market day no one gave the group a second glance. It was a familiar sight.[3]

At the King's Arms, the principal coaching inn of the town, the prisoners boarded the *Telegraph*, one of four daily coaches direct to Manchester. The four horse *Telegraph* carried four passengers inside and eleven outside. Wherever one sat coach travel lacked comfort. The inside passengers sat upright in what essentially was an unventilated box. On most coaches the outside seats were full width forward facing, with another, similar seat facing backwards. The seats were always narrow and sparsely padded. The only back-rest was an iron rail across the low part of the passenger's back. They were exposed to everything the English climate could do.[4] These outside seats were the lot of Emmett and his group.

At half past ten exactly the *Telegraph* left the King's Arms for Manchester, a journey of fifty-five miles in five eleven mile stages. For the first mile, because of the steep climb out of the town, and to save the horses, Emmett and his group walked behind the coach. Only on the relatively level ground of the new turnpike were they allowed onto their seats. They would find, before their journey was over, they would walk as many miles as they rode.

After the first of many stops at turnpike toll bars the coach had its first of many changes of horses at the Royal Oak in Garstang. In the highly competitive coaching trade the roadside coaching inns had to be extremely efficient. Horses were often changed in less than two minutes, the steaming horses led away to be fed and rested for a later return journey. Five minutes only were allowed for a quick refreshment set ready for passengers by the inn staff.

Already the roof passengers (the coach carried members of the public in addition to the convicts) would feel the effects of coach travel. Even on maintained turnpike roads they would be jolted unmercifully. On the roof seats there was little to hang on to – just a small handle by the side of the seat. It needed all the passengers' efforts to preserve their balance as the cumbersome coach rattled along. After half an hour's travel invariably one's legs lost all feeling.

In spite of De Quincey's view – 'the air, the freedom of prospect, the proximity to the horses, the elevation of seat – the outside of the mail had its incommutable advantages' – long-distance rooftop travel was a degrading endurance test.[5] In dry weather one was choked in dust, cold wet weather could mean – and occasionally did – even death from exposure.

On their journey however, at least the 'freedom of prospect' and 'the elevation of seat' did enable the convicts to view a richer and more varied countryside than they were used to in the uplands of east Lancashire. How soon the novelty palled in the face of discomfort and fatigue is not, of course, known.

In Chorley – so near yet so far from east Lancashire – the coach changed horses at the Gillibrand Arms in Market Street. From his seat on the coach Chambers would see the 'big chimney' of Water Street factory, the scene of his final blow against the powerlooms. Whether he saw the landlord's brother James Blade, the special constable at Water Street riot, is again not known. Neither is it known whether Chambers regretted his previous short visit to Chorley.

The coach continued over Chorley Moor to the broad streets of Bolton le Moors, then through increasingly built up smoky industrial towns and villages into the narrow congested streets of Manchester. Market Street was particularly crowded, almost impossible to get through, but almost five hours after leaving Lancaster the *Telegraph* halted at the Mosley Arms.

The roof passengers undoubtedly would have great difficulty in getting down from the roof and would need help from the coach guard.[6] Stiff, cold and bruised from constant jolting the fare-paying passengers would be pleased to enjoy hot food and a glass or two of mulled ale before continuing their journey. The convicts however were not allowed inside any inn. The best they could get would be bread and beef or cheese outside the tap-room door or shelter in the stables and they would eat their food whilst chained to any convenient ring-bolt fixed to the wall. They were not allowed intoxicants. Very probably, however, most escorts would allow a glass of ale rather than risk the not uncommon impure water.

At half past three the *Telegraph* (the same in name only, because both coach and horses were replaced) left on its long journey to London. An hour later a change of horses at the *Plough* in Stockport, on the way passing the huge silk mills and calico print works in the town. At Bullock Smithy (now Hazel Grove), then a long street of irregularly built cottages and inns, horses were again changed. The coach paused at Macclesfield at six o'clock and by the time it made its slow way over the bleak, high moors to Leek it was eight o'clock and dark.

Even in darkness there was a lot of traffic on the roads. Most people travelled by horse or on foot. The *Telegraph* was only one of fifty-four coaches a day from Manchester to London alone. Coaches continued through the night, passengers sleeping as best they could through the jolting and swaying, the sound of the post horn and the noise of passing traffic.[7] Stoppages at toll bars added to the misery.

A main road journey, such as Manchester to London, consisted of a mixture of local roads which varied widely in standards of construction and repair. There were few straight stretches so there were almost continuous changes in direction. There were only too few lengths of 'macadamised' roads of graded and properly compacted stone which were self-draining of surface water. No 'smooth' surface existed.

As the *Telegraph* drove towards Ashbourne in Derbyshire, it was leaving the 'lower ground' (the part nearest the provincial terminals) of its route and entering the 'middle ground'. This was normally that covered in the hours of darkness. (The 'upper ground' was the part of the journey nearest London.)[8] The beauties of the hills and woods around Ashbourne and the River Dove therefore went unseen by the passengers.

When Emmett and his fellow convicts walked up the steep hill into Brailsford, half way along the Derby road, they were less than a dozen miles south west of the village of Pentrich. Nine years before, Jeremiah Brandreth, the self-styled 'Nottingham Captain', led his 'insurrection' of fifty knitters and labourers on a march to Nottingham on the first stage of a march to London to overthrow the Government. They were dispersed by cavalry after Brandreth killed a man and later Brandreth and two others were hanged. In spite of the wearisome journey, Emmett, Baldwin and Chambers, as self-styled captains, must have thought themselves lucky not to have shared the same fate.

The *Telegraph* entered the paved, well-lit streets of Derby about midnight. They had travelled about 115 miles, almost half way to London, since leaving Lancaster almost fourteen hours before. Twenty minutes only was allowed for a meal, the guard sounded the post horn and the coach was on its way. Just beyond Shardlow they crossed the handsome stone Cavendish Bridge across the River Trent and entered Leicestershire, a flat fertile landscape with many quiet villages. The passengers huddled together in fitful sleep. Crushed closely together as they were – and also chained together – anyone sleeping leaned on his neighbour with all his weight. It was a miracle no one fell off.

After a two o'clock change of horses at the King's Arms at Loughborough, the coach rattled on the granite setts of Leicester's streets. At four o'clock the coach halted at the Stag and Pheasant Inn. Leicester was the busiest town in the 'middle ground'. The dozen or so coaching houses were as busy at four in the morning as most other towns during the day. Between seven at night and seven in the morning no less than forty passenger coaches, from all parts of the country, were in the town. During the same hours dozens of goods carriers, with teams of six or eight horses drawing huge wagons, came and went. At the Stag and Pheasant, as at all the other coaching houses, there was a tremendous bustle as ostlers, postboys, servants and passengers went their different ways. Emmett and his fellow convicts went out of sight in the stables.

By five o'clock the *Telegraph* was at the George in Market Harborough, then continued on to Northampton, Newport Pagnell and Woburn. By this time it was dawn and at the crossroads in the coaching village of Hockliffe, in Bedfordshire, the coach turned onto Watling Street which would take them through Dunstable, St. Albans and Barnet into London.

Barnet was an attractive hill-top village which looked over open country. In the High Street were more than twenty coaching inns. Barnet's position on the Great North Road eleven miles from London meant that every day one hundred and fifty coaches passed through the town. Barnet was the first and last change of horses out of London. For the *Telegraph* and its passengers, it was the final stage of this journey at least.

As the coach came down Barnet Hill into Finchley Common the roof passengers could see ahead the permanent haze of smoke hanging over London. The coach was part of a mid-morning flood of vehicles entering the city. Countless carts bringing in vegetables and other goods from the countryside merged with scores of long distance coaches and wagons from the north and west.

The entrance into London was a sight no other country in the world could parallel. There was a stupendous noise and tumult as thousands of carts, coaches, carriages, even omnibuses, passed along the macadamed streets. These streets soon became choked with traffic, horses and humanity. London's poor, the half naked children and wretched women, thronged the streets begging from the passing traffic, some taunting and mocking the prisoners. Huge warehouses and tenements towered above. Over all the smoke and dirt the coach passengers could see the huge dark dome of St. Paul's.

The *Telegraph* made its slow way through the congestion along the Edgware road, along majestic Oxford Street, then Holborn towards St. Paul's. A few hundred yards before, the coach turned off Holborn into aptly named Fetter Lane to the White Horse, its London terminus. It was about mid-day – over twenty-five hours since leaving Lancaster. A prison van awaited the coach and the seven convicts were quickly taken a few hundred yards to the dreaded Newgate Prison, almost under the shadow of St. Paul's.

Newgate, once described as '. . . massive, dark and solemn, arrests the eye and holds it . . . of all the London prisons except the Tower, it alone has an imposing aspect'.[9] Newgate's outer door was less than five feet high and was covered on top with formidable spikes. Another, massive oaken door, faced with iron, was alongside. Through the prison door, the lodge was a small sombre, high roofed, room. From there another heavy oaken, iron faced door led to the interior. Emmett and his fellow convicts were to lodge here for the night. The break was more for the benefit of the escorts than the prisoners.

Beyond the reception room was a gloomy passage leading to the reception cells. These were 13' 7" wide and 8' 10" high – larger than the Lancaster cells. There was a small table, a stool, a tap and water basin. On the floor was a rope mat on which to sleep. The seven convicts, Mr Wilkes and his assistant, although perhaps not particularly welcome, could rest until morning.[10]

At half past eight the following morning (Thursday) the daily coach to Canterbury (via Rochester and Chatham), the *Eagle*, left the Spread Eagle Inn, in Gracechurch Street, just a few hundred yards from Newgate. Unlike the ten miles an hour average of the *Telegraph*, the *Eagle* was a slow coach. It required seven hours to travel just thirty miles.

As the coach passed over the old London Bridge (the new London Bridge was being built by its side) Emmett and his group, still shackled to the roof seats, had an unforgettable view of the River Thames. The river was almost choked with shipping of all descriptions – timber ships from the Baltic, wine ships from Spain and Portugal, even Baltimore 'Yankee' clippers. As far as the eye could see there was a forest of masts and spars with just a narrow pathway of water through the middle. It was the busiest waterway in the world.

The coach soon gained the open country of Shooters Hill, continuing through the pretty village of Dartford into the county of Kent. Kent was truly the Garden of England. It was a land of orchards and hopfields, of wooded hills and rolling downs. A greater contrast with east Lancashire could not be imagined.

A prison hulk in Portsmouth harbour, with convicts going aboard. The Dolphin *prison hulk at Chatham would be a similar vessel.*

The coach was back onto the straight Watling Street, the Roman road from London to Dover. Many times however, the convicts walked behind the coach up the long low hills. Soon the River Medway came in sight, then through the village of Strood and the ancient cathedral city of Rochester, across the bridge over the Medway and into Chatham.

Chatham was a hive of industry. It had been a naval town since the days of Elizabeth the First. Here were built many of the ships which routed the Spanish Armada. For centuries the River Medway provided a sheltered area of water for naval vessels, protected by the shore batteries of Chatham and Sheerness. Across from the Royal Dockyard, in a great loop of the river, lay hundreds of men of war at anchor or undergoing repairs. Near the far, marshy shore, amongst them yet apart, was the filthy, decrepit hulk, the *Dolphin*, 'like a wicked Noah's Ark'.[11] The time was almost four o'clock. The 270 miles journey, started some fifty-four hours before, was almost at an end.

The convicts and their escort were ferried from the dockyard to the *Dolphin*. Once aboard the convicts were received as 'healthy' and signed for by the overseer, George Lang. Thomas Emmett became number 2005 in the 'Sworn Lists', (the hulk register). (Of his other fellow-rioters, Isaac Hindle with three others, arrived at the Dolphin on Friday 20th October. James Clayton, John Hoyle and Simeon Wright, with four others, arrived on Tuesday the 26th.)

The *Dolphin* was one of ten prison hulks within relatively easy reach of London and its prisons. They housed, at any one time, a total of 4,450 convicts.[12] The *Dolphin* was a twenty-seven year old ex-East Indiaman. Before becoming a hulk in 1824 she had been a fifty-four gun Royal Navy ship of the line. She was larger than most hulks, housing anything up to six hundred convicts. Now, her masts and rigging cut away, dirty and foul, and held by rusty chains off a stinking marshy shore, she was bereft of all her dignity.

Whichever the hulk, the reception of new prisoners never changed. New prisoners were mustered on the quarter-deck and received by the Captain. They were ordered to give any money they had to the Captain for safe keeping. Their cloaks and top coats were taken from them and their prison irons removed, all to be taken back by Wilkes to Lancaster Castle, who left as soon as the prisoners were taken to the forecastle. 'There every man was forced to strip and take a thorough bath in a large tub of water, after which each was handed an outfit consisting of a coarse grey jacket, waistcoat and trousers, a broad brimmed felt hat and a pair of heavily nailed shoes – before leaving the forecastle each man was double ironed with fourteen pound irons fitted by a blacksmith to the left wrist and the right ankle. They were then taken on deck to receive a hammock and a straw palliasse.'[13]

The clothes, hat and shoes were of any size. If lucky, convicts could later exchange with a comrade any that did not fit. The jackets and trousers were of a canvas-like material (the trousers universally known as 'cockchafers' because they rubbed the genital skin raw.) Neither were they new – they had belonged to prisoners who had been transported, and were still infected with their vermin.

The hulk barber again shaved heads, then armed military guards, with bayonets fixed, marched the laden and fettered prisoners below deck. 'In most of the hulks a passage ran down the middle of each deck, upper, middle and orlop (lower). On both sides were cells containing from ten to twenty prisoners opening on to the passage by a door with a grille, through which all which went on inside could be seen. In the bulk-head separating one cell from another was a lantern protected by an iron framework.'[14]

New prisoners were usually allocated to the lower deck. Here the air was at its foulest – hot and stinking even in winter. Here were kept the 'ne'er do wells' and the incorrigible. The sickly (of whom there were always many) were on the middle deck and the long-term prisoners, those who had served the greater part of their sentence without actual transportation, were on the upper deck, the most airy and clean of the three.

Permanent overcrowding, however, made proper classification impossible. No attempt was made at division or selection. Boys as young as nine or ten – pickpockets or petty thieves – were put with the most hardened criminals. Protesters against poverty and want from east Lancashire and poachers from the Shires went in with thieves and murderers from the stews of Seven Dials and Marylebone. The innocent wrongly convicted were housed with the most guilty.

Emmett and his group descended into hell. Nothing could prepare them for the sights which greeted them. They were to learn that from now on what happened to them was a total lottery. Sheer luck only would decide their fate.

As the new men were marched past the cells they were greeted with jeers, the clanking of chains and the cry 'New Chums, New Chums' and howls of mocking laughter. The inmates of the lower deck were the type of brutalised humanity of which Emmett, as a country 'yokel' never dreamed existed. The new men were put in the same cells. Immediately, the 'old hands', as they were known, would descend like locusts on the 'Johnny Raws'. Each cell had a leader, usually a brutal wretch devoid of human feeling – a man who had fought and bullied his way to the position.

As soon as a new man entered a cell the leader ordered him stripped and every article in his possession – money, personal keepsakes, what little he had – was taken from him. Sodomy was rife – in some hulks new men were gang-raped as a matter of course. Corruption abounded, the simple-minded 'Johnny Raws', who had yet to learn how to look after themselves, were preyed on and cheated by everyone. 'Old hands', warders, soldiers, officers, themselves mostly brutal and unfeeling by nature and experience, all treated the new prisoners with contempt.

Newcomers were tormented by forced quarrels and fights. Indecent and profane talk intimidated the modest. Even the issue of food was in the power of the 'old hands'. 'They called me a yokel and gave me a bad allowance of victuals. They took the best and biggest pieces for themselves and 'new chums' got lean or bone or whatever they liked to give them – if he [a new prisoner] does not do as they do, they pull him out of bed and make his life a burden. He must do and say as they do. If your heart is quite different to their ways, you must say and act as they do before them. If your heart is set against them they will endeavour to cheat you all they can.'[15] The forced use of a stinking, foul, always overflowing, water-closet in full view of prisoners and guards alike became the final, overwhelming, indignity for any 'new chum'. Compared to the hulks Lancaster Castle was a mere bagatelle.

Emmett and his group also soon became infested with vermin – fleas, bugs and lice. Their bodies, clothes, bedding alike, even the very walls of the hulk exuded vermin. Blankets were hardly ever washed or changed. It was little wonder hulks were regularly swept by epidemics of dysentery, cholera and typhus. The *Dolphin* herself, in 1826, suffered an epidemic of 'inflammation of the lungs' (probably tuberculosis). It was clear to the surgeons, 'In the majority of cases where death ensued, it appeared there had been existing disease'.[16] For all prisoners filth, fever and personal uncleanliness were inseparable. On many, sick and well alike, a depression of spirit would descend. It was not unknown for men to pine away and die.

The Royal Dockyard at Chatham, with a civilian workforce alone of 1,500 was the largest industrial enterprise in south east England. The dockyard imported 12,000 tons of foreign timber a year. In the period of Emmett's confinement on the *Dolphin* four Royal Navy ships totalling 5,328 tons were being built. The largest, the *Royal George*, a 120 gun 'first rater' of 2,616 tons, was launched in September 1827. In all ten warships were launched in the two years ending in 1827.[17]

The Hulks Act of 1776 'ordered and adjudged' that a person punished by transportation, should in his time on the hulks be kept at hard labour: 'such convicts, being Males might be employed with Benefit to the Public in raising Sand, Soil or Gravel from, and clearing, the River Thames'.[18] By 1826 this, and other types of work, had extended to any work for the Admiralty. At Chatham this meant unloading timber ships and coal barges, demolishing old property to make way for a new dock, removing stone ballast from ships, dismantling old ships, dredging mud and sand from the Medway and building earthen or stone defence ramparts. A few 'lucky' long term prisoners worked on farms in the area.

On the *Dolphin* every convict, young or old, fit or not, who could be spared worked in the dockyard every day except Sunday. He was paid a penny a day, that is sixpence per week. A number remained on board as cooks, servants to officers or to clean and sluice the hulk with seawater.

A typical working day started with 'All hands' called at five o'clock. After muster and breakfast of oatmeal skilly (gruel) at six, the prisoners were divided into gangs of ten. On leaving the hulk their irons were checked by armed soldiers acting as guards. Once rowed ashore, the gangs were allocated work. Ralph Rashleigh described a typical job '. . . without any consideration for any fitness for the work I was placed in a timber gang and found myself yoked with about twenty others to a large truck, each man being attached by a broad band which was fixed over one shoulder and under the opposite arm. The foreman of each gang [a civilian] was a veteran sailor of the Royal Navy, who was apt to visit on the convicts the same tyranny as he had been subject to from his officers when he was on shipboard.'[19]

All the labour was difficult and dangerous and accidents were frequent, particularly in the severe cold of winter. Convicts were not used to such heavy manual work. They were hampered further by their leg irons, which if too tight or too heavy cut off circulation and caused gangrenous sores. Convicts, however, were expendable. Nothing was thought if one was hurt, 'no more of than a dog or a cat'.

The convicts were at the mercy of the foreman. If anyone did not work hard enough, he was put on report and 'double-ironed', with pay stopped for up to four months. Work continued every day except if there was fog or thick mist. On those days, for fear men would escape over the marshes, all were confined to the hulk. On very wet days men broke up stones for macadamising roads.

In the dockyard at twelve noon the gangs were mustered, counted, then searched to prevent public stores, food, or tobacco being smuggled out of the dockyard (contact with friendly civilians made this possible). They then returned by boat to the hulk to have dinner in their cells. At twenty past one the convicts returned to shore to work until sunset (or six o'clock in summer). After muster and search they returned to the hulk. Once aboard, each gang was mustered yet again until the guards were satisfied all were present and nothing smuggled aboard. (Any guard who missed finding contraband was himself severely punished.) Once the convicts were 'tween decks, the hatches were battened down for the night and guards posted. Such routine became Emmett's lot for five winter months.

In winter, after being locked up for the night, the convicts were allowed to mix and converse. Discipline was relaxed. Firstly each cell ate, or messed together. Portions of bread, meat and potatoes, often indifferently cooked, were issued, the amount depending on the number of men in the cell. Everything depended on the cell-leader. If he was fair, everyone got an equal share – if not he and his cronies had first pick, the rest got their leavings.

The rest of the evening was usually spent in a 'free and easy'. Men could smoke and talk until ten o'clock. 'At Chatham men could go to any part of the hulk they pleased.'[20] (Emmett, no doubt took the opportunity to talk to his fellow rioters.) Sometimes a hundred or so convicts would gather in one area. Large kettles of tea were brewed. There would be dancing and singing to a fiddle. 'Flash' songs (songs interlarded with underworld cant or rhyming slang) were most popular. Men gambled with home-made dice, dominoes and cards. Other men washed and mended their clothes.

Pilfering and corruption continued to thrive. 'You can keep nothing, you have no place to keep anything in.'[21] Items stolen from prisoners were sold to guards. The money bought tea, sugar and tobacco. Robbing of the dead was commonplace. If a man died in his bed during the night, his body was searched by the others for hidden money or valuables. Only in the morning, when the hatches were raised, was the body, by then stark naked, removed. Many smoked tobacco in the belief it kept fever away. This, plus the stench of the bilges and unwashed humanity, made the air so foul one could hardly breathe. Candles went out in the fetid atmosphere. The guards who removed the hatches every morning were almost overcome by the rush of hot, noxious air.

In the evening 'free and easy', however, crime was the constant subject of conversation. Not for nothing were hulks described as 'seminars of profligacy and vice'. 'Some talked decently and properly, some talked of their trials and former convictions, some cursed, some swore, many talked profanely and indecently.'[22]

Thomas Dexter, sentenced in 1828 to seven years transportation, was on the *Dolphin*. He was asked by the Select Committee into Secondary Punishments, 'Was the language in the *Dolphin* much better than you heard in Newgate?'

'Not at all, when the prisoners were by themselves (no guards present) I should say the language was quite as bad as Newgate.' A final question: 'Do you think a man can learn much good in the hulks?'

'I'm sure he could not. Men must leave their hulk much worse than when they went into it.'[23]

The Reverend George Harker, chaplain of the *Dolphin* in 1827, also told the Committee that a 'small selection of the best religious publications has been made for the use of the men during their hours of relaxation from labour'. It must be said, however, that although a chaplain visited the hulk and there was a library of religious and secular books on every hulk, any efforts to gain knowledge or enjoy reading would have been useless when one was in such corrupt company as the lower deck. It would be a brave man indeed who stood out against the gang law which prevailed. If a man valued his skin, he would better fight, sing and gamble with the rest. This way of life, with all its abominations, continued for Emmett through the winter of 1826 and early 1827.[24]

Another burden a decent man had to bear was the uncertainty of his length of stay on the hulk. Because of the arbitrary system of selection and the availability, or otherwise, of ships, prisoners never knew when they would leave the hulk. When Capper, as Superintendent of the Convict Establishment, estimated he had a ship-load of convicts available he requested the Admiralty to charter a ship. Both these things could take some time.

The young, physically strong, long sentence men (for example, those transported for life) such as Emmett and his group were always sent to Australia at the first opportunity. Consequently, on 5th March 1827 Isaac Hindle, Simeon Wright, John Hoyle and James Chambers were transferred from the *Dolphin* to Plymouth. On 31st March Hindle, Wright and Hoyle sailed in the *Guildford* for Sydney, New South Wales. (James Chambers, however, did not arrive in Sydney until 1828.)

Meanwhile, on 30th March 1827 the 497 ton convict ship *Manlius*, a sturdy, square-rigged merchantman built in Quebec in 1825, sailed from Gravesend. She dropped anchor off Sheerness at the mouth of the Medway on 1st April.

On the *Dolphin* at about the same time, selected prisoners, Thomas Emmett, Josiah Baldwin, Joseph Clayton and Lawrence Hardman (amongst them also Oliver Collins), were called out for transfer to the *Manlius*.[25] The 'Bay' prisoners (as they were now known, after Botany Bay) were given a perfunctory examination by the surgeon, then addressed by the chaplain. In the custom of the day the chaplain told them not to wallow in, or rejoice in, their past, which had gone beyond recall, but to set forth on this new journey with joy in their hearts. He told them to accept their lot in life and be content to be rewarded in the life hereafter. This view was favoured by many Church of England vicars who believed the 'lower orders' incapable of managing their own affairs, that there must always be masters and men, governors and governed, because not all were born with equal capabilities.

The feelings of prisoners about to sail for Australia were said to be mixed. Some were anxious to leave England and take the chance to build a better life. Some, those transported for life, were naturally distressed to leave home and family behind for ever, never to see them again. Others were relieved to leave England's shores. They believed their 'character' was ruined and so could not bear the thought of ever facing friends and family again. Australia was the only place to go.

During the first days of April the 'Bay' prisoners were transported, by lighter, in small groups, to the *Manlius*. Emmett and his group went aboard on 4th April.[26] Like all the others, they were stripped of their pestiferous clothing and cleansed with buckets of seawater. All were clothed in the regulation blue kersey jackets and waistcoat, course linen shirt, duck trousers, yarn stockings and woollen caps. Their old clothes were often just thrown overboard. The ship's surgeon and master for understandable reasons were particularly anxious to receive no diseased persons aboard. The convicts were placed in cells below. Their bedding, one blanket.

On 16th April, some thirty miles and a world away, the Lord Mayor of London sat down, with six hundred guests, to dine in Guildhall. Prince Puckler-Muskau, a minor German princeling, was present. The Prince later noted in his diary: 'Tired with sitting six mortal hours at dinner – for once went to bed at midnight'.[27]

As the Prince lay replete in his bed, the *Manlius*, flying the red and white 'whip' (pennant) of a convict ship, prepared to set sail, with her miserable cargo, for New South Wales. It was 17th April 1827, one week short of a year since the beginning of the loom-breaking riots.

CHAPTER TWELVE

Thomas Emmett – On the *Manlius*

TRANSPORTATION over the seas was thoroughly English in concept; no other nation in Europe did the same. The Russia of the Czars, the only other country with a comparable view, exiled its citizens to Siberia, but within its borders.

Those in Britain who supported the principle of transportation believed it would do four things: expurgate, deter, reform and colonise. First, to clear Great Britain of the 'criminal classes' and so, in theory, rid, or at least greatly reduce, the country of crime. By doing so, it was believed, it would not only get rid of the guilty but deter the innocent remaining. Transportation would also enable a convict, once his debt to society was paid, to contribute to society by his own honest industry. Finally, whilst working as a labour force for the Government and free settlers, convicts would aid a colony's economic progress.

As the *Quarterly Review* put it in 1828: 'the entire removal of the individual to a new scene of life affords at once the only security to society against his future crimes and the contagion of his habits, and the only chance left for himself of regaining decency and respectability'.[1] The Recorder of Liverpool expressed it more succinctly: There was in the prisons, he declared, 'a vicious population, the removal of whom from the country was a measure of absolute necessity'.[2]

Such was the theory. In practice, because of poverty, inequality and unemployment, crime in early nineteenth-century Britain increased. Harsher laws simply created more transportable crimes. As the poor became poorer the law became more brutal to deter them from crime. Property was a god. Those without clothing who stole clothing, those without food who poached in private land were treated equally as savagely as those who assaulted and murdered. In practice also transportation inflicted grievous suffering on those who were not harsh unmitigated scoundrels of the lowest criminal type.[3]

Once aboard the 'Bay' ship the mental suffering of those treated harshly for their crime of reaction against injustice became absolute. It is reasonable to suppose that Emmett, as a simple country labourer, never in trouble with the law before, would now be in his lowest depths of despair. After five months' hell in the *Dolphin* in the company of the likes of Michael Bonell and Daniel Guinan and worse, he was, in the *Manlius* confined with others of the same ilk. (Bonell and Guinan had already sailed for New South Wales aboard the *Guildford* on 31st March.)

The mental anguish of Emmett and those of his kind was movingly expressed by a fellow Lancashire man, Thomas Holden, a Bolton handloom weaver. In 1812 Holden was charged with conspiring to riot. After he was sentenced at Lancaster to seven years transportation, Holden wrote, 'Dear Wife, I have received the hard sentence of Seven Years Transportation beyond the seas – to be sent from my Native Country perhaps never to see it again distresses me beyond comprehension and will Terminate with my life . . . to part with my dear Wife and Child, Parents and Friends to be no more, cut off in the Bloom of my Youth without doing the least wrong to any person on earth . . . O, my hard fate, May God have mercy on me, Yr affectionate Husband until Death.'[4]

Holden's last letter before he left for New South Wales ends despairingly, 'Dear and loving Wife, when I come to reflect on being banished from You and from my Native Country it almost breaks my Heart and all for not Doing the smallest Injury either to Government or subjects.'[5] Holden despaired so at leaving for seven years. One wonders at the depths of Emmett's despair as he left England for a life-time to a place, to him, on the outermost edge of the world.

The *Manlius* was a three masted, square-rigged ship of some 479 tons. She would be about a hundred feet long and thirty feet broad. The *Manlius* was a typical British merchantman of the day, such as might be seen in any port the world over. As a merchantman she was built for carrying capacity, not speed. Narrow and deep, flat-sided and flat-bottomed, without almost a hundred tons of ballast she wallowed in the slightest sea. The *Manlius* was a fairly new ship, built in Quebec in 1825, and this was her first voyage as a convict ship.[6] As no vessel was specially designed and built to carry convicts, the *Manlius*, when chartered by the Admiralty in February 1827 went to Deptford Royal Dockyard to have prison bulkheads and doorways, fitted in her holds.

Whilst she was at Deptford the *Manlius* was re-surveyed and re-affirmed as A1 classification, which meant she was in the highest state of repair and equipment. Although relatively small and slow, she was in the best possible condition – sea-worthy and well-found. The external appearance of the *Manlius* differed in no way now from an ordinary merchantman except for a box-like wooden barricade, loop-holed and fitted with strong doors, which ran across the deck the width of the ship. Inside, covered with iron bars, lay the main hatchway. Below this, in the lower deck, lay 176 male convicts, in leg-irons – and as a precaution to prevent escape during departure and the first few days of the voyage – chained to ring-bolts fixed to the bulkheads. Above, red-coated soldiers of the 39th Regiment (the Dorsetshires) armed with muskets, stood guard. (The military guard was a detachment, consisting of one captain, one subaltern, one sergeant and twenty rank and file, on its way to join the regiment in New South Wales.)

On the poop-deck, in common with any other ship going on a long journey, was a miniature farmyard. A number of coops held hens, ducks and geese, these to provide eggs and eventually fresh meat for the captain and his officers. Goats, sheep, pigs and a couple of milch cows, together with the hay and provender to feed them, took up more space on the afterdeck, the whole already bringing once familiar farmyard smells to the prisoners below.

At dawn on 17th April the Downs pilot boarded the *Manlius*. As the morning sky lightened and the mists cleared the *Manlius* weighed anchor and slowly gathered way. With a creaking of sheaves and rigging and a gentle flapping of sails the *Manlius* listed slightly as she felt the wind.

For most of the prisoners below, the new experience of being at sea was immensely frightening. Battened down, in cramped conditions, and in a semi-darkness lighted only by small oil lamps which themselves fouled the air, many men became sea-sick as the ship pitched and rolled as it rounded the North Foreland and entered the rougher waters of the English Channel. A day after leaving the Medway the *Manlius* arrived in the Downs and hove to off Deal. The pilot disembarked, taking with him, as a final action of contact with home and loved ones, last minute letters from crew, soldiers and prisoners.

The *Manlius* was now under the sole control of her master, Captain Johnson. Free to sail, she turned into the Channel and with sails bellying in the wind, she set out on her 15,000 mile journey to Port Jackson and Sydney. Down below the wretched prisoners, still in leg-irons, lay in pools of their own vomit as the ship bucked and crashed against the fresh seas. Sleep was impossible. Even standing was impossible, as with no 'sea-legs', the sick, panic-stricken men lost their balance as they tried to counter the rolling of the ship.

The prison quarters were down the main hatchway 'tween decks. Peter Cunningham, a Surgeon Superintendent who made several voyages to Van Diemen's Land and New South Wales in the 1820s, described a typical prison quarter on board a convict ship. 'Two rows of sleeping berths, one above the other, extend on each side of the between decks of the ship, each berth (separated by iron bars) being six foot square and calculated to hold four convicts, everyone thus possessing eighteen inches of space to sleep in . . . Strong wooden stanchions, thickly studded with nails, are fixed round the fore and main hatchways between decks. In each of which is a door with three padlocks, to let the convicts out and in, and to secure them at night. The convicts, by these means, have no access to the hold through the prison, a ladder being placed in each hatchway for them to go up and down by, which is pulled on deck at night. Scuttle-holes, to open and shut for the admission of air, are cut along the ship's sides; a large stove and funnel placed between decks, for warmth and ventilation; swing stoves and charcoal are put on board, to carry about into the damp corners; and in fact everything to secure health and proper comfort to the convicts during their voyage.'[7]

The prison was in effect a pen about sixty feet long, twenty-five feet wide and five feet ten inches high. It was guarded by soldiers at all times. Each oaken door was fitted with loopholes just large enough for a musket barrel so in case of trouble the soldiers could sweep the centre corridor of the prison with musketry shot. Notwithstanding the intentions for health and proper comfort, the prison was already a crowded, dark, foul-smelling 'coffin', dipping and lurching with every sea. Hemmed in by his sea-sick scum of the earth companions and guarded by equally terrified armed soldiers, Emmett must surely have been at his lowest ebb. He must have wondered, as Thomas Holden had, what he had done to deserve this fate.

Although the *Manlius* prison was newly constructed, it quickly became infested with the usual ship's rats, cockroaches and vermin. Because security took precedence over prisoners' comfort, the poor ventilation, together with 176 bodies crammed in a confined space, quickly caused the prison to become foul and insanitary. It was already little different from the *Dolphin* hulk. In spite of the Admiralty's detailed instructions on cleanliness and ventilation (notices of which were posted up for the prisoners to observe) the prison was so overcrowded as to be impossible to keep clean.

When the *Manlius* reached 'blue water', that is out of the English Channel and beyond the rough waters of the Bay of Biscay, the prisoners' irons were removed. At long last they were allowed on deck for exercise and fresh air. For some, including Emmett, it would be the first time for at least seven months they did not feel the weight of iron on their legs. Their chafed, broken, often ulcerated, flesh would for once be given chance to heal. Most would carry the scars to their grave. Offenders against the strict regulations of behaviour, however, were liable to be put back into close or double irons, that is handcuffs and leg-irons, for periods stretching from one day, or for serious offenders the rest of the voyage.

David Conway, the *Manlius*' Surgeon Superintendent, was ultimately responsible for the prisoners' health, conduct and welfare. His powers in most instances overrode those of Captain Johnson who was concerned solely with the running and navigation of the ship. Conway's powers and responsibilities were absolute. For disciplinary matters he even overrode the officer in charge of the military guard.

As Surgeon Superintendent, Conway was engaged by and paid by the contractors. Most surgeons however found convict service understandably unattractive. The exacting responsibility for up to two hundred criminals on a long voyage, in various climates and under particularly unpleasant conditions, did not attract the best of qualified surgeons. With more lucrative and congenial opportunities for the well-qualified, either in private practice or official posts, it is not surprising that the qualifications and character of most convict ship surgeons were usually of a low standard. Many such surgeons were either inexperienced poverty-stricken novices, embittered failures or alcoholics. Many of the better ones who served were naval surgeons on half-pay.

Inexperienced or drunkard as many were, the proportion of surgeons who treated the convicts humanely was relatively high. This is shown by the number of convict ships which arrived in Van Diemen's Land and New South Wales with few or no deaths on board.[8] The *Manlius* convicts were fortunate in that Conway was evidently humane and conscientious. All through the voyage he concerned himself about the convicts' diet and its effect on the sick. Of seventy-three persons Conway listed as sick (over 40% of the 176 convicts aboard), just two died. Although according to the Admiralty 'Instructions for Surgeon Superintendents on Board Convict Ships', Conway was not supposed to accept sick prisoners from the hulk, it was inevitable after at least five months in such disease-ridden conditions, that most convicts were at least sickly and weak. Conway himself entered in his journal, '. . . a great many of the prisoners were diseased with having suffered much in the hulks'.[9] Conway must have been kept very busy, certainly in the first week or two of the voyage.

During this early part of the voyage, Conway organised the hospital. This was in the forward part of the ship. A bulkhead separated it from the prison and two doors fitted with locks kept out intruders. It would hold about a dozen men.

Conway next appointed convicts in good health, who were fit and trustworthy, to act as attendants to the sick. He selected men, to work on a rota basis, to cleanse with seawater the 'tween decks water-closets. (His instructions advised, however, 'he is to cause the convicts to use the seats of ease on deck as much as possible, in preference to the water-closets'.)[10]

Surgeon Superintendents, in general, needed to be very careful about whom they chose for any position of responsibility. They would not, for example, use hardened thieves and the incorrigible (in the underworld slang, the sons of St. Peter: 'every finger a fish-hook'). It is, therefore, possible that Emmett and people like him – who were not professional criminals, would be given such a position. For Emmett this would be an opportunity, perhaps the only one so far, to prove himself different.

Conway also inspected all the convicts daily to ascertain the first symptoms of 'fever, flux or scurvy' and visited the sick in hospital twice a day. Anyone considered not sick enough for hospital, for example, those with venereal disease or ulcerated legs, stayed in his bunk.

By now the convicts spent as much time on deck as weather and circumstances permitted. When the weather was fine they were on deck the whole of the day and even dined on deck. The convicts were kept busy in various ways. Under the supervision of the crew, gangs scraped and swabbed the deck. Others used the minimum of two hours' exercise per day allowed by Admiralty regulations by constantly walking round the deck in file. Men were encouraged to dance to keep limbs supple, albeit at all times the convicts were on deck, all the military guard were on duty to guard against mutiny.

Another part of Conway's multifarious duties was to ascertain those 'who can read, those who can read and write and those who can do neither'. He had then to 'use his best endeavours to establish schools for the convicts where circumstances permitted'.[11] Conway was fortunate that he had on board a convict named George Joll, a thirty-two year old schoolmaster under sentence of transportation for fourteen years. It was established practice on convict ships to use any convict who had such experience and ability to teach his fellow-convicts. It is highly probable George Joll was given this job. Also on board were three convict clerks, William Hitchen, Robert Jelf and William Kerridge, and a printer, William Aldis. No doubt these men assisted.[12]

Inevitably early in the voyage the scourge of dysentery appeared. Dysentery was endemic in the hulks, so sickly convicts brought it with them to the ship. In spite of Surgeon Conway's efforts his treatment, in the manner of medical knowledge of the times, could only be rudimentary. Very little was known about the probable causes of dysentery, typhus and cholera and other infectious diseases, therefore it was certain dysentery would appear in the crowded stinking 'tween decks. During the voyage Conway was to have at least twenty-one convicts in hospital with dysentery (only the more serious cases) and two would die. (The official issue of two bedpans and two 'close-stool' pans per ship, regardless of numbers aboard, gives some indication of the sanitation problems in the hospital.)

Ironically, the first person on the *Manlius* to lose his life was the ship's first officer, washed overboard on 15th May during a storm as the ship neared the Canary Islands. The whole of the voyage, as if disease and overcrowding were not enough, was to be plagued with bad weather, with few respites of calm.

Several days after the loss of the first officer, the look-out spotted the 12,000 feet Rico del Tiede on the island of Tenerife, in the Spanish Canary Islands. The words 'land in sight' quickly went round the ship. For the convicts, however, it meant being put back into leg-irons and kept down below in the prison. A day later the *Manlius* dropped anchor in Santa Cruz harbour. Immediately bum-boats laden with welcome fresh fruit and vegetables came alongside. Captain Johnson arranged for fresh beef, pork, and poultry to be purchased, to replace the 'farmyard' stock long since eaten.

Sufficient wine also was purchased for Captain Johnson and his officers and passengers. (The *Manlius* had two – a Mr Cruickshanks and Quartermaster Benjamin Lloyd, of the 39th Regiment, who was joining the Regimental depot at Sydney.)

The convicts shackled below had at least the gratification of the strange, warm tropical scents blowing from the shore. The lucky ones near the scuttle-holes could see the fruit and vegetable sellers as they bargained with soldiers and crew. Beyond lay the tempting, glorious sight of white buildings and waving palm trees round the harbour. The Admiralty had a strict rule that any monies or property convicts possessed on arrival on the ship was to be delivered to the Captain for his keeping. This however, did not stop (and probably encouraged) petty thieving amongst convicts. No doubt at least some convicts were able later to barter something with the crew for fruit.

The *Manlius* stayed two days at Santa Cruz before setting sail on the three thousand mile run to Rio de Janeiro in Brazil. The convicts were brought out on deck again only when the *Manlius* was out of sight of land. As the ship journeyed nearer the Equator, conditions in the prison worsened considerably. At best the prison was ill-ventilated and now under the blazing sun, even with hatches open, the stench of sweating humanity, water-closets and bilge-water would be unbearable. Hot pitch bubbled from deck seams and burnt flesh where it fell. Water was always scarce – just two pints a day were issued and this putrid and warm. Night-time indeed was a nightmare.

The convicts were on deck as much as possible. Although deck-scraping and swabbing and laundry work continued there were too many to be occupied all the time. No 'proper' employment using tools could be found for the convicts because of the risk of tools being used as weapons, in, for example, a mutiny. Consequently the boredom of the long sea voyage was alleviated by gambling, petty thieving and quarrelling.

In good weather fishing was allowed. A hooked strip of canvas greased in fat would attract bonitos and 'sea-lawyers', the sharks which trailed behind the ship's stern. In the circumstances these made excellent eating and a change from the staple brined or salt beef (known as 'salt-horse' by convicts and crew alike, and it probably was).

Despite working-parties, fishing and the school, there was much idleness and boredom amongst the convicts as the ship made its way over the vast seas 'forever advancing, forever in the same place'. Gambling stood high in the long list of convict vices and inevitably led to more thieving and more quarrels. Gambling became a mania. Men gambled for anything – food, tobacco, even their clothes. Dice were made out of bone from the salt beef; cards from anything a man could lay his hands on – bibles and prayer-books were particularly useful.

Peter Cunningham stated: 'Gambling is a prevailing vice and requires great exertion to keep it under; dice, cards, pitch and toss, soon become general; and to such a height of infatuation will this vice be carried that I have known a country simpleton go three whole days without food, having gambled away his rations for the period. Until gambling is stopped thieving will be carried on, because the fellow who loses his own dinner will always insure one out of another fellow's mess, unless he is a very sorry thief indeed.'[13] Two things were certain for any country 'simpleton'. He would need to be more than a very sorry thief to even survive, and if he could not play cards when he boarded the ship he would be an expert when he left.

Other distractions of course existed. Singing and dancing on deck were encouraged, although it was usually the 'flash'type so dear to the London criminals. Crew members could always be relied on to provide the fiddles for accompaniment. Crew members provided other services. Josiah Baldwin, amongst others no doubt, took the opportunity to have a mermaid tattooed on his left arm. Another favourite pastime was to stage plays, or more often mock trials. These were often a parody of their own in which the 'judge', probably the biggest villain aboard, 'robed in a patchwork quilt with a swab combed over his head for a wig, his face made up with red lead, chalk and stove blacking, would volley denunciations (amongst great hilarity from the audience) at the cowering 'prisoner'.'[14]

The dreary monotony, when even the flying fish and the schools of dolphins became commonplace, was broken for a time when the ship reached the Equator. The ship's crew would perform the ceremony of 'Crossing the Line' in which 'Father Neptune' would come aboard to initiate those who had never crossed the Equator before. The ceremony took place on the main deck and on a convict ship it would be necessary – as fear of mutiny was never far away – to have again all military guards on duty. Father Neptune appeared '. . . fearsome in swab-wig and iron trident, shells and dried starfish entangled in his oakum beard and stinking to heaven – the sea-god would bear down on the neophytes flanked by his grinning Jack-tar "mermaids" holding buckets of soap and gunk. The initiates were clipped with scissors and lathered with a mop, "shaved" and then ducked in a tub of sea-water.'[15] Obviously only trusted convicts took part but it was a welcome means of lessening the tension which grew from boredom.

As the *Manlius* sailed through the tropics the perennial problem of dysentery worsened and Surgeon Conway's tiny hospital filled with patients. On 24th June convict William Weaver, from Essex, died. Five days later another convict – Richard Mansfield of Middlesex – died. Each was buried at sea after a short service by Conway.[16]

In the 1820s many convict ships followed the route of the Canary Islands, then Rio de Janeiro and then the long sail, helped by the prevailing Westerlies, direct to Australia. All ships called at the Canaries, most called at Rio de Janeiro, with some calling at Cape Town, either in addition to, or instead of, Rio de Janeiro. Nothing is known of *Manlius*' actual route in 1827 except for Conway's ambiguous comment: 'we experienced very severe weather before we got into the latitude of the Cape and from thence to Sydney nothing but gales and heavy seas . . . '[17] What is certain, however, is that it would be necessary for *Manlius* to call at one or even both of these ports for re-victualling in preparation for the long final stage of her journey.

When bad weather struck *Manlius* the idle basking in the sun would come swiftly to an end. In bad weather the convicts were kept, chained and locked in the darkness 'tween decks day and night. The violent motion of the ship made sleep impossible and the terrified convicts could do nothing except listen to the crashing of the waves and the tortured creaking of the ship's timbers.

With the hatches and the scuttle-holes closed the prison became utterly foul. Windsails were fitted above the hatchway and ventilators to bring in air, but they were not enough. Conway did his best. 'The greatest attention to ventilation and moving the windsails about the prisoners was paid . . . as many of the prisoners as could be got on deck and out of the wet were doing so even during the severe weather.'[18]

In spite of this, the condition of the convicts (and also the military and the crew) was appalling. Water broke on every deck as the ship rolled in the seas. The whole of the ship was wet. Water seeped through the ship's seams and it was impossible to keep anything dry. Bunks and bedding were soaked through. Worse, bedding could not be brought up on deck, in the normal practice, to clean and air to get rid of vermin.

It was not uncommon for seas to crash through the hatchways and down into the prison, leaving convicts knee-deep in swirling water filthy with the refuse of the bilges. The fetid, damp atmosphere, in such overcrowded conditions bred more vermin and disease. The closed hatchways and scuttle holes excluded all air and light, so, devoid of oxygen, lamps and swing stoves (for heating) would not burn, leaving all in the wet darkness.

Thirty years before 1827, a Dr Vanderkamp, a missionary, described a similar voyage in a convict ship. '. . . the loathsomeness of the convicts' situation in perfect darkness was beyond description. The prison – with its dreary darkness, heat and putrid effluvia – with the clank of chains affords the strongest idea of Hell and of the damned which could be conceived.'[19]

As the voyage went on, not surprisingly fevers and scurvy made their appearance. Surgeons were instructed to issue daily to each convict lime-juice mixed with sugar and port wine to prevent scurvy (partly caused by vitamin deficiency), but this was never completely effective. A constant supply of fresh fruit and vegetables was necessary – of which, of course, there was always only a limited supply on board.

Other food, however, was in ample supply. 'The rations are good and abundant', wrote Surgeon Cunningham in 1825, 'The common diet of the convicts is certainly more than is requisite to keep them in health, as they have no work to do'.[20] The food was as good as, if not better in many respects, that issued in either the army or the navy. Complaints by convicts about food were relatively few.[21]

The convicts were divided into 'messes' of six men. Each group elected its own mess captain (in practice, as in the hulks, the strongest with his cronies took over). The mess captain, again as in the hulks, drew the daily ration and each mess was responsible for cooking and sharing it. In the 1820s each convict was allowed a pound of salt beef or pork a day, with three quarters of a pound of bread, plum pudding or pease pudding twice a week and a pot of gruel, made with Scotch barley every morning. This was supplemented by occasional issues of rice, suet, flour and butter. There was tea and sugar daily and three quarts, when in good supply, of water a day. An occasional treat was 'red port wine' (nine bottles per hundred men).

On board *Manlius* however, Conway was not too satisfied about his convicts' diet. He recorded in his journal, 'There is ample food but not sufficiently made [prepared]. The prisoners have nothing by way of breakfast unless three times a week – Monday, Thursday and Saturday the days which oatmeal is served out. It is astonishing to see how they watch these days on which they have the oatmeal. It is made into a thick porridge.' Because of this Conway believed, 'Raisins or currants may be done away with and oatmeal given in their stead, as also a portion of the pease, as they do not eat a third of them [raisins and currants], the rest is thrown overboard. When raisins and currants are served out there is always quarrelling as one mess divides to each his share, another mess mixes them up with their flour direct as they get them. This, I feel, has tended to cause much pain in many of the cases of dysentery, if not in some instances to cause the complaint from the sharp pieces of wood and small stones which one invariably mixed with them.'[22]

Unfortunately, the system of having mess captains on board ship meant little had changed from life in the hulk. The hell of the *Dolphin* was exchanged for the hell of the *Manlius*. The brutal, vicious cell-leader who had fought and bullied his way to the top in the *Dolphin* did the same in the *Manlius*. Men were, if anything, more corrupted in the *Manlius* – a spell in the *Dolphin* had ensured that. The once 'Johnny Raws', such as Thomas Emmett, had for sheer survival's sake, learned how to look after themselves.

However William Johnson as Captain, or indeed David Conway as surgeon, saw the convicts on deck, the real world down in the prison hold was still a personal nightmare for such as Thomas Emmett. He – and others – were herded twenty-four hours a day with depraved and degenerate men who had the most unimaginable depths of indecency and criminality. To survive he had to be as they were. What he had been before mattered not. 'He was now a prisoner and – thrust into a suffocating barracoon – he lost his self-respect and became what his gaolers took him to be – a wild beast to be locked under bolts and bars, lest he should break out and tear them.'[23]

On the *Manlius*, sometime about 9th August, land was at last sighted. The interminable storm tossed journey in the Southern Hemisphere winter was almost over. Everyone on board, convicts, guards, crew and all, watched as the ship passed by a low lying, brown scrubby land, sloping down to a white sandy shore. This was the coast of southern Australia. Once through the dangerous, rocky, Bass Straits between the coast and the island of Van Diemen's Land, the ship was never out of sight of land as she made her way along the coast of New South Wales.

Immediately after sighting land Captain Johnson ordered the *Manlius* to be prepared for port. 'Lag-ship' (convict slang for convict ship) or not, the *Manlius* would be as presentable as possible when she arrived. The convicts were set to clean and fumigate the prison, the hospital and themselves. Blankets and clothing were washed (dipped first in a tub of urine to help kill vermin). Decks, as always, were thoroughly scraped and swabbed. The crew was kept busy painting woodwork, varnishing the bright work and repairing and tarring the rigging. The men of the '39th' cleaned their equipment and polished their brasses.

Conway would have time for little else but to complete reports and catch up with his multiplicity of paperwork in readiness for arrival. He was required to record in his journal his observations on the general condition and state of health of the convicts. By this stage of the journey he would no doubt also know the 'character' of his charges. Clearly, a favourable report would stand any convict in good stead on arrival.

There was an air of expectancy about the ship. Convicts received new clothing for use on arrival – a jacket, waistcoat, 'trowsers', two shirts, a cap and a pair of shoes. When all the work was finished they were, as was customary when nearing a port, kept in irons below. The crew 'made and mended' their shore uniform of white duck trousers, striped shirt and coloured neckerchief. They brought out their traditional shiny black tarpaulin hats and brass buckled shoes.

Two days later the *Manlius* passed Botany Bay (the actual settlement was at Sydney, seven miles up the coast). An elegant white lighthouse high on the rocks on the southern entrance to Port Jackson, the harbour in which Sydney lay, soon came into view. An hour or so later the *Manlius* passed between two ragged, creamy-brown, sandstone cliffs 250 feet high and three quarters of a mile apart. Known as the Heads, these formed the entrance to one of the finest harbours in the world.

A pilot came on board to take the ship the final seven miles. The harbour was almost land locked and those on deck had the sensation of being on an inland lake with little bays with sandy beaches on either side. It was as beautiful as a dream. The ship slowly made its way to Sydney Cove, which was between two spits of land, Bennelong Point and Dawes Point.[24] The *Manlius* hove to and dropped anchor at the entrance to Sydney Cove, several hundred yards from its wharves and warehouses. On the rising ground behind lay the whitewashed dwelling-houses, mansions and government buildings of Sydney. It was a cold dry August day.

The journey from England took 114 days, almost four months. In spite of the persistent bad weather it was one of the quicker voyages to New South Wales in 1827. Of seventeen convict ships to Sydney that year, the average time taken was 120 days.[25]

The *Manlius*, and Thomas Emmett, arrived in Sydney, New South Wales on Saturday, 11th August 1827. It was one week short of a year since Thomas Emmett stood trial.

CHAPTER THIRTEEN

On the *Harmony*

As felon transportees Mary Hindle and Ann Entwistle should, in theory, have been separated from the rest of the prisoners after the trial. Each sleeping room in the Female Felons' tower was intended to accommodate three prisoners. It is inevitable, however, that Hindle and Entwistle shared their room with several of the other female transportees at present in the castle.

In spite of the usual drop in numbers after the assizes Lancaster Castle was still overcrowded. Although the total had dropped from the record high of 578 in 1826 to 525 (in the quarter ending March 1827) the castle filled up with vagrants and deliberate offenders seeking relief from the winter cold and hunger.[1] Because prison discipline was lax and the buildings poorly designed for the constant vigilance necessary there were constant problems with the inmates.

The castle was also used as a dumping ground by Lancashire asylums for their problem cases. (Mentally unstable vagrants were a not uncommon feature of Lancashire's, or indeed England's, roads.) The insane and the violent, therefore, were mixed willy-nilly with convicted prisoners and those awaiting trial. Female prison staff were too few and overworked to have proper control. (Mrs Cecilia Leech, the matron in charge of female prisoners, complained when asking for an assistant that she had worked for seven years from six in the morning to nine at night seven days a week for twenty pounds a year.)[2]

Amongst this mess of overcrowding and atmosphere of fear and tension Hindle and Entwistle awaited the future. It is very possible however, that forty-six year old Ann Entwistle was not unduly distressed. She had been in prison twice before and – as she had told her escort at Helmshore – she had no fear of prison and would at least be better fed. With winter upon them, and perhaps little comprehension of the future, Entwistle would have few worries.

Mary Hindle, however, as far as is known, was of different calibre. Her husband George was a woollen manufacturer. As Mary Holden of Haslingden, she was married at Haslingden Parish Church in 1819 by the Reverend Gray. He baptised their daughter in 1820. Her home in Pleasant Street, Haslingden, a street of small manufacturers and tradesmen, was a 'Club' house – a sign of working-class wealth and respectabilility.[3] Her father-in-law, Abraham Hindle, was a respected businessman in Haslingden – a churchwarden in 1826. Of course Mary Hindle may have been 'no better than she should be'. She certainly frequented public houses – and made bets with others who did – but her background and upbringing seems that of a respectable family.

It is very possible, in her case, that Judge Park felt a dreadful example had to be made, not of a petty criminal such as Ann Entwistle, where the effect would not be quite the same, but of a usually honourable, decent, person, in order to impress on other usually honourable, decent persons not to think of breaking the law. It is noteworthy that of the eight male transportees only Emmett, a single man, and James Chambers, a family man, had no previous convictions. Perhaps the same logic applied to them.

It is possible Judge Park was concerned for Mary Hindle's future and reasoned that transportation would give her the opportunity to have a new life away from bad associates. Whatever his reasoning, Judge Park's sentence of transportation for life on Mary Hindle, a married woman with a six year old child, seems particularly savage.

Her sentence seems even more so when the totals and types of female offenders are considered. In the history of transportation to Australia from 1787 to 1842 approximately 8% (2,000) of 25,000 female convicts were transported for life. Of the 25,000 females transported for periods of either seven, ten, fourteen years or life, at least 91% of a sample were sentenced for theft, burglary, robbery, forgery, perjury, murder, manslaughter, assault, and so on. The remaining 9% were not recorded. Offences for riot and machine breaking were too few to feature in the sample.[4] Up to 1827 it is probable that Mary Hindle and Ann Entwistle were the only two English female rioters and machine breakers transported to Australia. (It is also likely that Ann Entwistle, at 4 feet 8¾ inches, was the smallest female rioter ever transported to Australia.)

Mary Hindle's character witness did not turn up at court. It is not known who he or she was. The absence of a character witness was always a strong disadvantage to a defendant. Judge Park, in spite of his reputation for 'his good sense and strict impartiality' and as a judge, 'the extreme anxiety he displayed for his client,' was of course helped in his judgement by an independent opinion of a defendant's character.[5] Mary Hindle was doubly unfortunate – a character witness who did not turn up was worse than none at all.

After the trial, however, many people believed Mary Hindle had been unjustly treated. On 10th October 1826 John Holgate, a Helmshore factory owner, sent a petition signed by thirty-four 'very respectable inhabitants' (including William Turner) to Robert Peel. On 23rd October Peel's secretary replied: 'I am directed to acquaint you that the prisoner's case is of such a nature that he cannot recommend her to His Majesty as a fit object for any extension of the Royal Mercy'.[6] Other petitions by the Reverend Gray, her husband George and her late father's employer, cotton manufacturer John Rostron of Holcombe (who also offered her a job for life) were also turned down. The law demonstrated its mercy when thirty death sentences were commuted to imprisonment. With the transportees, it demonstrated its power.

Mary Hindle, with Ann Entwistle, remained in custody to await a ship to Australia. Separated from her husband and child, in the company of the sick, insane, the violent and ne'er-do-wells, and now with hope of a pardon gone, Mary Hindle's own sanity must have been at risk. Dr John Smith, the prison surgeon, speaking of the prison as a whole, later wrote that he 'frequently observed prisoners under depression. From time to time suicide attempts have taken place'.[7] It would not be surprising if Mary Hindle was in that category.

Two of her fellow-rioters were much luckier. When Alice Grimshaw and Margaret Yates were given three months' imprisonment on a non-capital charge they went to Preston House of Correction to serve their sentences. They stayed there under the benign rule of Governor William Liddel until released in November 1826. Liddel's care of his prisoners was even more lax than the care of those at Lancaster. On 29th March 1827 Liddel was charged by the County Justices with dereliction of duty. Amongst many other things he 'had not prevented male and female prisoners from communicating'; 'been inattentive to cleanliness'; 'played cards with his turnkeys and convicted prisoners' and, in addition, 'his general habits were those of intoxication'.[8] Grimshaw and Yates were fortunate indeed to serve their sentence under such an indulgent master.

At the same time, Betty Howorth, at seventeen the youngest to be sentenced to death, and Ann Ingham (who almost certainly was present at Chatterton) completed their three months' imprisonment at Lancaster. They returned to the cold and semi-starvation of home. In February 1827 Betty Marsden left, her six months completed. Five women rioters remained. Mary Hindle, Ann Entwistle, Betty Cunliffe, Johanna Oldham and Phoebe Tomlinson. These last three left in August 1827.[9]

As the women lay in their sleeping rooms the spring 1827 assizes brought a reminder of the riot. George Heys, of Haslingden, the captain at the New Inn and Lower Booth, and almost certainly known to Mary Hindle, was amongst four rioters brought to trial. After the riots Heys fled, first to Manchester, then Liverpool. There he worked at his trade of navvy (navigator – construction labourer) on the new docks until arrested there by the indefatigible John Kay, constable of Blackburn.

Described as, 'an emaciated looking wretch, age of twenty-eight but looking forty,' Heys described how he sent one pound to his wife so she could go to Liverpool to be with him. His wife was 'ill of a fever' and could not go.[10] Heys told the court that, at the time of the riots, he and his wife and four children had nothing to eat and he was out looking for work. His character witness, Thomas Rostron, a Haslingden weaver, said he had known Heys since he was a child. 'I never heard anything bad said against him and I know he was always willing to work for such wages as he could get.'[11]

The jury found Heys guilty but recommended mercy 'on account of the distress of the times'. The judge was equally merciful. Heys received three months' imprisonment. He would be back with his wife and family by June.[12] Next, John Fairbrother and Lawrence Rostron were quickly acquitted for their part in the riots at Woodhill and Lower Booth respectively.

Finally William Barnes of Haslingden stood accused of breaking windows at Chatterton. Robert Ashworth, a special constable, told how he arrested Barnes in a public house in Haslingden a week after the riot. Barnes was defiant. 'Yes, I was at Aitkens', he said, 'There was no flinching there. We did as much as we could and I did as well as anyone'. Thomas Rostron, this time a reluctant witness for the prosecution, told the court that though Barnes was present at Chatterton, he did not actually see him assist the mob. John Rothwell, another weaver, who had known Barnes for seven years, acted as character witness. He knew Barnes as a very quiet man and a good neighbour.

Fifty-seven year old Barnes was as truculent in court as he was at Chatterton. When asked if he had anything to say, he replied, 'I leave myself at the mercy of the court. You can do as you please'.[13] Barnes was the only rioter to be defiant at his trial.

Although, at his age, he could chance saying 'Do as you please', he at least showed he was not intimidated. The judge acquitted him.

Lancaster Castle was at all times damp and poorly ventilated. In winter, of course, conditions worsened. Pulmonary and catarrhal complaints were common. Dysentery was practically endemic. Early in 1827 *cholera morbus* appeared, presumably because the wells which supplied the castle drinking water were contaminated by human faeces. The condition of prisoners was, in general so poor that imprisonment for long periods, say over a year, was permanently detrimental to health.

Sometime during her stay at Lancaster Mary Hindle's own health began to suffer. Possibly as a result of years of lack of proper food and warmth, now combined with overcrowding and bad ventilation, she began, to add to her misery, to have repeated attacks of 'pulmonary inflammation' (pleurisy). This was probably in addition to tuberculosis. During an attack, pain in her left breast and difficulty in breathing plus constant coughing made sleep impossible. Dr Smith, with the limited means at his disposal, could do little but put her in the female infirmary and try to ease the pain with a solution of antimony and nitrates.

In 1827 Lancaster Castle housed, in addition to debtors and vagrants, two classes of prisoner, those awaiting trial and those sentenced to death or transportation and hard labour. Only the second class was required to work. Those on hard labour normally operated the treadmill to operate the looms on which other prisoners wove the cloth to make prison clothing. Others were cotton winders, waste-pickers, tailors, shoemakers, and so on.

Mary Hindle and Ann Entwistle were not required to work. The permanent overcrowding and shortage of staff, however, meant that Matron Leech was forced to use trustworthy first class prisoners on such jobs as supervisory cleaners, cooking in the kitchen and assisting the nurse (a paid employee) in the female infirmary. How well Mary Hindle behaved, or was able to work is not known. It is feasible her conduct would be such that she would be employed when she was fit. The alternative would be idleness and intense boredom. In winter, prison nights were intolerably long. The overcrowded sleeping rooms were candle lit from dusk until nine p.m. and then in total darkness until eight a.m.

The sour stink of unwashed bodies made the crowded nights worse. Prison rules for personal cleanliness were hardly enough in the circumstances. 'Every prisoner shall wash himself [herself] thoroughly once a day, and his [her] feet at least once a week. He [she] shall also, if the Surgeon so advises, be placed in a tepid bath at least once a month.'[14] At best life was uncomfortable, at worst it was a nightmare.

At least the food improved in 1827. Because Surgeon Smith believed the cholera and diarrhoea outbreaks of 1826 were at least assisted by the poor diet, the portions of stew, boiled beef, potatoes and cheese were increased. They were supplemented by red and white herrings and cows' heads. Whether this was completely responsible or not, deaths dropped from ten in 1826 to five in 1827. In March 1827, however, dysentery worsened, affecting almost all prisoners. Diarrhoea remained a plague, and a female prisoner died of *cholera morbus*.[15]

Mary Hindle and Ann Entwistle spent almost nine months in these conditions awaiting the unknown future. Ships carrying female convicts to Australia were less frequent than those for males. Of twenty-five convict ships sailing in 1827 just six carried females.

There were no hulks for females, therefore they invariably waited for long periods in prison for a ship. Unknown to Mary Hindle and Ann Entwistle, two ships sailed whilst they were waiting – the *Princess Charlotte* for New South Wales on 31st March and the *Persian* for Van Diemen's Land on 13th April.

The day after the *Persian* sailed, the Home Office wrote to the High Sheriff's Office at the castle. They were to remove their female transportees 'with convenient speed, on board the Ship *Harmony* lying at Woolwich in the River Thames and there delivered to the Contractors or Master of the said Ship'.[16] The castle was allowed fourteen days in which to deliver the prisoners.

By mid-April ten other female transportees had joined Mary Hindle and Ann Entwistle. As was customary the head gaoler, Thomas Higgin, personally notified the transportees. The prison chaplain, the Reverend James Rowley, accompanied him to address a few words of consolation. Most Church of England clerygymen believed that if convicts behaved themselves they could, in time, redeem the character they had lost. To suffer in the cause of redemption would help cleanse their guilt. In this way he advised them to humbly accept their new lot in life. (What, if anything, the Reverend Rowley said to Ann Entwistle, a Roman Catholic, is not known.)

The prisoners were divided into two groups of six each. Six went on 25th April – exactly a year since the riots at Middle Mill and the New Inn – and the others the following day. On the morning of their departure the prisoners were examined by Dr Smith. Home Office regulations required him to ensure that 'they shall be found free from any putrid or infectious Distemper, and fit to be removed from the Gaol'.[17]

Dr Smith would need to decide whether Mary Hindle was physically fit to travel 250 miles on the outside of a stagecoach. Very possibly, the longer she stayed at Lancaster the more her health would be affected. As he himself was later to comment about prison conditions: 'Pulmonary complaints are observable amongst those who have undergone a long imprisonment'.[18] Mary Hindle, was however, by order of the court, a transportee. The two factors combined gave Dr Smith no option but to pass her fit to travel.

Some care was taken, however, of the convicts on their journey. The Home Office required that 'the convicts must be cleanly and properly clothed and each of them provided with the Articles of Wearing Apparel as undermentioned:

One New Woollen Jacket or Gown
One New Cotton Jacket or Gown
One New Cotton Petticoat
Two New Flannel Petticoats
Three New Shifts
Two New Neckhandkerchiefs, Coloured
Three New Pairs of Stockings (Two pair of which Worsted)
Two New Pair of Shoes.'[19]

The clothing not actually worn by the convicts was bundled up and taken on the stagecoach.[20]

Mary Hindle's journey from Lancaster to London would be very similar to that of Thomas Emmett. In April it would, at least, be warmer. Nothing, however, could spare Mary Hindle and her fellow-travellers the shame and humiliation of travelling

Mary Hindle and Ann Entwistle leave Lancaster Prison for Woolwich, April 1827.

chained together on top of the stagecoach.

Whether Mary Hindle saw her husband and daughter before she left Lancaster is not known. It is hardly likely that life and the authorities would be so cruel that she did not, although prison rules allowed her visitors only every three weeks. Full of guilt and shame at losing her 'character' she also had the unendurable burden of leaving her family, never, as far as she knew, to see them again. For a woman such as Mary Hindle the sentence of transportation was of exquisite cruelty, a torture with no ending.

She also had pitifully few legal rights. Women were doubly disadvantaged. They were the legal chattels of their husbands. However little working-class men had, their women had even less. They could not own property, nor sign any legal contracts. They had no rights over their own children. They had no social or legal status in a completely masculine world. Mary Hindle could do nothing, if her husband could not, or would not, help her. She was entirely dependent on the kindness of such people as John Holgate.

After the mental anguish of leaving family and friends behind came the indignities only women had to undergo. When calling at coaching inns en route to London access to lavatories would, in all probability, be forbidden. Stables and backyards would meet their needs. A pump or a well would supply water. Much would depend on the decency of the male escorts but even they could not stop the inevitable jeers and lewd comments of every idler. Too often female convicts invited contempt rather than pity. Some female convicts were coarse and crude themselves and well able to return in kind any indecent language. For a decent woman it was only the beginning of a journey calculated to debase and mortify.

When the coach arrived in London the convicts boarded a lighter at one of the busy wharves near London Bridge. They sailed down the River Thames towards Woolwich through the congested mass of river traffic which was one of the wonders of the maritime world. On either side of the river ships large and small were lined in row after row at the docks and wharves. Tyne colliers discharged coal to feed a million coal fires. Dutch schuyts unloaded fish at Billingsgate wharf. Busy steam packets ferried passengers across the river. The whole was a mass of noise and confusion – a scene of wonder to the Lancashire convicts.

The ten mile journey to Woolwich took the lighter along Limehouse Reach, past the Royal Dockyard at Deptford, and the dockyard at Blackwall where the 120 feet high masting shed (higher than any factory the convicts had ever seen) towered over the area. From there onwards desolate marshland lay on either side of the river until they reached the town of Woolwich.

Woolwich was a wholly naval and military town. On the rising ground behind, the elegant quarter mile long frontage of the Royal Artillery Barracks was prominent. The town was also the home of the Royal Military Academy and the Royal Marine Barracks. The famed Royal Arsenal extended for half a mile along the river bank. The Royal Dockyard however was the leading establishment, employing nearly a thousand men and boys. The yard built and repaired naval ships. There was a large inner and outer basin and dry docks as well as slipways for building. The merchantman, now convict ship, *Harmony,* lay in an adjacent wharf.

The 373-ton *Harmony*, like the *Manlius*, was a newcomer to the convict trade. (She was to make a second voyage, to Van Diemen's Land, in 1829). After her holds were fitted with prison bulkheads, doorways and so on at Deptford in March and early April, she moved to Woolwich to await her cargo. Her Surgeon Superintendent, William McDowell, joined her at Woolwich on 16th April.

The *Harmony* was smaller than most convict ships. Of the eighty-eight which sailed from England to New South Wales in the period 1820 to 1829 inclusive, only three were smaller – and those by just a few tons. She was probably about one hundred feet long and thirty broad. She was a sturdy ship, however, built in St. John's, Newfoundland in 1818. Probably because of her age she was classified E1, which meant when surveyed for insurance purposes no defects were found and she was deemed capable of carrying a dry cargo safely. The numeral signified she was 'well-found' in equipment.

The Home Office notified gaols holding female transportees as soon as the *Harmony* arrived at Woolwich. Although Lancaster Castle was perhaps one of those in England furthest away from London, their prisoners were amongst the first to arrive. Ever-crowded and always cost-conscious, Lancaster's policy was to pass onto someone else, as soon as possible, the responsibility and cost of feeding and keeping convicts.

Mary Hindle and her group arrived on 26th April. Each was examined by McDowell and received and signed for by *Harmony*'s master Richard Middleton. Mary Hindle became ship's convict number thirty-two. She and the rest languished in fetters in the dark and gloomy prison 'tween decks for almost six weeks before *Harmony*'s complement of eighty convicts arrived and she was ready to sail.

Many female transportees were from the thieves' kitchens of England's larger towns and cities. London and its immediate area provided at least 25 per cent – many from the foul rookeries of Seven Dials, Marylebone and St. Giles. The next largest group invariably came from Lancashire. (In *Harmony*'s case, 15 per cent.)[21] For many, particularly those from the slums of London, crime was a way of life and only source of income. Some were alcoholic wrecks who haunted the gin-shops selling themselves for a tot of gin. At least one in five were professed prostitutes, 'on the town'. At least 83 per cent of all female transportees were sentenced for theft of property – robbery, larceny or burglary. Most of the rest were for offences against the person – assault, murder or manslaughter – with a few perjurers, coiners and vagrants.

Many were professional criminals with special 'talents': 'skinners', who enticed children to go with them and then stripped them of their clothes or alternatively, as prostitutes, stripped drunken customers and sold their clothes; 'till-friskers', who emptied tills whilst a partner distracted the shopkeeper, and so on. Their behaviour and attitudes contrasted completely with those who had offended through poverty and suffering. Lancashire and London had barely a language in common – the cant language used by London criminals in particular was incomprehensible to others.

By the beginning of June *Harmony* had eighty 'she-lags' aboard. Forty-six were transported for seven years, fourteen for fourteen years and twenty for life.[22] In addition were three children.[23]

Just a day or so before she sailed David Middleton welcomed aboard a distinguished passenger, Lieutenant Colonel James Thomas Morisset of the 48th Regiment (Northamptonshire). Colonel Morisset was already well known – and feared – by convicts in New South Wales. He was returning there with his new wife Emily and baby after two years in London. Morisset had applied for the post of commandant of Norfolk Island penal settlement. He was previously commandant at Newcastle where 'He was a terror to the convicts, infamous for the harshness of his punishments'.[24] Morisset was obsessed with 'keeping the scoundrels in order', and as the New South Wales government was keen to make Norfolk Island more feared as a punishment centre than ever, Morisset was their ideal man.

Although a military dandy, resplendent in his own scarlet and gold uniform, Morisset was frightful at close hand. In 1817 in the Peninsular War he was wounded by an exploding mine. 'His mouth was diagonally upward – one eye was normal but the other protruded like a staring pebble and never seemed to move.' The cheek bone and jaw had been shattered to fragments and had re-knit to form a swollen mass 'like a yellow over-ripe melon'. He would defiantly thrust his cheek forward in communication as though daring his interlocutor to look away. Morisset wore his wound like a badge of honour.'[25]

Fearsome in looks, demeanour and reputation, Morisset's presence on *Harmony* must have put the fear of God into the female convicts. It so happened he was the only military man aboard. Female convict ships did not carry a guard of soldiers.

On 4th June 1827 the *Harmony* took aboard the river pilot, slipped her moorings and moved slowly down the river. The Thames was a busy highway, at all times full of shipping so a river pilot was essential. At the fishing village and port of Gravesend she changed pilots and made for Sheerness, where the Downs pilot took over. At Deal, the final contact with England, the *Harmony* came under the control of Captain Middleton and she gathered way for her run down the English Channel. By this time *Harmony*, a slow ship, was left behind by the scores of other, faster, ships which left the Thames at the same time.

With the sole difference of having no military guards, female convict ships had the same regulations and conditions as the male. The surgeon was responsible for the convicts, the master for the running of the ship. When the *Harmony* reached the open sea the convicts were released from their irons and the daily routine established. As on the male convict ships the females were divided into messes of six each. Each mess had its own cooking and eating utensils and a kettle for tea making. In theory, the prisoners elected their own mess captain or, on female ships, matron. In practice, as on the male convict ships, the strongest and most vicious seized the position for the power it gave them.

After a few days at sea McDowell appointed half a dozen convicts as 'matrons of the deck', with responsibilities for keeping the prison clean and carrying out his orders. Similarly to male convict ships, to alleviate boredom, schools were encouraged. Mary Hindle could read and write so possibly she helped to teach others.

Several factors determined the sort of voyage the convicts would have. Not least were the personalities and competence of the surgeon and master. Admiralty regulations advised the surgeon 'to receive the cordial cooperation of the master in the execution of the duties entrusted to you'. Likewise the master was required to 'comply with the surgeon's regulations regarding the management of the prisoners and permit them on deck as ordered'.[26]

If the master was brutal (and there were many such in the merchant service) and the surgeon incompetent or weak, the convicts were doubly unfortunate. Naturally, a strong conscientious surgeon took a lot of the discomfort out of the voyage, regardless of the character of the master. If both surgeon and master were brutal, incompetent, or simply incompatible, the voyage, certainly for females, could be one of unlimited horror.

There was also the nature of the crew. On a ship the size of *Harmony* they would number approximately thirty. Most merchant seamen were, in the 1820s, notoriously the dregs of society, little better than many convicts. They were hard-drinking, hard-swearing and often illiterate. They lived aboard ship in cramped squalor and were generally tough, quarrelsome and amoral. Their indiscipline was notorious. Place such men on a ship with female convicts on a sixteen-week voyage and it was inevitable fornication would thrive.

Prevention of fornication was an insoluble problem on all female convict ships. Right from the beginning of transportation to the end, 'the desire of the women to be with the men was so uncontrollable that neither shame nor fear of punishment could deter them from making their way to the apartments of the seamen'.[27] Decent surgeons and masters were powerless, regardless of regulations, to prevent it in the face of the unruliness of most convicts and the insubordination of most seamen.

Anything could happen. In 1824 surgeon James Hall, on the *Brothers*, was knocked down, beaten and kicked by six female convicts at the instigation of the chief mate, for trying to suppress fornication. In contrast, in 1826 on the *Providence*, surgeon Matthew Burnside was dismissed from the convict service for cohabiting with one of his female convicts throughout the voyage and for inviting others to drink in his cabin. The ship's master was also dismissed for colluding with Burnside.[28]

As always, life for convicts, particularly females, was an absolute lottery. There is no record of the experience of the convicts on *Harmony* but sexual intercourse between at least some and crew members was inevitable. Because many female convicts were prostitutes and loose-living it was assumed by most seamen that all were. Sexual harrassment was part of the system. Decent women lived in constant fear of rape.

At worst, convicts such as Mary Hindle would need, for sheer self-protection, to have a 'regular' cohabitee, such as a ship's officer or mate. This would be some security against the attentions of the more degenerate of the crew. Very possibly, however, with such a distinguished passenger and his wife aboard, more effort than usual would be made by *Harmony*'s surgeon and master to keep immorality under control. Neither would want an adverse report made against them by a man such as Morisset.

Not surprisingly, considering their way of life, some convicts came aboard with venereal disease. Even at Woolwich, on 1st May, five weeks before *Harmony* sailed, McDowell treated twenty-six year old Charlotte Dawson and forty year old Martha Hibbert for chancre (venereal ulcer). Fortunately McDowell was not too busy treating the sick during the voyage. Only nine persons became sick enough for hospital treatment. (Three of these he treated twice.)

Unfortunately for Mary Hindle her 'pulmonary inflammation' (pleurisy) returned when *Harmony* was fifteen days at sea. The cause, no doubt, was the unbearably fetid air and the overcrowded conditions below decks. Also the *Harmony*, because of her small size, would certainly be a 'wet ship', taking water as she rolled and pitched in heavy seas.

The voyage on *Harmony* was McDowell's second. In 1825 he was in charge of 210 male convicts on the *Lady East*, en route for Van Diemen's Land. When the ship arrived at Hobart many convicts complained of gross ill-treatment and excessive punishment (flogging) at McDowell's hands. An official enquiry exonerated McDowell, concluding that 'the prisoners were very insubordinate and he had inflicted no punishment beyond that normal for preserving order and discipline'.[29] McDowell himself therefore boarded *Harmony* with a reputation.

Harmony, in contrast, was a quiet ship. McDowell recorded no hint of anything amiss and no convict appears to have complained about him. McDowell's treatment of Mary Hindle and his detailed recording of it, indicates a caring and professional attitude towards her during her stay in the ship's hospital. His journal states: 'at sea June 19th 74 degrees in the shade . . . Mary Hindle . . . complained of pain in her left breast attended with a difficulty of breathing. Pain increased on her drawing a faint inspiration or by pressure on the cartlidge ends of her ribs or even lying in a horizontal position. No fever. Pulse a little quicker than usual and smaller. Bowels regular – applied a large blister to her breast.' (This was probably a mustard plaster to 'draw out' the inflammation.)[30]

The following day, 'Breathing and pain in her breast greatly reduced from blister and feels much better. Had blister dressed and continued with nitrates and antimonical solution.' (This to stimulate the secretions in her chest and so ease the coughing.)

On 21st June however, 'Dysphemia and pain in her breast rather worse and says she did not sleep well during night. Pulse small and quick. Skin hot. Tongue rather dry and complains of coughing in night.' On the 22nd, though, 'She considers herself nearly well in comparison to what she was before. Blister dropped and nitrates and antimonical solution given.' McDowell must also have 'bled' her (applied a leech). He noted 'Pain in breast greatly relieved from bleeding'.[31]

On 23rd June she still had pain and difficulty in breathing. The following day however, McDowell wrote: 'No complaint this morning but a little debilitated. Continued antimonical and nitrate solution.'[32] She then convalesced in hospital until discharged on 30th June.

By this time *Harmony* was at the Cape Verde Islands and the temperature in the high seventies. More than Mary Hindle were affected by the conditions. On 3rd July convicts Margaret Cain and Esther McDonald were admitted briefly to hospital with a diagnosed pulmonary inflammation. This time McDowell was less concerned. McDonald, he tartly noted, was 'a very discontented woman, her debilitated condition more from the heat than from her disease'.[33] (It was 79 degrees in the shade.)

As *Harmony* crossed the Southern Ocean on her final run to Australia Mary Hindle again fell ill. She was admitted to hospital on 11th August and stayed there until 20th August.

Five weeks later, in the early hours of Thursday 27th September, *Harmony* passed through the Heads and entered Port Jackson. By then she was in the company of *Prince Regent*, carrying 180 male convicts, which left Woolwich five days after *Harmony*. It was unusual for two convict ships to arrive at Sydney at the same time so '. . . the metropolis was thrown into a bustle the whole of the day'.[34]

McDowell's relations with Middleton on the voyage must have been acrimonious to say the least. When McDowell presented his report and convict indents to the Governor he formally complained that Middleton had short served the convicts' rations. Sir Ralph Darling agreed with the findings of an official inquiry that, 'although McDowell's conduct had been irritating, the master's proceedings had been most unbecoming and improper'. McDowell's complaint was upheld and Middleton did not again command a convict ship.[35]

As a result of her two stays in hospital and the general consequences of Middleton's short rations, Mary Hindle had a more wretched voyage than most. Of sexual matters nothing is known; of storms or otherwise nothing is known; but for Mary Hindle, arrival at Sydney must have been something of a relief – mixed with anxiety for the future.

Australia's seasons are opposite to Britain's; its September is late spring. Whatever Mary Hindle knew or did not know of 'Botany Bay' and her life to come, at least for her health's sake she would have two summers.

CHAPTER FOURTEEN

A Lucky Break

AS soon as practicable after the arrival of *Manlius* in Sydney Captain Johnson and Surgeon Conway left the ship for Government House. Here Captain Johnson presented the ship's log-book for the Governor's inspection.[1] Surgeon Conway presented his report and the Convict Indents, a list of all those given into his charge.

For Conway it was an important mission. He had to satisfy the Governor that the convicts were in a clean, healthy state and that no unnecessary expenditure was made of 'medicines, medical comforts and necessaries' in his charge. As a Surgeon Superintendent, Conway was granted a gratuity for each of the convicts arriving safely. He needed a certificate from the Governor to obtain his pay when he returned to England. He also had to apply to the Governor for permission to secure a passage home.

It is therefore perhaps understandable that when submitting his complaint about the quality of the convicts' food on board *Manlius* Conway ended his report: 'If having given my apprehensions on the question of diet and it does not meet with your approval, I hope you will consider it done with the best motives'.[2] Conway was taking no chances.

Only when the Governor and his staff were satisfied with every detail of the ship's papers was official sanction given for landing the convicts. A day was appointed for the Colonial Secretary, or his deputy, to go on board *Manlius* and examine the convicts. Because of the weekend this was probably Monday 13th August. No-one, neither crew nor military, let alone the convicts, could leave the ship before then. Neither could anyone board her.

On Sunday, Conway led his final Divine Service, disturbed only by the usual throng of fruit-sellers and curious onlookers calling from small boats surrounding the ship. On deck for the first time, the convicts had a tantalising glimpse of Sydney town and the sounds and smells of dry land.

On Monday morning the official news of *Manlius*' arrival appeared in the 'Shipping Intelligence' report of the *Sydney Gazette*. 'On Saturday last arrived from England whence she sailed on the 17th April last, the ship *Manlius*, Captain Johnson. She brings 172 male prisoners. Passengers, Quarter-master Lloyd, 39th Regiment, Dr Conway and Mr Cruickshanks.'[3] (To be described as a passenger would surely bring a wry smile to Dr Conway's face.) This formal announcement meant that employers or would-be employers could apply to the government's Assignment Board for convict labour.

Sometime on Monday morning the Port Health Officer gave the *Manlius* a clean bill of health. Immediately afterwards, the Chief Superintendent of Convicts and a bevy of minor clerks came aboard. The convicts were mustered on deck in small groups in the presence of Captain Johnson and Surgeon Conway.

Each convict was questioned and his records checked. Conway was required to describe the conduct of each man during the voyage and whether he had any infirmity which might affect his future employment. The interview, however, was not one-sided. Convicts were given the opportunity to lodge any complaints about the voyage. 'Have you received your rations?'; 'Have you any complaint to make against the Captain, his officers and crew?'; 'Have you any illness or infirmity?'. Each convict gave to the panel his name, age, place and date of trial, his sentence, his native place and his trade. His height was measured and a clerk wrote a detailed physical description.[4]

Thomas Emmett, Josiah Baldwin, Joseph Clayton and Lawrence Hardman must have been of more than usual interest to the panel. In 1827 'political prisoners' such as the rioters were rare. Eight out of ten convicts were thieves, with most of the rest offenders against the person, that is assault, rape, manslaughter, murder, and so on. Over the whole period of transportation to New South Wales from 1788 to 1849 only a 'minuscule fraction' could be classified as 'protest' offences, such as rioting and machinery-breaking.[5]

Emmett was unusual on other counts. He was (alone of his fellow rioters) a first offender. (Almost two thirds of transported convicts had previous convictions.) It was also rare for a first offender to be transported for life – seven or fourteen year transportation was the norm. Emmett could also read and write. Of the other three only Joseph Clayton could do so. Despite his being only 5' 3½" tall – only Josiah Baldwin was smaller, by half an inch – Emmett's personal attributes, skills and behaviour would be welcomed by the interviewing panel. He would be a welcome change to the all too common reprobates, and a good choice for assignment to a 'good' employer. There is no record of Surgeon Conway's remarks concerning Emmett, or indeed how he behaved on the *Manlius*, but it is fair to assume Conway did not comment adversely on him.

Assignment was a matter for the government and it was the practice to place convicts where they would be most useful. The essential work for the colony's economy was done on the farming establishments so they had priority. The government itself was an employer and convicts who had 'a depraved character' (there were also those in authority who believed *all* convicts were depraved) were usually placed in government service. These were worked, in gangs, on the hardest of labour on the roads, bridges and harbours of the colony.

The muster of the convicts could take several days, particularly if complaints were numerous or protracted. The convicts were kept below, still in leg-irons until the Assignment Board made arrangements for their reception and distribution. By government regulation written application for convict servants was necessary. A list of applicants and their requirements was kept and convicts assigned to employers according to the quantity of land the applicant possessed. Applicants for domestic servants needed no property qualification, although strictly speaking all assignments of convicts as domestic servants in Sydney ceased in March 1826.

These preliminary arrangements took time. Emmett and the rest of the convicts stayed below on *Manlius* for thirteen long days – until Friday 24th August – before they set foot on solid earth.

At an early hour the convicts were again mustered on deck and sorted into groups. They were taken ashore in rowing boats or lighters. The solid earth they had longed for seemed to move under them as they stood unsteadily on the quayside. The constant motion of the ship at sea remained with them for some little time.

The convicts immediately became the centre of attraction of every idler in Sydney. Once again questions were asked. 'Who are you?'; 'Where are you from?'; 'What's the news from England?'; 'Anyone from Lancashire?' For the convicts, relieved at last to be ashore after the crowded, stinking weeks afloat, Sydney was a bewildering revelation. Noisy, drunken men and women from the pot-houses and grog-shops of the Rocks, the nearby convict quarters, taunted and abused the newcomers.

The newcomers were to discover that drunkenness and licentiousness were the curse of Sydney. Mr Ernest Augustus Slade, a former magistrate for the port and town of Sydney, was later to say, 'You see drunken people in all directions, men and women fighting in the street and the most disgusting scenes of all descriptions'. Slade likened the Rocks to the stews and slums of St. Giles in London, but: 'I should call St. Giles a paradise compared to the Rocks'.[6] Once again the new convicts had swapped one hell for another.

In 1827 there was, however, another Sydney. The town had a population of some 12,000, including many free settlers. At first glance it had all the sights of a well-off English provincial town. There were long wide streets lined with whitewashed two storey cottages with verandahs in front enclosed by a neat wooden paling. Elegant street lights, lit by whale-oil, stood every fifty yards. Standing back from the streets were white freestone or brick mansion houses, these roofed, incongruously, with wood shingles.

Peter Cunningham was impressed by 'the number of parrots and other birds of strange note and plumage which you observe hanging at so many doors . . . At the corners of the streets, and before many doors, fruit stalls are to be seen, teeming, in their seasons, with oranges, lemons, limes, figs, grapes, peaches, nectarines, etc., etc., at very moderate prices.'[7]

In contrast, Cunningham noted, 'the government gangs of convicts marching backwards and forwards from their work in single military file – with perhaps the jail gang straddling sulkily by in their jingling leg-chains – tell a tale too plain to be misunderstood'.[8]

The convicts from *Manlius* were soon aware they were in a country far different from England as they observed these things as they marched four abreast, chained together, up the hill from the quay to Hyde Park Barracks a mile away. The convict barracks stood on the edge of Hyde Park, an area of common land, then used for military exercises, horse racing and cricket.

The three storey building built in 1819 of soft red brick, was designed to house the convicts working for the government in Sydney. The frontage was of three main sections, the centre section surmounted by a triangular stone pediment ornamented by a crown and a large clock. It was, for those with eyes to see, an architectural gem. It was also large enough to house, if necessary, 800 convicts.

Inside, on each floor, were four large airy wards, making twelve in all. Six wards were 65 feet by 19 feet, the other six, 35 feet by 19 feet. In each were long rows of hammocks slung on strong wooden rails fixed on vertical stanchions. Seventy men slept in each large room, thirty-five in the small. Each ward was in the charge of a watchman who was supposedly responsible for the conduct of the occupants. As new arrivals, however, Emmett and his colleagues were put into a long dormitory 80 feet by 17 feet and slept on mattresses fitted to a simple raised wooden platform.

The usual occupants of the barracks were those convicts employed on government service gangs, those returned, by order of magistrates in the country areas, for punishment for committing further offences whilst on assignment and newly arrived convicts, such as Emmett and his colleagues, awaiting assignment.

Discipline within the barracks was, in 1827, almost totally absent. Corruption was rife. Drunkenness and going absent without leave were common crimes. Some convicts came and went as they pleased, bribing staff to turn a blind eye. Once again, as 'new chums', the new arrivals were exploited by the 'old lags'. Once again they were robbed of their new clothes and footwear. Once again there was sodomy. And once again there was no redress.

The barracks were at least clean and the food good. Water troughs, towels and soap were available and barbers were employed to shave the convicts twice a week. Breakfast was porridge, dinner beef stew and vegetables, served in small tubs, one each for a mess of six men. The Chief Engineer (in charge of the road parties to which most of the inmates belonged) inspected the messes several times a week and attended to any complaints about the food. Every Sunday morning the convicts mustered for church attendance, their general appearance 'cleanly and decent'.

After four days, on Tuesday 28th August, the *Manlius* convicts were mustered again. The Assignment Board representatives, reading from the newly compiled assignment books, announced to the convicts the names of their new masters and the places to which they would go.

Emmett was assigned to the Australian Agricultural Company at Port Stephens, a hundred miles north of Sydney. New Prisoner 27/1506, Emmett had got a lucky break. The worst of the nightmare was over. For any convict assignment was always a lottery. It was a matter of merest chance whether one got a brutal or a kindly master. A bad master could, and often did, by cruelty and injustice make an assigned convict's life unbearable. On the other hand, if an employer was decent, convict life lost many of its terrors.

The Australian Agricultural Company was, or tried to be, a decent employer. It was also a large, well-regulated establishment. The directors of the Company believed it was in their own interests to make their convict servants as comfortable as possible, on the principle that: 'where a man behaves well, to make him forget if possible, he is a convict'.[9]

Emmett, however, was to be separated from his fellow-rioters. Although hardly likely as a group to riot and destroy machinery in New South Wales, the group was dispersed over the colony as a matter of policy. Of the four, only Joseph Clayton had a trade (he was a wheelwright). Emmett, Baldwin and Hardman were each listed on the *Manlius* Indents as 'farmsman'. (In England they would be described as farmers or farm labourers.)[10]

Ironically, Clayton, probably because of his two previous convictions in England, plus possibly further offences either on *Dolphin* or *Manlius*, was disposed of in a group of twelve to the Chief Engineer's Department in Sydney. From then on, until his sudden death, aged 37, on 12th April 1834, Clayton worked in a gang building roads and bridges in the Sydney area. Although unchained, the gangs were closely guarded by soldiers and in the charge of brutal ex-convict overseers. Clayton was to spend the rest of his life in the company of the incorrigible and unemployable, to be inevitably levelled down to the worst in disposition and corruption.

Josiah Baldwin, Emmett's fellow-captain in Rossendale, went to the farming establishment of J.S. Harrison at Penrith, thirty miles from Sydney. Baldwin, who also had two previous offences in England, was, within twelve months, back in Sydney gaol. Lawrence Hardman went to Bathurst, over 125 miles west of Sydney, to the farming establishment of a Mr J. W. Sturgeon. He later went to Berrima, near Goulburn.

Oliver Collins, Emmett's companion on the stagecoach from Lancaster to Chatham, went from bad to worse. It is not known where Collins was assigned in 1827, but by 1828 he was at the penal settlement at Moreton Bay (now Brisbane, Queensland). Here went the 'doubly damned', the most extreme punishment short of death. Collins clearly committed a serious offence in the colony to have merited this move.

Collins' fate could not have been more different from Emmett's. Collins went to Moreton Bay during the regime of the Commandant, Captain Patrick Logan. In a cruel system, Logan had the worst reputation in Australia for cruelty. Logan had men flogged to death for the pleasure it gave him. He drove hundreds to their grave by working them, in irons, half-starved, in the heat of the day, until they dropped. At Moreton Bay, Collins, like numbers unknown, disappeared into the mists of Australia's history.[11]

For those such as Emmett, Baldwin and Hardman, assigned to a private employer, there were government regulations for their protection. Each employer was bound to supply specified amounts of food and clothing. (Those regulations were, however, very difficult to enforce over such a huge area as New South Wales.) Employers were allowed to 'indulge' their convicts with tea, sugar, milk or tobacco, as an incentive to good conduct, or as a reward for it. There were no prescribed hours of work. The usual hours were dawn to sunset. Sunday was an inviolable day of rest. There were no regulations about housing convicts. Men lived in outhouses or made do in shingle-roofed huts as best they could.

Over a year each convict would receive two new jackets, two pairs of 'trowsers', three linen or cotton shirts, three pairs of shoes of 'stout and durable leather' and one hat or cap. This clothing, at a cost of twenty shillings to the employer, was supplied by the government.

Assigned convicts usually worked as field labourers (or farmmen), shepherds, drovers, bullock-drivers, or to anything their employer decided. They were not ironed, nor indeed, under close supervision. (For shepherds guarding huge flocks of sheep in the outback, loneliness and fear of the bush was the biggest enemy.)

Although government regulation decreed that an employer or his agent should collect his assigned convicts from Sydney, it was not uncommon for men to be sent alone to their new place. (Australia was a prison without bars from which it was almost impossible to escape so as 'new chums' most arrived because there was no alternative.) In 1819 a youth of seventeen, transported for stealing a hat, was given, in Sydney, a note for his new master, a farmer four hundred miles away in the interior. He went alone, unguarded. The Tolpuddle Martyr, George Loveless, in 1834, was sent on foot from Sydney to Strathallan, three hundred miles away. He was given a blanket and rations. He was fourteen days on the way.[12]

For assigned convicts fates could be very different – one could be a well-fed domestic servant living in the family household or the wretched slave of a harsh master and flogged for the smallest offence. In general, however, most conceded that overall a decent assigned convict improved his life by coming to New South Wales. The Reverend John Dunmore Lang, a Church of Scotland minister who was in New South Wales during the 1820s, in answer to the question, 'What is the condition of the assigned servant compared with the field labourer in England?', replied, 'He is better clothed and better fed, and as comfortably lodged; he is under personal restraint, not being allowed to leave his master's property without a pass, but he has a great many comforts which may render his situation by no means irksome or severe'.[13]

There were many humane employers who gave convicts a home of their own or allowed them to keep animals in exchange for good conduct. In spite of this, assignment was still a form of slavery. There was a restraint on freedom of action and many suffered extremely the degradation of being 'owned'. Some assigned men were moved around over the years to many different employers. A man had no control over his own life. Hopelessness too often turned into bitterness.

In theory the assignment regulations provided protection for the convict against a cruel or oppressive master, but there was always the threat of a flogging or imprisonment. Being in a public house on a Sunday could mean twelve lashes with the cat o' nine tails. Insolence to a master could mean fifty. Such punishments were ordered, and witnessed by, a local magistrate who often had his own convict labour and was in full sympathy with his fellow-farmers.

At Maitland, a small settlement some forty miles from Port Stephens, for example, in the thirty days of September 1833, eighteen convicts were flogged, mostly for 'neglect of duties', drunkenness, or absconding. They shared a total of 698 lashes, with ten receiving fifty each. (One such, Henry Valentine, for absconding, arrived on *Manlius*.) The magistrate, Mr P.N. Anley, J.P., was required by law to submit a monthly return to Sydney. His final entry read, 'No.18; John Orr, neglect of duty, twelve lashes (a boy); cried out very much'.[14]

In London in 1837, James Macarthur, a New South Wales businessman and a director of the Australian Agricultural Company, told the Select Committee on Transportation his approach towards his own convict labour. 'If a convict is well behaved he will be kindly treated. If you take a number of convicts the greater proportion will be ill-behaved; their pilfering and misconduct would render them unprofitable as compared with free labour.'[15]

Speaking of his Company's assignment of convicts from newly arrived ships in the late 1820s, Macarthur went on, 'When a lot of convicts were received from a ship they were at once put to some very hard labour, such as felling and burning timber, which was a severe punishment to them. We kept them at that kind of work for a considerable time – and so broke them in; made them well-disposed. It taught them the difference between good and bad, and the advantage of regular and orderly behaviour. Out of fifteen (of one such group) we threw out the exceptional characters and kept only the best. We did not reject them until we tried every means of making them useful. The rejected convicts were either punished by flogging or sent to the penal settlement or road gangs.'[16] In fact, the quality of most convicts was such that

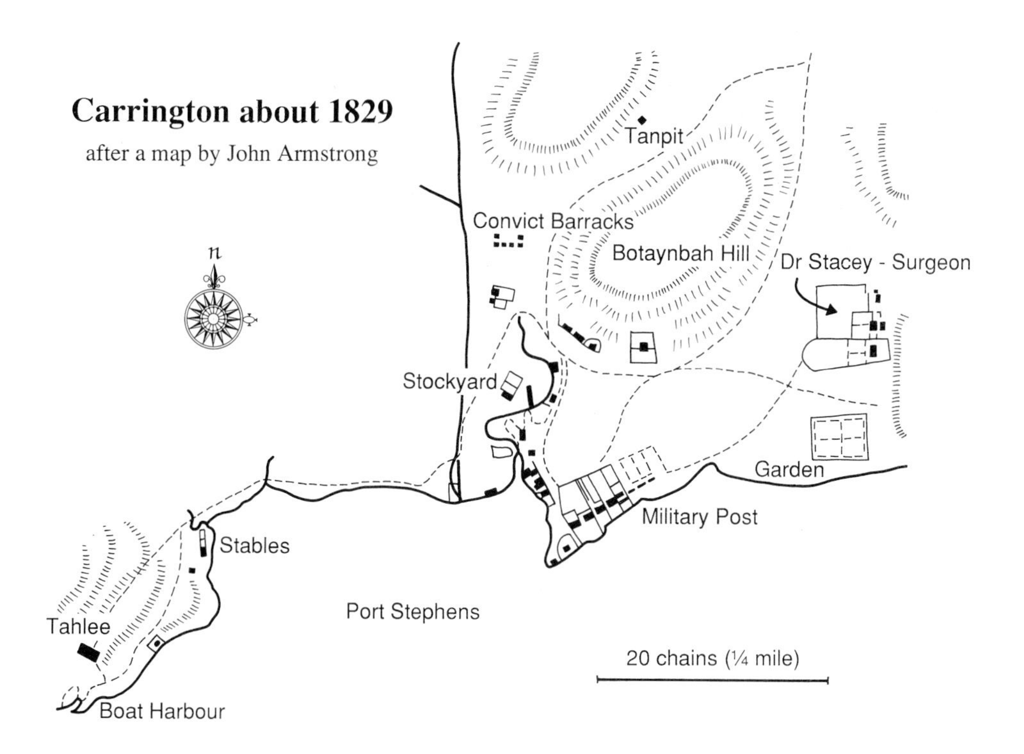

In August 1827 Thomas Emmett was assigned as a gardener to the Australian Agricultural Company's main settlement at Carrabean (later renamed Carrington) on the northern shore of Port Stephens. He lived in the convict barracks and would probably work in Dr Stacey's garden.

This map is based on original records held by the Australian National University Archives of Business and Labour and is reproduced by kind permission of P. A. Pemberton, author of *Pure Merinos and Others*

the Australian Agricultural Company was constantly complaining to the government about the numbers being short and many of the individuals 'useless'.

In 1827 James Macarthur, with his brother and brother in law, was the senior member of the management committee of the Australian Agricultural Company. The Company was formed in London in April 1824. Its main purpose was to raise fine woolled sheep, of the purest and finest breed, on a one million acre government grant in New South Wales. It was a Company based on sound moral principles. It was the hope of the Company 'that their servants (those free and salaried) should not only assist in the punishment and reformation of British criminals, but also diffuse useful knowledge throughout the colony, encourage migration of useful settlers and female servants and promote a system of rural industry'.[17] Thus the Company intended that 'most of their shepherds and labourers would be assigned convicts, supervised by free and experienced persons, many of them from Europe on seven year contracts'.[18]

In January 1826 Robert Dawson, the Company's agent in New South Wales, established the Company's main settlement at Carrabean (renamed Carrington in 1831) on the northern shore of the sheltered, natural harbour of Port Stephens. He then took up the whole grant on one million acres in one block stretching north from Carrabean to the Manning River. A village and boat harbour were built at Carrabean. Farms, and later settlements, were built at Booral and Stroud, in the river valleys which stretched north towards the Manning.[19] Sheep stations were established on the hilly western side of the grant area. The rest of the area was good agricultural and pastoral land, thinly wooded and well watered.

In 1827 more land at Carrabean was cleared and spacious stores and workshops created. Landing facilities were improved. (For a few years from 1816 Carrabean had been a centre for cedarwood cutters, and vessels laden with cedarwood sailed direct to England.)

Meanwhile, in Sydney, in late August 1827 Thomas Emmett, now finally separated from his fellow-rioters, was marched in irons from Hyde Park Barracks to Sydney Cove. Those assigned to the Australian Agricultural Company were some fifteen in number and all, except for the clerk, Robert Jelf, were designated as labourers. The group was put down into the hold of the twice-weekly packet ship from Sydney to Newcastle and Port Stephens.

The seventy-five mile voyage to the old penal settlement of Newcastle took about twelve hours. Here, other convicts disembarked, destined for the notorious coal-mines.[20] Port Stephens lay fifty miles further north and within hours the ship passed between the twin headlands of Yacaaba Head and Tamaree Head and entered the calm, blue-water harbour and tied up at the jetty at Carrabean.

The settlement consisted of some thirty detached houses built for the Company's tradesmen, supervisors and overseers. In addition there were saw-mills, sheep-pens, stock-yards, stables, warehouses and so on. The whole covered an area approximately one mile square. The boat harbour and jetty was set slightly apart from the main residential area. On disembarking, Emmett and his group marched half a mile along the sea edge, then inland to the convict barracks on the outer edge of the settlement.

The convict barracks consisted of six huts enclosed by a wall. In 1827 they held approximately a hundred men. The barracks were sufficiently far away from the settlement to avoid any inconvenience or annoyance to the Company's married tradesmen, overseers and indentured servants, but not so far away as to be beyond the hearing and control of their overseers and guards should any disturbance occur. The housing for a military guard of eight soldiers under a corporal was also placed near enough to give any assistance if required.

The quality and usefulness of Emmett's group is not known, but it was possibly little different from previous ones sent to Carrabean. Richard Dawson held no high opinion of convict labour. He believed their skills and behaviour left much to be desired. Of a party of Irish convicts assigned in April 1826, he spoke of 'the little they can do'. The following month, of an assignment of boys fifteen to eighteen years of age, only two or three were made useful, after much trouble, in mason's work. Most of another group of eleven men were 'only tolerable labourers', and so on. In October 1827 when Dawson complained to John Macarthur (James's brother) that he 'desired something besides boys, cripples and Manchester weavers and spinners', it is just possible he was referring to Emmett's group.[21]

For Emmett, however, Carrabean convict barracks must have been a haven of peace after the uncertainties of life on the *Dolphin*, the *Manlius* and in Hyde Park Barracks. How much so, depended on Emmett's abilities and willingness to work.

CHAPTER FIFTEEN

A Family Story

THOMAS Emmet arrived at Carrabean at a bad time for the Australian Agricultural Company. Robert Dawson's constant disputes with George Slade, the Company's accountant led to his summary dismissal by Dawson. This led to a financial crisis at the very time the estates were expanding rapidly. As a result Dawson himself was dismissed. Eventually, in December 1829 Sir William Parry R.M., Arctic explorer and Hydrographer Royal to the Admiralty, arrived at Carrabean as the Company's new Commissioner.[1]

Parry quickly reorganised the administration and management of the Company estates. (Carrabean was renamed Carrington.) He also believed in, and so continued, the Company's moral and religious principle that its convicts should be reformed as well as punished. Parry did his best to impress upon the convicts the necessity of obtaining salvation through piety. He distributed a great number of Bibles, prayer books and religious tracts, but, as he feared, for little result. He found, by contrast, that most of the convict workers, their wives and their children barbarized their lives with their drinking, their promiscuity and their profane language. 'What can be done with these people?', he asked in despair.[2]

There were, of course, successes. The words on the tombstone of the convict Suzanna Craven at St. John's Church, Stroud, gives some idea of the vision of the world taught to the convicts and the free servants of the Company. 'She learned through divine grace the vanity of the world and no longer looked for happiness but, convinced of her sinful and lost estate, eagerly sought to be saved through Jesus Christ.'[3]

Most of those Parry and later his successor, Henry Dumaresq (Commissioner 1834 to 1838) were concerned about, however, worked in the pastoral out-stations and farms. Within the boundaries of Carrington and Stroud there was at least some propriety and discipline amongst the better convicts.

The pastoral districts were troubled, as anywhere else in New South Wales, with disorderly 'old hands' and lawless bushrangers. As free settlers developed more land the aborigines resisted, at least for a short time until they moved elsewhere or were subdued. The Company's shepherds were in constant fear, both of the bush itself with its lonely spaces and of wandering hostile aborigines. (In July 1830 one of Emmett's 1827 party of fifteen from *Manlius*, one James Tongue, was killed by aborigines in the bush.)

In contrast, convict life in Carrington was relatively peaceful. During 1827, the year of Emmett's arrival, the Company was busy building up its stock of fine Merino sheep. For example, a total of 964 French and Saxon ewes and rams arrived at Carrington. (These were a hardier strain than the original Spanish Merinos.) Forty-four free settlers – shepherds, labourers and artisans and their families – a total of eighty-eight persons, came with them.

One such free settler was John Baker. He arrived on 24th November 1827, with his wife and two young sons, contracted at a salary of £30 per year to serve as a gardener. Baker, undoubtedly, replaced Thomas Allen, a gardener who should have come to Carrington in November 1825. For reasons unknown, however, Thomas Allen was discharged by the Company when his ship was at Rio de Janiero, en route.

By 1829 Carrington possessed a large botanical garden. The garden, as far as is known, was built and developed by Baker. Amongst other things it was to provide Dr James Stacey, the Company surgeon, with medicinal plants and herbs. Thomas Emmett, at least in 1828, was employed in the botanical gardens.[4] It is reasonable to suppose that Emmett was a member of the convict gang, supervised by Baker and his overseers, which constructed and maintained the garden.

From his assignment to the Company on 28th August 1827 to 30th April 1835, Emmett must have satisfactorily conformed to the rule and disciplines of the Company. It says much of Emmett that he survived the Company's 'breaking in' period, to quote James Macarthur's evidence to the Select Committee on Transportation, 'of very hard labour such as felling and burning timber'. Emmett had clearly become well-disposed to the advantages of regular and orderly behaviour. He had already learned, in prison, in the *Dolphin*, and the *Manlius*, the unforgettable lesson that to survive one submitted to authority.

On 30th April 1835, therefore, Emmett's 'ticket of leave' was recommended by Port Stephens Magistrates Bench. It was conditional on his remaining in the district of Port Stephens (Carrington). Six months later, on 26th September, the recommendation was confirmed by the Colonial Secretary's Office for publication in the Government Gazette.[5] Perhaps not only Emmett's good behaviour was considered. A note in the recommendation record shows he had had a stroke and 'lost the use of one side and his arm'. He would now, even at thirty-one years of age, be of little use to the Company.

A ticket of leave was a statement of exemption from working for any particular employer. It was the first of three stages towards any convict's absolute freedom. The second stage was a 'Conditional Pardon'. This gave the right to live and work anywhere in New South Wales but not to return to Britain. The third, a rare occurrence indeed, was an 'Absolute Pardon', granted personally by the Governor. This restored all a person's rights, including, if desired, to return to Britain. At the full expiration of a convict's sentence he or she was also free to return to Britain. Very few took up the offer.

In theory, therefore, Emmett, as a ticket of leave holder, no longer had to work as an assigned convict for the Company. He could, if he wished, work for himself, or whomever or wherever he pleased, within New South Wales. The ticket of leave was renewed every year and could be revoked at any time for any offence, but at least it held out hope for a convict who behaved well.

Emmett got his ticket after eight years, the minimum time for a 'life' sentence. (Male convicts transported for seven years could apply after four years, those transported for fourteen years, after six.) After getting his ticket, Emmett decided, or indeed was forced by his disability, to stay on at Carrington. The Company was a good employer. There was a surgeon and a hospital. There were, for those who wished, evening classes for convicts, schools and a church. Although by 1835 Carrington was declining in importance and 'going downhill' (Stroud, as more central to the pastoral operations, had been the Company headquarters since 1831) it was popular with the convicts. Many other ticket of leave men, as well as Emmett, decided to stay (sixty-two in 1836).[6]

There is no record of how Emmett earned money to live. Some limited gardening or labouring work was perhaps possible. From the scanty records available it is known however that in 1836 Emmett had money (an unknown amount) issued to him from the savings bank.[7]

The Australian Agricultural Company's humane and liberal principles in dealing with convicts ensured that those who behaved themselves got wages. Sir William Parry, in 1838, declared, 'People [convicts] who possess a skill that raises them above a common labourer or who were trustworthy, whom you could put over others, were given wages in addition to their free food, clothing and housing. It was well worthwhile to give a man £10 or £15 a year to look after a dozen others.'[8]

Emmett was at Carrington eight years when he gained his ticket of leave. He would, by then, be an 'old hand' and see many newly arrived convicts pass through the Carrington reception centre. (By 1837 there were 464 agricultural convicts plus 122 coal mining convicts employed by the Company.)[9] His experience, his length of service, and his work as a gardener quite possibly put him in the 'skilled' or 'trustworthy' category described by Sir William Parry. Emmett, therefore, was probably secure at Carrington and, with money, had neither need nor desire to leave.

There was no Company policy on marriage for ticket of leave men, although it was encouraged for moral or social reasons. The Company employed a chaplain and there was a church at Stroud. There is no record of any marriage by Thomas Emmett but it is known that he and a Deborah Wall had a son, also called Thomas. He was born on 2nd September 1838 at Maitland. Little is known of Deborah Wall. She was possibly the daughter, or widow, of a free settler, or more likely of an emancipist (an ex-convict who had served his term).

It is known, however, that Deborah Wall did not marry Thomas Emmett. In May 1838, four months before the younger Thomas Emmett was born, she married a Thomas Phillips of Maitland. On Thomas's baptism certificate his name is spelt 'Aymot', written probably as Deborah pronounced Emmett.[10]

On 1st October 1842 Sir George Gipps, Knight, Captain General and Governor in Chief of New South Wales, at Government House, Sydney, signed and sealed the conditional pardon of convict 27/1506 Thomas Emmett.

Emmett now, in addition to his ticket of leave privileges had the rights of citizenship within the colony. As a reminder to his vulnerability to the full weight of the law, the formal language of his pardon concluded: 'provided always and on Condition for and during the space of his original Sentence – otherwise the said Thomas Emmett shall be subject to all the Pains and Penalties of Re-appearing in Great Britain and Ireland for and during the Terms of his original Sentence or Order of Transportation; or, as if this Remission had never been granted.'[11] Thomas Emmett was still not to return to England.

Emmett was the first of the male rioters to get a ticket of leave and conditional pardon. Josiah Baldwin waited until May 1836 for his ticket of leave and 1847 for his conditional pardon – a full twenty years after his arrival in New South Wales. It took Lawrence Hardman twelve years (until October 1839) to gain his ticket of leave, and a further six (1847) for his conditional pardon. Of the two who came on the *Guildford*, Isaac Hindle waited even longer – until August 1840 – for his ticket of leave. He received his conditional pardon in Sydney in 1845. John Hoyle (Red John) got his ticket in February 1837 and his conditional pardon on the same day as Hindle in 1845.

Unlike Emmett, who had a permanent situation with a reputable public company, all four of these men worked for different masters in different districts scattered throughout the wilder, more remote, parts of New South Wales. Unlike Emmett, all four had previous convictions in England, and certainly Baldwin at least, had spent time in gaol in Sydney. There is no hard evidence, but for these four a lack of permanency, many different masters, good or bad, plus perhaps further offences, may explain the delay in their receiving tickets of leave.

Thomas Emmett enjoyed the privileges and rights of his conditional pardon for six and a half years. On 15th March 1849, at the age of forty-two, Thomas Emmett died. His death certificate states his abode was Carrington, his place of burial simply 'on the estate of the Australian Agricultural Company, County of Gloucester' (in which stood Port Stephens, Carrington, Stroud, and so on.)[12]

Thomas Emmett spent over half his life in New South Wales. In spite of the relative peace of his later years and a pleasant climate and the paternalism of the Company, his early years of poverty in Lancashire, the traumas and hardships of the hulks and his voyage to New South Wales clearly took their toll of his health.

Whether Emmett regretted his part in the riots will never be known. He was then not to know just how much his actions would change his life. Neither was he to know that during his years of exile, life in east Lancashire with its harsh winters and hunger, would continue to be just as hard.

There is no doubt that Emmett's quality of life at Carrington was much better than anything he could have hoped for in east Lancashire. Sir William Parry himself was quite sure. 'On the estate of the Australian Agricultural Company the condition of the convict, as regards clothing, lodging and feeding was in many respects superior to the condition of many of the agricultural classes in England. Of course men are deprived of having their families with them – but in other respects I think they are very well off indeed.'[13] It is highly likely Thomas Emmett agreed with Sir William.

Emmett saw many changes in the twenty-two years he was at Carrington. The Company expanded, but not without its problems of drought, low wool prices and, in 1847, when the assignment system ended, a labour shortage which forced them to advertise for emigrants. Emmett also saw a rise and fall of convict labour in the Company. In 1836 there were 95 agricultural convicts, in 1837, 464. In 1843, the year of his conditional pardon, there were 131. By 1847 when transportation to New South Wales ended, just four were left. At the time of Emmett's death in 1849 just 33 ticket of leave men were on the books. By 1850 all 465 employees were free settlers.[14]

The younger Thomas Emmett was ten and a half years old when his father died. Nothing is known of his childhood or youth. Neither is it known if he ever saw or even knew his father. As a native born Australian of convict descent, Thomas Emmett was a 'Currency lad', so called from the slang term meaning notes or coin only good in the colony, unlike the 'Sterling', free English born, settlers. Currency lads, in appearance and behaviour, were almost a distinctive group in the colony. By 1835 visitors to Australia were noting that the native born Australians were very different from those born in England. 'The strange way in which they spoke and how the heat of the sun and the hot winds made currency lads and lasses into hard-faced, grim-visaged, dry countenanced human beings on which the bloom of youth quickly faded.'[15] Currency lads were notable for their pride, independence and freedom from the Old World social constraints. Some were wanderers, constantly on the 'wallaby track'. Most of them carried no identification, and, being free did not need to. To them their father's 'ticket', restricting his movements, was a symbol of servitude. Thomas Emmett, no doubt, would be such a person.

When government geologists reported alluvial gold near what is now Bathurst, New South Wales in 1823 the news was suppressed. In 1841 when the Reverend W. B. Clarke showed a small quantity of gold to Sir George Gipps, the Governor of New South Wales, he was told very forcefully, 'Put it away or we shall have our throats cut'.[16] The Governor's concern was understandable. With a convict majority in New South Wales a gold rush could have been uncontrollable with possible tragic consequences. In 1851, however, the inevitable happened.

In January of that year a former New South Wales stockman Edmund Hammond Hargraves returned to Sydney from the Californian gold fields. From his experiences there he was convinced he could find gold in Australia equal in quality and quantity to any in California. Hargraves soon discovered gold at Ophir near Bathurst. The finding, in July 1851, at the Turon River field, of the Kerr Hundredweight (1,272 ounces of gold) sparked off a gold rush which lasted ten years and transformed life in New South Wales and the economic structure of Australia itself.

In 1852, when Thomas Emmett was not yet fourteen, a relatively local event possibly transformed his life. In March Thomas Renwick and Thomas Lawrie, both sons of long-time Company servants, discovered seven ounces of gold in five hours on the banks of the Peel River in the Company's Goonoo Goonoo pastoral estate, only a hundred miles from Maitland. The find was not far from Hanging Rock, where there would soon be major diggings.

The effect was electric. An Australian writer, Thomas Alexander Broune, under the pseudonym Rolf Boldrewood, wrote graphically of such a discovery. 'The whole country was full of absconders and deserters, servants, shepherds, shopmen, soldiers and sailors – all running away from their work and making in a blind sort of way for the diggings, like a lot of caterpillars on the march. Some of them you'd see dragging a hand cart with another chap and they having all their goods, tools and clothes on it. Soldiers, sailors, clergymen and doctors, old hands and new chums, merchants and lawyers. They all seemed as if they couldn't keep away from the diggings for their lives.'[17]

The Australian Agricultural Company, as well as many others, lost employees and their families to the gold fever. The news of the discoveries would certainly be known in Maitland but nothing is known of Thomas Emmett's reaction. What is known, however, is that in 1862, at the age of twenty-four, he was prospecting for gold at Lambing Flat (now Young) New South Wales.

Lambing Flat became notorious for the anti-Chinese riots which occurred there in 1861. Known in 1830 as Burrangong Creek, gold was discovered in 1860 on a nearby small plain or flat used as a lambing place. The name Lambing Flat was given to the settlement which developed. At one time 17,000 people, including many Chinese, worked the field. In June 1861 a 3,000 strong mob attacked the Chinese miners. The Riot Act was read and troops called in to restore order.

Thomas Emmett, son of Thomas Emmett and Deborah Wall, born 1838, died 1882. Ths portrait was painted in the gold fields by a Chinese itinerant artist. The original is in the possession of Mrs Gill Peasley of New South Wales

Mrs Peasley

Thomas Emmett was certainly at Lambing Flat in March 1862. There he married Maria Jane Tindall, just sixteen years old. On 4th August 1852, their son Alfred William was born.[18]

Lambing Flat produced its peak production of 124,648 ounces of gold in 1862 and it declined rapidly from 1865. Emmett was one of thousands who then moved on to the newly discovered fields at Emu Creek (now Grenfell), New South Wales. His second son, William Henry was born there in 1865. Emmett must have been one of the original seekers after gold at Emu Creek because only as late as November 1866 did a government mining registrar record that a 'rambling street' had just been formed.[19]

As early as 1867 the settlement was named Grenfell in honour of T.G. Grenfell, a gold commissioner shot by bush rangers in December 1866. From 1867 to 1869 Grenfell, with a yield of over 40,000 ounces a year, was the leading producer of gold in New South Wales.[20] Emmett and his family stayed at Grenfell until at least September 1872.

At Grenfell Emmett and his wife lost their two oldest children. In June 1865 his eldest son died, aged three. In August 1869 his second son, born in Grenfell, died aged four. Life in the gold fields was harsh and living conditions primitive. Families lived in 'humpies' – huts made of brush and bark stripped from eucalyptus trees. A contemporary account describes a typical digger's camp. 'Along the broad sloping valley were the straggling huts and tents of the diggers. Within the tent might be a piece of bark nailed on four posts driven into the ground for a table, and the same sort of thing on stretchers to sleep and sit upon – perhaps a pickle case for a seat, an old sardine box for a salt cellar, a herring tin for a sugar basin . . .'[21]

Miners and their families lived on 'bush-fare' of mutton or beef, tea with sugar and 'damper' (unleavened bread) baked in ashes. The toll in human life was high. Many, and possibly Emmett's two children, died of disease brought about by the insanitary living conditions and the poor diet. It is noteworthy that Emmett's children died in winter, the 'wet season', when conditions would be at their worst and the children most vulnerable to childhood diseases.

During their stay at Grenfell, Emmett and his wife had a third boy, Thomas Matthew (after Thomas the convict?) in 1868. (Thomas Matthew was to die, aged seven, in 1875.) A girl, Eva Jane, was born in September 1870 and a boy, Arthur, in September 1872.

In December 1874 however, their sixth child Maria was born at Parkes, New South Wales. Emmett, like thousands of others with gold fever who found the distant hills always green, moved on to Parkes in 1874 when important finds of alluvial gold were made. The next move took them to Blowering near Tumut, New South Wales, where Florence Gertrude was born in March 1877. The next child, Alice Maud May, was born, surprisingly, at Sydney in June 1879.

In 1882 Emmett and his family were at Temora, New South Wales, a town established when gold was discovered in 1880. Emmett's twenty years as a gold miner had, however, taken their toll. On 16th May, at Temora, he died, aged forty-four, from a lung complaint caused by the mine dust. Tragically, his youngest child Isabella Theresa was born on 19th May – three days after his death. Maria Jane Emmett, at the age of thirty-six was left in very poor circumstances, with six children ranging from twelve years to a new born baby.[22]

Thomas Emmett, convict 27/1506 of Lancashire, was part of the good and evil of transportation to the colony of Australia. His son Thomas was representative of the pioneer spirit which was part of the development of Australia as an industrial nation in its own right. The link between the elder Thomas Emmett and present day Australia is sustained by the Peasley family of New South Wales. Alice Maud May Emmett, born in Sydney in 1879, married George Benjamin Warden at Cootamundra, New South Wales in 1900. She died, a widow, in Sydney in 1950. She had two daughters. Her second child Zillah May married Roy Hedly Tennyson Woods. Their eldest child and only daughter Jill married Leslie Peasley. Jill Peasley, of New South Wales, is the great great grandaughter of convict 27/1506 Thomas Emmett.

By coincidence, Leslie Peasley's great great grandfather William was transported to New South Wales in 1837. William Peasley's father, in 1809, married a Marie Jackson of Burnley, Lancashire. Burnley is not seven miles from Haslingden, the scene of Thomas Emmett's violent reaction to his poverty and deprivation which led to his transportation.

CHAPTER SIXTEEN

A New Life

THE *Harmony* took 115 days to sail the 16,000 miles from Woolwich to Sydney. She lay in Sydney Cove a further sixteen days before Surgeon McDowell was formally released from his duties. During this period the female convicts were 'disposed of' in much the same way as male convicts, that is they were mustered on deck in the presence of McDowell and Captain Middleton for examination and interview prior to assignment.

Most female convicts, low-living and professional criminals as they were, were hardly good material as servants in the 'respectable' middle-class households of Sydney and New South Wales. Throughout Sydney society there was a constant fund of horror stories about female (and male) convict servant behaviour. Lewdness, insults and drunkenness were the norm. Parents were plagued by fears of their children corrupted by immoral women employed as nannies or servants. Because most female convicts were known thieves (over 80%), everything in the house – pantry, dressing-tables, desks, even the mistress's sewing-basket and certainly the wine-cellar – had to be locked up.

Small wonder good convict servant women were at a premium in Sydney. Such was the corruption of servants by other servants, decent-minded female convicts could only be obtained from a newly arrived ship – unless, and it was possible, she had already been corrupted on the voyage.

When ships such as Harmony arrived those employers entitled to receive female convicts were notified, at least officially, by a notice in the Government Gazette, to apply on a particular date. Influential individuals in need of a good servant, however, disregarded the official system. They instead contacted the ship's surgeon as soon as the ship arrived. The surgeon was asked to recommend the name or names of convicts of good character and conduct. The women were then applied for, by name, by the individual employer. Such was the demand, often many applications were made for the same women. Clearly those Sydney residents with influence, or friends on the Assignment Board, got the most valuable convicts. All this was done in spite of a rule in force since 1826 that no assigned servants were to reside in Sydney.

There is no doubt that Mary Hindle and Ann Entwistle as non-criminal, 'political' offenders would, in the eyes of potential employers, be far better servants than the great majority on board *Harmony*. As far as is known neither misbehaved on the voyage, neither, according to McDowell's convict indent, did any have former convictions. (Ann Entwistle's admitted stay in Preston House of Correction before 1826 must have been conveniently forgotten.)[1] Mary Hindle could also read and write

– clearly an advantage. Ann Entwistle was noted on her indent simply as 'can read'. (Perhaps she learned on the ship.)

Mr John Nicholson, Harbour Master and Superintendent of Sydney dockyard was, in 1827, in need of a good female servant. Nicholson lived with his wife Eliza and five children at Darling Harbour, Sydney. The children's ages ranged from two to nine years. There is no doubt Nicholson asked McDowell to recommend a good servant. There is no doubt McDowell recommended Mary Hindle. Her past record and basic good character was known to McDowell. Her behaviour on board *Harmony* was known to him. As a doctor he also knew Mary Hindle's health would not be strong enough to stand a long journey to a rural assignment. Neither would her health withstand the harsh extremes of the climate. An assignment by the sea, in Sydney itself, was more suitable. Nicholson required a laundress, therefore McDowell described Mary Hindle, on her convict indent, as a laundress.

On 13th October 1827 the female convicts were mustered on *Harmony* for the last time, and in groups, were taken ashore by lighter. Once on Circular Quay the women immediately entered the hell on earth that was the traditional greeting of those who frequented the gin shops and brothels of the harbour and the thieves' kitchen of the Rocks. The common view in Sydney of female convicts, no less than that in England, was that all were prostitutes and whores, inviting contempt rather than pity. This time therefore, the idlers and pimps came to leer and ogle as well as taunt and abuse.

A female convict in New South Wales had no rights except the right to be fed and clothed. She was no better than a slave. The assignment system – for the great majority – was just as much a lottery as for men, with sexual abuse making it worse than ever. Any free settler or convict could take a common law convict wife and throw her out when he tired of her. Those not prostitutes already were forced into it. Prostitution was part of the system. So called 'employers' were on the quayside looking for convicts to work as prostitutes. A ship-load of new chum 'she-lags' therefore attracted intense interest.

Mary Hindle was fortunate. As she arrived on Circular Quay she was met, by prior arrangement, by Nicholson's man-servant William Heyes. She was already assigned to Nicholson. Mary Hindle's journey, on foot, with Heyes to the home of her new master at Darling Harbour was only some half mile away through the streets of Sydney. Compared to the rest of Sydney, Darling Harbour was quiet and placid. On its gentle slopes stood the elegant houses and business premises of Sydney's merchants and civil officials. Mary Hindle was fortunate indeed.

Mary Hindle's life as a convict servant would not be easy. Much would depend on the benevolence of Mr and Mrs Nicholson. However humanely treated, though, Mary Hindle would always be a convict. Obedience would be enforced, if necessary. Even the children of the household had power over her. As the Reverend Bishop William Ullathorpe testified: 'They [settlers' children] are aware of the condition of these servants; they look down on them with contempt'.[2] Whatever Mary Hindle's life in the Nicholson household was like, it would be sheer heaven compared to that of 90% of her fellow-convicts. Her good character and background had succeeded in making assignment less of a lottery for her than for most.

Whilst on the quayside Mary Hindle was separated from Ann Entwistle. In much the same manner, however, and on the same principles, Ann Entwistle was assigned, as a laundress, to Gregory Hazard, a printer and bookbinder in Princess Street,

Sydney. In 1827 Hazard was twenty-eight years old, his wife Helena twenty-four. They had two girls aged one and four and a boy aged two.

As a laundress, Ann Entwistle's duties in the Hazard home would be similar to those of Mary Hindle's in the Nicholsons'. Hazard had two employees, both bookbinders. At forty-six Ann Entwistle was the oldest in the home and business by some seventeen years. Hazard and his wife were free settlers, arriving in Sydney barely twelve months before. John Nicholson, in contrast, had lived in New South Wales ten years. How well Gregory Hazard, or more to the point, Helena Hazard, could handle convict servants remained to be seen.

Within twelve months there must have been problems between the Hazards and Ann Entwistle. The 1828 Census of New South Wales shows Ann Entwistle at the Female Factory, Parramatta.[3] It is not known when or exactly why she left the Hazards' employ. For one reason or another Ann Entwistle did not succeed as a domestic servant.[4]

If Ann Entwistle was a typical handloom weaver, it is highly likely she had no domestic skills. In weaving families long hours at the loom ensured no time or inclination for anything other than weaving. Harriet Martineau expressed a disdainful English middle-class view: 'Women brought up to weaving know little else. They are not taught to sew or knit so they are fit for nothing when bad times come.'[5]

Perhaps Ann Entwistle was in this category and was too old, unwilling or unable to learn. It is, of course, possible she was rejected for drunkenness or prostitution. Whatever the reason, the Hazards evidently requested (as was their right as employers) the government to remove Ann Entwistle to the Female Factory at Parramatta.

In 1827 Parramatta, fifteen miles up the Parramatta River from Sydney, was a small market town. Like many an English market town Parramatta had an open square, magnificent town houses and pretty detached cottages complete with gardens. St. John's Church was modelled on the double-spired Reculver Church in Kent, often the last thing emigrants saw as they left the coast of England. Parramatta was also Australian. It had a soldiers' barracks, a convicts' barracks and a gaol, all rather prominent. It was full of redcoats, convicts, male and female, and aborigines.

The Female Factory stood by a stream a quarter of a mile from St. John's Church. It was the second building to have the name. The first factory was simply a loft some sixty feet by twenty feet above a gaol. There was neither security nor discipline. Convicts of both sexes came and went as they pleased. The whole was a source of debauchery and scandal. In 1821 a new Female Factory was built. It was a three storey structure, complete with cupola, clock and a security wall. Inside the wall were courtyards and a large garden. The factory was designed to hold three hundred female convicts. Designed by Francis Greenway, the same convict architect who built the Hyde Park convict barracks, the factory was another Colonial Georgian architectural showpiece.

The factory was intended as a temporary residence for new arrivals and, in theory, those between assignments. To this place came also those rejected from the assignment 'slave-market' of Sydney Cove. The very old, the unattractive, the sick, the pregnant, those with children, the absolutely incorrigible, as well as the decent awaiting collection by their assigned employer, all came to the factory. (Twenty-two, almost 40%, of *Harmony*'s convicts were at the factory in 1828.) In addition, there were those such as Ann Entwistle – rejected by their employers for general unsuitability or drunkenness, or immorality – or all three.

In 1828 the Female Factory held 537 convicts – almost double its capacity – bringing overcrowding in addition to the perennial problems of indiscipline and vice. The inmates were divided into three classes. The first class were those sent to await assignment or returned from assignment without grievous complaint from a master or mistress. These were composed of 'those without blame, being given every indulgence consistent with good order.'[6] The second class, by far the largest, were those with children and those returned from assignment because they were pregnant. The third class were the villainous, depraved and unemployable. In the same class were assigned servants under Colonial Sentence – that is sentenced by a magistrate to serve imprisonment in the factory for some offence.

The classes lived in separate dormitories. There were 'living' or dining rooms, a hospital and cells for solitary confinement. The whole was run by a female superintendent (matron) who used, in a system of favouritism, the 'best' convicts as monitoresses in charge of rooms, and as servants or cooks.

The factory was also the first, and in 1828, the only weaving establishment in Australia. Convicts were set to work to card and spin woollen yarn. The yarn was woven into the coarse 'Parramatta' cloth worn by male convicts. The finished cloth was washed in the nearby river and spread to dry and bleach on 'tenting' grounds by the river bank.

The factory was built, in theory, to control female convicts and prevent immorality. A forbidding structure, a moat and a high wall were intended to prevent all contact between inmates and outsiders, 'until such times as they should either be married or assigned as domestic servants or married persons'.[7] In the late 1820s however conditions were little better than in the old days. Male convicts still came and went freely. Some female convicts did not stay in the factory but lived with male convicts in Parramatta. Females fresh from the ship awaiting assignment were still robbed and exploited by the 'old hands', much as Emmett and his fellows were in the Convict Barracks.

For women, was added sexual abuse and harassment. Thomas Reid, surgeon on the female transport *Morley* visited his former charges in the factory in 1821. He described how they gathered round him, weeping incoherently, and told him that when they arrived the previous evening 'they were surrounded by hordes of idle fellows, convicts – provided with bottles of spirits – for the purpose of forming a banquet "according to custom" which they assured themselves of enjoying without interruption, as a prelude to excesses which decency forbids to mention'.[8]

When Ann Entwistle arrived at the factory she entered the 'first class' of inmate. This says much for her probable good conduct whilst in the Hazard household. She was fortunate. All assigned labour within the factory was drawn from the first class. She could work – and be paid. Duties such as monitoress, laundress, messenger, midwife, needlewoman or schoolmistress are examples. The pay was good – from 6d per day as a monitoress up to 1s. 9d. per day as a midwife. By comparison although women in Sydney earned two shillings per day, they paid board and lodging which factory women did not.

In 1828 Ann Entwistle would be one of the few skilled handloom weavers in New South Wales. In the factory her weaving skills – those learnt at such cost to her domestic skills – would come into their own. For her work she would receive two thirds of her pay immediately with the remaining one third accruing until she should leave the factory.

As a 'first class' inmate and working for pay, Ann Entwistle was possibly not involved in the general indiscipline and vice which was the hallmark of the factory. She did, however, get off to a bad start. On 7th April 1828, shortly after her arrival at the factory, the matron, Mrs Ann Gordon, sentenced her to twenty-four hours' solitary confinement on bread and water 'for taking, without authority, bread from the dining-hall'.[9] Thereafter she may have opted for a quiet life – that much is unknown. At forty-seven and already going grey, she was much older than most female convicts. (Of the other twenty-two females from *Harmony* at the factory in 1828, the average age was just over twenty-five.) She would therefore be better able to conform to the rules and less likely to be influenced into indiscipline.

Another role of the Female Factory was that of marriage bureau. Marriage was not only morally desirable but was considered by the New South Wales Government to be necessary for the well-being of the colony's economy. Only first class inmates were given access to this outside world. The government officially encouraged them to marry by assigning them to free, emancipated or ticket of leave husbands.

Another method was much more degrading. Single settlers or ex-convicts often went to Parramatta for a 'factory lass'. The only prior requirement was a written application to the matron. 'A bizarre scene: the women lined up in their coarse flannel dresses, some scowling and some hopefully primping; the "Coelebs" or bachelor, often an elderly and tongue-tied "stringybark" from the back-country, hesitating his way along the ranks; the matron reeling off the women's characters and records. After muttering the awkward "yes", recalled one witness to this colonial mating ritual, the bride-elect flies round to her pals, bidding hasty adieus and the bridegroom leads her out. "It's a bargain you've got, old stringybark," cries one. Hubbub and confusion mark the exit of the couple – the clothes of the convicts are returned to her, and dressed like a free woman she hies with her suitor of an hour to the church.'[10]

It was possibly in this manner that Ann Entwistle met and married her second husband. He was a fifty-eight year old widower, John Butcher, a 'Free by Servitude' man (that is, completed his term of transportation). The banns for the marriage were read in St. John's Church, Parramatta some time between April and June 1830. John Butcher (also known as John Arnold) was one of the earliest convicts in the colony, arriving in the *William and Anne* in 1791, three years after the 1788 first fleet of convict ships.[11] By her marriage Ann Entwistle should have seen the last of the Female Factory. The couple lived in Parramatta and it was six years later, on 3rd June 1836, when the Parramatta Magistrates Bench recommended her ticket of leave and allowed her to remain in Parramatta.[12]

Although a ticket of leave is evidence of good conduct, for some reason Ann Entwistle was late in getting hers. In March 1829 a Government Order modified the regulation for granting tickets of leave to female convicts: 'that they shall be allowed that indulgence after the following periods of uninterrupted good conduct in service or as monitoresses in the factory viz: under sentence for seven years, after two years; for fourteen years, after three years; and for life, after four years. Women returned to the first class of the factory will not be considered as having forfeited their claim to a ticket of leave, as a return to this class implies that the individual has not been guilty of any fault.'[13] An explanation for the delay could be that Ann Entwistle did not after all see the last of the Female Factory but perforce returned there and lost her first class status.

In 1838 marriage banns were again read for Ann Entwistle. The groom was a fifty-eight year old widower, Richard Birking or Burkin. Ann's age was recorded as fifty-seven. Birking (Burkin) was a free man who came to New South Wales on the ship *Fame* in 1817. For her first marriage Ann had required the Governor's consent; none was needed for this second.[14]

On 1st February 1843, at the age of sixty-two Ann Entwistle (Birking) was granted her conditional pardon.[15] She had waited sixteen years. From then on she and Richard Birking had twelve more years of marriage, until in 1855 Richard Birking died. The last record of Ann shows that she died in Sydney in 1868 at the age of eighty-seven. Her true age is unclear. The *Harmony* Indents and her first and second marriage certificate give her year of birth as 1781, whereas other documents range from 1773 to 1801. It is possible Ann herself did not know her true year of birth.[16]

Ann Entwistle survived a lifetime granted to few women. In Lancashire she survived almost forty years of long hours at the handloom, raising three children in years of both plenty and want, part of the time as a widow. She had been in a House of Correction for some petty offence. She had the exhilaration of several days of riot and destruction, escaping from custody and being fired on by the military.[17] She survived imprisonment, trial and sentence of death. She survived the voyage of the *Harmony* (leaving three children in England), and a period of assignment, outside and inside the Female Factory. She married three times – outliving all three – and died at eighty-seven. At 4 ft. 8¾ inches, she was tiny – but tough. At her death, her face small-pox pitted, hair grey, her forehead scarred and the first finger of her right hand crushed, there was much evidence of how life had treated her.[18]

The actions of relatively well-behaved female convicts were rarely recorded in the annals of New South Wales. There was much contemporary criticism of the morals and behaviour of female convicts. They were stereotyped by chauvinistic observers as prostitutes and criminals and therefore, in their eyes, fit only for the recording of their wrongdoing. Although no doubt brutalised by her experiences and her treatment by a sexist society, Ann Entwistle – and thousands of others – courageously survived her misfortunes. She was truly a remarkable woman by any standard.

Mary Hindle's life as a servant in a decent household in Sydney would be very different from that of Ann Entwistle. There would, however, be two initial problems. Firstly, of acceptance of Mary Hindle by the Nicholson family, and secondly, of Mary Hindle's own acceptance of her new life and its disciplines.

No doubt Eliza Nicholson was aware of the reputation of most female convicts, and aware of – or even experienced – the horror stories of convict servant behaviour. Mary Hindle, therefore, would be thoroughly schooled in her duties and closely watched before she was accepted into the family. A rioter, however, is not a thief or a whore. Whatever happened to Mary Hindle between April 1826 and October 1827, she at least before then experienced respectability. If she had any spirit she would have overcome the effects of the base company she had kept, and also overcome the prejudices against her.

For her part Mary Hindle, as a handloom weaver, would have a similar lack of domestic skills to Ann Entwistle, and so would find it hard to cope with domestic chores. Mary Hindle – and the Nicholsons – must have survived the 'probationary' period, as there is no record of her working anywhere else. At a time when the Government was experiencing great difficulty in disposing of female convicts because of their general bad reputation and intractability, the Nicholsons had a good servant in Mary Hindle. She was from a non-criminal background, she could read and write (only one third of convicts were literate) and at twenty-eight was mature, yet young enough to adapt to her new life.

Mary Hindle also benefited. Her working conditions, regular food and benign treatment contrasted with that of female convicts in rural areas. Here many were treated as badly as, if not worse than, slaves. They were often ill-treated and raped, then when pregnant or guilty of some trifling offence, sent to the Female Factory. The factory, depending on the 'class', was no real punishment, but the corruption there held its own terrors for any decent woman.

Many in New South Wales, including Major Ernest Augustus Slade, a magistrate, firmly believed female convict servants such as Mary Hindle were much better off than free servants in England. He painted a rosy picture to the Select Committee on Transportation. 'On their entrance into service they are treated in every respect the same as servants in England; they have tea, sugar, beer; they have rum on washing days, they have meat, bread, butter and everything in abundance; the majority receive wages and the indulgence of going out the same as servants do in England.'[19] Slade, of course, was talking about good convict servants with good masters.

Darling Harbour was less than a mile from the brothels and grog shops of the Rocks and Circular Quay. In their abasement and degeneracy they were the very antithesis of the secure life in Darling Harbour. As with Thomas Emmett, Mary Hindle would know from her prison and ship experiences that one survived by submitting to the authorities. She also knew that by keeping a still tongue and doing her master's – and mistress's – bidding, she would be all right. The most her future offered was that if she kept away from the temptations offered by the Rocks and elsewhere and kept out of trouble, she would, after four years, get the qualified freedom of her ticket of leave. Whether Mary Hindle learned the other lesson of survival for female convicts in New South Wales of getting herself the protection of a man, convict or otherwise, is not known.

In October 1828 Eliza Nicholson gave birth to a second girl, bringing the family to six. With boys aged ten and nine, a girl aged seven, boys aged five and three, and now a baby, there was plenty of work and washing for Mary Hindle. The presence of the seven year old girl must have been especially poignant to her. Her own daughter, Elizabeth, left in England and perhaps never to be seen again, was nine years old in 1828.

Physically and materially, however, Mary Hindle would live comparatively well – certainly better than her family and friends in Haslingden. As described by Slade, her food, supplied free, would be 'in abundance'. Mutton and lamb, washed down with beer or tea, was food for the poorest. Her 'pulmonary inflammation', in this dry, mild 'Mediterranean' climate, would soon disappear. As with Thomas Emmett, in her assignment to a decent employer, Mary Hindle had been given an opportunity to 'reform' from her past crimes and regain her character and worth.

Like thousands of other female convicts in New South Wales, Mary Hindle's subsequent life and fate is shrouded in mystery. Like thousands of her contemporaries nothing is known of her activities simply because they were not unlawful. She never attracted the attention of convict officialdom.

What is known, however, is that between 1829 and 1837 her husband George and daughter Elizabeth came from England to New South Wales.[20] This in itself is remarkable. Husbands who went to their convict wives were few and far between. Often the passage money was beyond their means.[21]

In a letter dated 25th May 1838, Mary Hindle wrote to Sir George Gipps and requested a free pardon. This would absolve her completely, restore all her rights and allow her to return to England. In her letter she stated her husband and two children (one born in the colony?) were with her. (This would considerably strengthen her case.)[22]

From hereon, however, Mary Hindle remains a mystery. Her name is not on any records after the date of her application. Where she lived or worked at that time is not known. There is no record of a reply from Sir George Gipps. Neither is there a record of a ticket of leave nor a conditional pardon.[23] Mary Hindle simply disappears into the unrecorded realms of Australian history.

The story of the fate of Mary Hindle, Ann Entwistle and thousands like them, suffers from several disadvantages. Firstly, convict records were ill-kept, secondly, only 'crimes and passions' were recorded; good behaviour or long service was not. Thirdly, in the 1850s many convict records were destroyed when convict ancestry amongst politicians became a contentious issue. Finally, and most importantly, female convicts had few legal or civil rights in a discriminating society. Military officers, judges, magistrates, parsons, and all so-called 'respectable' people considered all female convicts as prostitutes and incorrigible thieves and so inconsequential as human beings. Most contemporaries seldom recorded anything other than criticism of female convicts. In their eyes, 'convict men might in the end redeem themselves through work and penance, but women almost never'.[24]

In New South Wales – and elsewhere in Australia – there were thousands of unknown, plodding convicts caught up with, and in fear of, a deadening authority. They learned to survive by keeping quiet, by 'getting by', almost in secret. As political convicts Mary Hindle and Ann Entwistle had a better chance than most of 'getting by' and so redeeming themselves.

CHAPTER SEVENTEEN

Surely not in Vain

IN east Lancashire after the riots little changed. For the weavers, matters went worse; for at least some of the manufacturers, things improved. David Whitehead of Rossendale succinctly summed up their views. 'We had to prove at Lancaster Assizes that the powerlooms were riotously broken, which we did, and got damages awarded. The money was collected from the inhabitants, and we were paid. In the meantime we got new looms and set them to work as fast as we could, after which we had good trade for some time.'[1]

He added, somewhat self-righteously, 'Glory be to God – his care has ever been over me – he hath made our enemies as naught, lighter than chaff. Our factory and all we have is the Lord's and he hath taken care of it.'[2]

At Lancaster, Judges Parke and Scarlett also took care of the manufacturers. The manufacturers' civil actions for compensation took place in the Sheriff's Court. The defendants were the Hundred of Blackburn, the Hundred of Salford, and in the case of Henry Sudell's factory at Chorley, the Hundred of Leyland. All the plaintiffs' actions were successful. In defended cases the judges overruled defence objections that the factories could have been defended. 'Such resistance, if attempted, could only have been attended with bloodshed.'[3]

Compensation was based on a comparison between the valuation made by the plaintiff and a sum thought proper by a local magistrate acting on behalf of the Hundred. The total cost to Blackburn Hundred came to over £11,500, to Salford Hundred £4,458, to Leyland Hundred just £483. Individual payments per loom destroyed varied, no doubt because of damage to windows, doors, dressing machines and so on. Compensation, considering the cost of a new powerloom at ten pounds, was not ungenerous. (Richard Rostron of Dearden Clough, considering he removed all warps, weft and cloth from his looms and left his doors open in readiness, seemed most generously compensated at £1,500 for fifty-eight looms destroyed, an average of twenty-six pounds per loom against a general average of fifteen pounds.) The manufacturers gained in another sense. The powerlooms installed in the early 1820s were replaced by more modern, more efficient looms.

The payment of the compensation became a vexed public question. A letter writer to the *Manchester Mercury*, on 23rd May 1826, begged to be informed which Act of Parliament authorised the various Hundreds to pay for the damage. He got no answer. The burden of payment, by a levy on each Hundred general and poor rate, fell on many who had already little or no money and also had nothing to do with the riots in the first place. David Whitehead, however, had little sympathy. Speaking of 'those

A commemoration of the work done by distressed handloom weavers in the months after the riots. Those engaged on rock breaking and removing were mostly inmates at Blackburn workhouse. This stone is in Revidge Road, Blackburn

Mr H. Hartley JP

who should have known better', he wrote, 'Finding that the County must pay for the damage done and they [the local people] must each pay their share, they learnt the lesson by their folly, which they will not soon forget. For those who pay for their own education retain it all the better.'[4]

For the poor the reality was very different. The levy was applied to the occupier, not the owner, of every cottage, house and property in each Hundred. (The levy was enforced on all but those on poor relief so the poor supported the very poor.) The total payment for the seventy-seven townships within Blackburn Hundred came to £13,960. To add to the inequity the levy, for no logical reason, was not evenly calculated for each township.

At a time when many handloom weavers were earning five or six shillings a week at the most and some getting four or five shillings poor relief, with none in Blackburn earning more than eight shillings a week, the levy was a further tribulation. The additional payments for a family of a man, wife and three children, for example, in Blackburn (population 27,091) approximated to 6s. 10½d.

In the nearby hamlet of Ramsgreave (population 515) it was 13s. 9d.; in Haslingden (7,776) 5s. 1¼d.; Rishton (919) 14s. 2d.; Oswaldtwistle (5,597) 6s. 1¾d.; Cliviger (near Burnley) (1,598) 15s. 0d.; Padiham (3,529) 5s. 6¼d., and so on. Any of these totals amounted to one, even two weeks' income per family.[5]

For those who could not pay, the workhouse – 'the gaol for being poor' – further beckoned. Blackburn workhouse, as were many others, was extended – in Blackburn's case to take in a further four hundred. Workhouse Committees, ever mindful of running costs, required their inmates to work. Cloth was woven on handlooms for sale to selected manufacturers. Able-bodied men capable of hard work were sent to break stones for MacAdam's road construction schemes. Selected young females filled 'the lamentable deficiency of female servants in respectable houses in the area.'[6]

Those handloom weavers on road construction suffered more than their public display of pauperism. The repetitive physical effort of handloom weaving developed strong muscular shoulders, arms and legs. They, however, needed soft hands with which to handle weft and warps. Time spent on stone breaking or similar occupations so hardened their hands as to make them unsuitable, at least for a time, to weave properly. As indoor workers, even exposure to the wind and rain quickly made them ill.

Those not in the workhouse but on poor relief still worked either on the roads or at the handloom. The arrangements varied between townships. At Great Harwood men working on the roads had the choice of a shilling a day or eight pounds of oatmeal. Most took the oatmeal.[7] Oswaldtwistle Poor Law Overseers' account book illustrates the efforts, rough and ready at times, to keep local people out of the workhouse and to give them work at home. Entries for 1827 include:

June 28th: 'To see James Bury [the powerloom manufacturer at White Ash] if he will employ James Lonsdale's wife at weaving; if not to give him [Lonsdale] an order to the workhouse'. On the same day: 'If Edmund Hacking of Treacle Row should apply to the overseer for relief during the next fortnight he is to have an order for the workhouse. We give him something bye and bye'.

Handlooms were given or lent to selected persons:

August 9th: 'John Westell to have a pair of looms and no more pay. Livered [delivered] a pair of looms August 10th'.[8]

On the same day: 'James Tomlinson to have a pair of looms and weft. Livered looms and machine. To com [come] no more'.

Oswaldtwistle was a small town and all seemed to be known to the overseers. They did not shirk from moral judgements:

August 23rd: 'John Smith promised not to trouble the town no more this winter [that is, ask for relief]. This is a rascal'.

On the same day: 'John Grimshaw – I think he should do something towards his wife'.

October 18th: 'Mary Oldham not to have any more pay'.

On the same day: 'Jane Crossley not to have any more pay. With child. She says he is dead in Scotland'. [Possibly meaning husband.]

November 15th: 'Mr George Yates [manufacturer] promises to find a house and a pair of looms for 1s. 6d. per week if the Town will pay it for Thomas Fielding, wife and child. The Overseer must remove her immediately from the workhouse.'

January 10th 1828: 'To buy Benjamin Holland one pair of looms and he promises to never trouble the town no more'.

Women suffered in other ways. In what appears to be a situation similar to Jane Crossley's:

November 15th 1827: 'See about Miranda Cuthbert being removed [to workhouse] as she is pregnant. She works at Mr Walmesley's mill'.[9]

In this pendulum existence between starvation and semi-starvation, work and no work, income had to be carefully measured against expenditure. The stakes were nothing less than life and death. Moses Heap, a Rossendale handloom weaver, told of an elderly couple who went to buy a week's food and the weft for the next piece. 'The old man said, "Let's have hafe a peaund o' swine fat to mek a sad cake for't tay." His wife rebuked him with some astonishment. "Hafe a peaund o' swine fat un no roavings [weft] in't heause? Nay, Loll [Laurence] thad'll never do!" '[10]

By 1827 the work of the London Relief Committee drew to an end. Their work, their nation-wide appeals and the appeals to Parliament of the handloom weavers themselves began to draw a wider public attention to the 'most dreadful distress' in east Lancashire. The general public now acknowledged this distress even exceeded the general poverty and misery which was the common lot of the labouring classes throughout the country.

Even before the 1826 riots a House of Commons Select Committee on Emigration discussed wholesale emigration to the Colonies, including New South Wales, as one solution to the perennial problem of unemployment in the United Kingdom. As the riots impressed a new impetus on the particular problems of east Lancashire, William Fielden, of Blackburn, a former putter-out, and now described as a 'Master Manufacturer' gave evidence to the Committee.

William Fielden did not impress the Committee. On March 29th 1827, when asked his view, as a local man and a manufacturer, as to the principal causes of the low state of the handloom weaving trade, he found it 'very difficult to account for what it may arise from – there were too great a combination of causes'.[11]

William Fielden seemed more concerned with the manufacturers. 'The handloom was entirely at an end as a means of subsistence – and the powerloom would be the cause of saving the manufacturers of this Kingdom. Without the powerloom the manufacturers would be annihilated entirely . . . The redundant population – the handloom weavers – appears to me to be a permanent evil with no remedy.'[12] (At least some handloom weavers already agreed with him about powerlooms. A Darwen handloom weavers' petition, in July 1826 said that 'it is necessary for some other species of labour besides handloom weaving to be introduced to this district in order to raise the inhabitants from their present state of distress – nothing presents itself of equal advantage to the powerloom'.)[13]

William Fielden also gave his opinion to the Committee that although relief from the London Committee and poor relief had been necessary to preserve people from starvation, the relief had in fact a 'mischievous effect' in encouraging over production of manufactured goods; that is, the money was used to buy weft with which to weave more cloth. This further reduced the prices and therefore weavers' wages. Therefore, in Fielden's opinion the relief contributed to the distress.

Fielden's evidence and opinion about the ultimate destination of the London Relief Committee's money was disquieting to say the least: '. . . in local families [local gentry] where sums of money from the Relief Committee were sent for distribution to the poor, the overseers [poor law] came to request that the distribution of clothes should not be given until the poor people had paid their quotas [levy] for the destruction of the powerloom – otherwise their new clothing would be sold up together with the rest of their furniture and their apparel.'[14] Fielden clearly believed the levy could not be paid without the Relief Committee money. The inference, therefore, was that some, at least, of the Relief Committee's donations, given by benefactors throughout the country, went to the Lancashire County Treasury and thence to the manufacturers as compensation.

In further evidence Fielden told the Committee he had no opinions on how immediately to relieve the 'most dreadful distress', except a general stimulus in trade or emigration of the 'surplus' handloom weavers. When questioned further on emigration, he intimated the County Treasury would not raise funds for grants to promote emigration. He also considered handloom weavers would not, 'in the least', contemplate the idea of emigration.

Unfortunately for the public image of east Lancashire public men and manufacturers, William Fielden came across, in his replies to questions, as either complacent or indifferent to the problems besetting his area. He offered little of substance to the Committee. He did, however, fear, as did many other manufacturers, that emigration of weavers to other lands, the United States in particular, meant future competition from those countries – an opinion of little immediate value to the Committee.

William Fielden gave his evidence on 29th March 1827 exactly six weeks after yet another 'Petition from the Starving Weavers of Blackburn' was presented to the House of Commons by Joseph Hume M.P. The weavers made yet another desperate plea: 'We are human beings and worship the same God. Whyfore then should we be so oppressed in our native land?' The petition was 'ordered to lie on the table and to be printed'.[15]

The views of the petitioners when the Abstract Accounts for the newly built Blackburn Parish Church were published on 31st May 1827, go unrecorded. The church was consecrated on 13th September 1826 by the Bishop of Chester and cost £38,025. 15s. 7d.[16] The churchwardens, however, wanted the church to be heated and lighted. This required a 'church rate' on Blackburn ratepayers, not all of whom were members of the Established Church. An angry meeting called it 'uncalled for, inexpedient, and in the present circumstances of the operatives of Blackburn, cruel in the extreme'.[17] A poll held the week after the consecration was carried, however, in favour of the rate.

William Hulton, a magistrate and landed proprietor of Little Hulton, near Bolton, gave evidence to the House of Commons Committee on the same day as William Fielden. Hulton's concern and distress was evident from the beginning. 'I would like to state my strong opinion in contradistinction to the witness Fielden about the contribution of the London Relief Committee. Nothing but their donations saved us from famine – the practical result has been that in my area no riot or disturbance has occurred.'[18] (Perhaps Hulton was implying that if Fielden and his Blackburn colleagues had been more generous in their outlook the riots may not have occurred.)

William Hulton's evidence of his own and his wife's visits to homes of the poor in his area was in sharp contrast to the blandness of William Fielden. Hulton declared, 'I have witnessed things I have not conceived existed in a civilized country.' In emotional tones which deeply moved his listeners, he spoke of visiting a cottage. 'We there found on one side of the fire a very old man apparently dying, on the other side a young man about eighteen, with a child on his knee, whose mother had just died and been buried and evidently that young man and child were suffering from want... We were about to leave and the woman accompanying us said, "Sir, you have not seen all." We went upstairs and we found another young man, the widower, and on

A handloom weaver's cottage in Pippin Street, Blackburn. Note the side loomshop erected at a later date
Blackburn Library Local Studies Collection, No. 2950

turning down the rags which he was unable to move himself, we found another man who was dying and who did die in the course of the day.'[19] He also told of a widow and three children who had not tasted oatmeal and water – their only food – for forty-eight hours. Many had none at all in twenty-four hours.

William Hulton's evidence also deeply moved the country. Many, whether in authority or not, at last realized how many people, not just in Lancashire, were made defenceless against economic and technological change. The country began to see that misery and distress need not, nor should not, be an unavoidable consequence of such.

When asked his views on emigration by the Committee, Hulton, in complete contrast to Fielden, firmly believed emigration would at least partly solve the problem of over-production and over-crowding. 'I would be very happy for people to get the chance and I'm sure they would willing if it is explained to them.'[20] In contrast again to Fielden, he believed the parish would gain in paying people to emigrate, 'even at £30 per family of five'.

The Reverend J. W. Whittaker of Blackburn, in a letter to the Committee, also contradicted William Fielden about emigration. After telling the Committee that in one week in April 1827 no fewer than fifty families left Blackburn for Philadelphia, he added, 'It's high time the Government took up the subject of emigration as part of the country's policy. Emigration would prevent the convulsions we saw last year.'

As Fielden, however, he saw emigrants as potential competitors, yet in a different way. 'They become Americans, nor do they retain much regard for their native country. It would therefore be better to emigrate to the Colonies.'[21]

The Bishop of Chester, as Chairman of the London Relief Committee's activities in Lancashire and north Cheshire, finally sealed, in the eyes of the country, the reputations and attitudes of east Lancashire manufacturers. When asked by the Committee if manufacturers cared little for their labourers, he replied, 'The more respectable are an extremely humane body of men, with great interest in the spiritual and bodily welfare of their employees. There is a class of manufacturers, however, who care for nothing but how they make the greatest sum of money in the least time. The least respectable are a very considerable proportion of the whole in point of numbers.'[22]

Neither had the handloom weaver any doubts, either about manufacturers or emigration. Joseph Hodgson, a Blackburn handloom weaver, and poet, a man not previously noted for any Radical opinions, wrote in his 'Weaver's Complaint about the Decline of the Handloom Weaver':

> Ye Weavers of Blackburn, give ear to my song
> When I sing of Tyrants, I seldom do wrong
> For if they Transport me to Canada's wild shore
> I then shall have Freedom, when I have sailed o'er
> Free from Slavery
> Fetters and Knavery
> Never tormented with Tyrants again![23]

The increasing governmental and public changes in attitude made no immediate impact on east Lancashire. The area was quiet. As William Fielden told the House of Commons Committee, 'the disposition to destroy the powerloom had died away'. In fact, yet another 1827 House of Commons Committee – The Select Committee on the Causes of Increase in the Number of Criminal Commitments and Convictions in England and Wales, was, in the circumstances, surprised how 'quiet' Lancashire was.

After expressing concern and apprehension about the general increase in commitments throughout the United Kingdom, the Report referred to Lancashire, and William Hulton's evidence to the Committee on Emigration, and also 'the dreadful state of its population during 1826 and part of 1827'. 'Anyone . . . will surely expect that every moral restraint must have been dissolved amongst men of whom so great a portion were on the point of being starved to death.' The Report gave Lancashire's criminal commitment returns for 1825, 1826 and 1827 as 2,132; 2,374; and 2,459, respectively: '. . . an increase certainly less than might have been expected . . . Nor can too much praise be given to those who bore, without committing any breach of the law, sufferings, which for intensity could hardly be surpassed.'[24]

This Committee had recognised, and was concerned about, Lancashire's social and economic problems. The Committee also recognised the deficiencies of the office of High Constable for each Hundred. By now his 'duties' mostly amounted to a sinecure so the Committee recommended 'the office be made more efficient and available to a general system of organised police'.[25] There were to be no more 'disputes and dishonour' about the role of peacekeepers within any county in the United Kingdom.

(It was over ten years, August 1839, before an 'Act for the Establishment of County and District Constables by the Authority of Justice of the Peace' was introduced and a further year before, in Lancashire, justices appointed a Chief Constable, two Assistant Chief Constables, thirteen Superintendents and five hundred Constables.[26])

During the 1830s the numbers on poor relief reduced but slowly. A total of 256 in Great Harwood in 1826 dropped in 1830 to 131; in 1831 to 120; 1832 to 115; 1833 to 105.[27] Other changes however were rushing headlong. The improvements in powerloom technology and production engineering, plus the total commitment to powerlooms by the larger manufacturers, brought a rapid increase. From 12,150 powerlooms in Lancashire in 1820 the numbers rose to 46,000 by 1829 and 89,000 by 1835.[28] It was truly the age of steam. The number of cotton factories in Lancashire grew from 344 in 1819 to 974 in 1841.

The smaller manufacturer had no option but to follow. Some were as reluctant as the handloom weavers to leave the old ways. John Ashworth of Holt Mill, Rossendale, told the House of Commons Select Committee on Handloom Weavers' Petitions in 1835 of 'a very respectable gentleman in Rossendale' (John Ormerod of Tunstead) who believed he could weave bockings as cheaply by hand as by power. Ashworth added, 'but he [Ormerod] says "I have got my bark out to sea, and now I must sail or sink"'.[29]

Gradually, reluctantly, the handloom weavers and their families were drawn into

Emmett Row, the cottages at Holden Wood, Helmshore, built around 1822 to house workers at Abraham Emmett's factory. Thomas Emmett probably lived in the end cottage (down the steps), nearest the factory.

the factory system. The larger manufacturers such as William Greg who had factories in Styal (Cheshire), Bury and Lancaster were glad to employ them. 'I gave much employment to handloom weavers, partly from consideration of their condition and partly because they were accustomed to care and minute attention to their work.' William Greg told the House of Commons Select Committee on Manufactures, Commerce and Shipping, 'In my opinion handloom weavers are better off working sixty-nine hours a week for ten shillings than working fifteen hours a day at home'.[30]

Factory work was contrary to all the instincts and traditions of the handloom weaver. Where possible the head of the household continued on his handloom, vowing to have nothing to do with the 'steamloom'. For him the term 'steam-loom' was synonymous with bad taste and inferior work. Some still saw themselves, as they had once been – respected members of an elite society – but this was fading fast as their wives and children, almost literally, slaved in the factories.

Since well before the first Factory Act in 1802, the conditions and working hours in cotton factories had been abominable. Subsequent Acts were inadequately enforced and easily evaded by unscrupulous employers. The 1819 Cotton Mills Act forbade the employment of children under nine years of age and those under sixteen not to work more than twelve hours a day. Many children of east Lancashire handloom weavers worked in factories which ignored the law. Even before the 1826 riots, in 1823, a Justice of the Peace, Charles Whitaker, and the Reverend James Quartley, were appointed by Lancashire Quarter Sessions Justices of the Peace to visit and inspect factories in Blackburn Hundred. They reported back to the 1825 Quarter Sessions.

The inspectors did not meet with 'a single instance' in which the 1819 Act was complied with, although some violations were less in some cases than others. Many factories were dirty and ill-ventilated and many children under nine years old were employed. At Bannister Eccles' Jubilee Street factory in Blackburn, at least two seven year olds (Mary Counsell and Mary Ann Haslam) were spoken to. The inspectors found James Houghton's Park Place factory 'very dirty', but no one under nine years old was seen. A boy aged seven (John Grimshaw) was spoken to at Messrs Joseph Walmsley's at Grimshaw (near Darwen) and a girl aged six (Betty Waterhouse) at Messrs James Livesey's at Hoghton Bottoms (near Blackburn). The inspectors' comments on this factory were not untypical: 'There are 207 persons employed, and a great number are very young. Alice Waterhouse, Jenny Doherty, Maria Smith, Mary Brierley and many others are evidently not nine years old, but they say they do not know their ages'.[31] (Children were often told by parents and foremen not to tell inspectors their true age.)

Hours of work ranged from 'irregular' to seventy-eight a week. Seventy-two hours was the most common. Abraham Emmett's (that is, Thomas Emmett's uncle's) newly built factory at Holden Wood, Haslingden, one of these. Bannister Eccles' workforce often worked up to thirteen hours a day because of 'a fraud upon the workpeople'. A clock was affixed to, and worked by the steam engine. The steam engine worked normally at twenty-three strokes a minute. At this speed the clock was geared to keep the correct time. When the steam engine was under load it worked at twenty-one times a minute thus slowing the clock by six minutes per hour. 'Thus the workpeople are confined an extra hour a day and are only paid for normal hours of working.'[32] Each man, woman and child was cheated of six hours' pay per week.

The Factory Act of 1833 continued to prohibit the employment of children under nine years, and the working week of children from nine to thirteen was limited to forty-eight hours. Young persons between thirteen and eighteen were limited to sixty-nine. Life for adults was simply 'bed and work, work and bed.' It was common, for example, for 'a cotton spinner to work from 6 a.m. to 8 p.m., stopping at 4 p.m. on Saturdays (eighty hours), for an average wage of 22s. 0d. to 24s. 9d. per week.[33]

Little wonder Edward Gibbon Wakefield, whilst in Newgate Prison in 1833 for his abduction and marriage to William Turner's niece, was moved to write: 'Peter Moreau and his wife are dead, aged twenty-five years. Too much work has killed them. We say – work like a negro; like a galley slave; we ought to say work like a freeman.' Thus quoting Paul Louis Courier, Wakefield went on: 'I say, work like a Lancashire weaver. There is no such work in France or America, even among slaves – American slaves or convicts in New South Wales are fat and happy compared to very many free-born Englishmen.'[34]

Many more Acts of Parliament and many more years of effort by reformers were to come before the factory workers were rescued from a state of suffering and degradation, 'which', Michael Sadler M.P. told the House of Commons in March 1832, 'it is conceived, the industrious classes in hardly any other country endure, or ever had experienced and which cannot much longer be tolerated'.[35] Even so the hours of labour remained at sixty per week until 1875. The 'Half-Time' system, instituted in 1844 for children to attend school as well as work, lasted until 1921, when twelve year olds were no longer allowed to work in factories for half a day each day.

When Michael Sadler spoke those words the triumph of the factory system was already assured. The Lancashire cotton industry soon recovered from its long and severe depressions. Trade expanded more rapidly than any other industry in Great Britain. As the numbers of powerlooms increased and their quality improved, the demand for hand woven goods declined until only specialist 'fancy' (brocades, satins, silk) handloom weavers had work of any kind.

'Bad trade', for hand and powerloom alike, continued its customary cyclic pattern. 1842 was particularly bad. William Beesley, the Accrington Chartist, said at a meeting near Clitheroe 'There are some brave fellows in that place but God help them, they are in a miserable condition, being all of them handloom weavers'.[36] The distress throughout Lancashire and northern Cheshire was so severe it resulted in the biggest demonstrations and riots since 1826. Thousands of factory operatives came out on strike. In Preston, on 12th August 1842, four were shot dead by 72nd Highlanders brought in to clear rioters from the streets. On 15th August rioters in Blackburn forced most factories to close. For fifty miles around Manchester strikers went from factory to factory 'turning out the hands', then, to ensure the factory remained closed, drew the plugs from the boilers. This released the water out of the steam boiler, making it temporarily useless.

David Whitehead's Lower Mill, Rawtenstall, was visited by the strikers. (His other, Higher Mill, burned down in 1841.) This time, however, although work stopped for a fortnight, David Whitehead escaped disaster. 'When they came [the strikers] the engineer said, "You cannot draw the plug, you cannot find it, but I will draw it for you." He drew the plug and they all went away without doing any damage whatsoever.'[37] (The engineer was shrewd enough to know the alternative could have been serious damage to the boiler and perhaps factory property.) There were few handloom

Edward Eccles of Chapels, near Darwen, weaving silk on a handloom around 1900. He was one of the last Lancashire handloom weavers and came from a family who had woven for generations. His uncle played an active part in the riot at Top Factory and lived for some time on Darwen Moors to avoid prosecution

Photograph reproduced by kind permission of Mr J. Garland.

weavers amongst the plug-drawers and rioters. Sixteen years later the new industrial proletariat of factory operatives were the violent reactors against distress.

By now there were comparatively few handloom weavers, in any case, as the numbers of powerlooms increased. By 1851, for instance, the census for Oswaldtwistle recorded 1,272 'weavers', of whom 77% were powerloom weavers, and only 23% classified themselves as handloom weavers, 9% of whom were specialist (silk) weavers. There had been a seventeen-fold increase in the numbers of powerloom weavers since 1826.

The small groups of independent handloom weavers persistently working at their trade against all odds became a mere handful after the 1860s. The importation of cheap silk from France plus the havoc caused by the Cotton Famine due to the American Civil War, sealed their fate. 'Fielden Brothers of Todmorden still retained fifty-three old handloom weavers on their books in 1861, but they stopped giving out work in that year and pensioned off the survivors.'[38] A few lingered on, almost as curiosities, in Rossendale, into the 1890s and, in the Chapels area of Darwen, even into the twentieth century. Here, in 1911, ninety-five year old Edward Eccles wove silk in his cellar loom shop. Known locally as 'the last of the old handloom weavers' he remembered the 1826 riots, in which his uncle took an active part.[39]

Richard Marsden, a contemporary historian, wrote a most eloquent epitaph to the handloom weaver. 'Thus passed away a type of industry, picturesque far beyond its successor, that from 1750 to 1850 found employment for several millions of people.'[40]

In later years another historian, speaking of Rossendale, wrote, 'However real the personal sufferings of the displaced workers, the new machinery had come to stay. The rapid growth of the population, together with improvements in relative comforts falsified in a wider view the gloomy foreboding of the handloom weaver. In spite of periods of bad trade, the general prosperity of the people increased so greatly that the district [Rossendale] earned for itself the name of the Golden Valley.'[41]

The journey from the 'Golden Age' of the handloom weaver to the 'Golden Valley' of the powerloom weaver was long and hard. It was accompanied by distress and suffering of a depth and scale unparalleled in England's social and economic history.

The 1826 riots were unsuccessful in that, to quote David Whitehead, 'the new looms were set to work as soon as they could'. The 1826 riots were successful, however, in that, in spite of the horrors of early factory work, they forced successive governments to concern themselves more with how people lived and worked. The rioters, therefore, helped force the pace of the social reforms of the early Victorian age. Their sufferings were surely not in vain.

Notes

Chapter One

1. 'Lancashire Church Survey, Blackburn Hundred, 1650', *Lancashire and Cheshire Record Society*, vol. 1 (1878–9), pp. 167–8.
2. K. Gray, *Some Contributions to the Early History of Nonconformity in Rossendale* (unpublished M.A. thesis, University College of Wales, 1942), p. 89.
3. Jon Elliott (ed.), *David Whitehead of Rossendale, 1790–1860* (Rawtenstall, 1973), p. 3.
4. W. Radcliffe, *Origin of the New System of Manufacture, Commonly Called 'Power Loom Weaving'* (Stockport, 1828), pp. 9–10.
5. E. Hopwood, *A History of the Lancashire Cotton Industry and the Amalgamated Weavers' Association: the Lancashire Weavers' Story* (Amalgamated Weavers' Assoc., 1969), p. 10.
6. C. Aspin, *James Hargreaves and the Spinning Jenny* (Helmshore Local History Society, 1964), p. 42.
7. S. J. Chapman, *The Lancashire Cotton Industry: a Study in Economic Development* (Manchester U.P., 1904), p. 53.
8. Radcliffe, *Origin of the New System*, p. 60.
9. W. Thom, *Rhymes and Recollections of a Hand Loom Weaver* (Glasgow, 1845), p. 9.
10. Radcliffe, *Origin of the New System*, p. 65.
11. Ibid., p. 10.
12. B. Lewis, *Life in a Cotton Town: Blackburn, 1818–1848* (Carnegie, 1985), p. 5.
13. G. C. Miller, *Blackburn Worthies of Yesterday* (Blackburn Times, 1959), p. 322.
14. T. Newbigging, *Lancashire Characters and Places* (Brook & Chrystal, 1891), p. 148.
15. Ibid., p. 148.
16. Hopwood, *A History of the Lancashire Cotton Industry*, p. 19.
17. Archibald Prentice, Manchester historian, quoted in E. P. Thompson, *The Making of the English Working Class* (Penguin, 1974), p. 308.
18. Public Record Office (P.R.O.), H.O. 42/110 1811, quoted in J. L. and B. Hammond, *The Skilled Labourer 1760–1832* (1919, reprinted Chivers, 1965), p. 83.
19. Named after the mythical Ned Ludd, a Nottingham apprentice who destroyed his master's stocking-frames in the course of a dispute. 'Luddite' thereafter described anyone who destroyed machinery as a form of industrial protest.
20. C. B. Whyatt, T*he Baptists and Social Conditions in Lancashire, 1760–1832* (unpublished M.A. thesis, Manchester University, 1948), p. 89.
21. Ibid., p. 15.
22. Blackburn Reformers and Radicals (a contingent of whom arrived at St Peter's Field just before the massacre) were especially bitter. A Blackburn manufacturer, Hugh Hornby Birley,

commanded a troop of Manchester Yeomanry on the Field that day. He, it was claimed, never had any sense of guilt or remorse. He died, still held in odium by many, in 1845 and was buried in St Peter's Churchyard, overlooking what had been St Peter's Field.

23. W. O. Henderson, *Industrial Britain under the Regency, 1814–1818: the Diaries of Escher, Bodmer, May & de Gallois* (Frank Cass, 1968), p. 34.
24. Ibid., p. 137.
25. J. S. Lyons, *The Lancashire Cotton Industry and the Introduction of the Power Loom, 1815–1850* (unpublished Ph.D. thesis, University of California, Berkeley, 1977), p. 167.
26. Hansard Parliamentary Debates KLI, 497, quoted in R. J. White, *Waterloo to Peterloo* (Peregrine Books, 1968), p. 60.
27. Whyatt, *Baptists*, p. 227.
28. P.R.O., H.O. 42/194, quoted in Hammond, *Skilled Labourer*, p. 122.
29. *Blackburn Mail*, 20 November 1822.
30. P.R.O., H.O. 40/18, quoted in J. L. and B. Hammond, *The Town Labourer, 1760–1832* (1917, reprinted Longman, 1978), pp. 204–5
31. Evidence of James Grimshaw, hand-loom manufacturer of Barrowford and Colne, to House of Commons Select Committee on Manufactures Commerce and Shipping, 1833 (690) vi, p. 748.
32. Ibid, p. 748.
33. 'Diary of William Varley of Higham', in W. Bennett, *History of Burnley*, vol. 3 (Burnley Corporation, 1971), pp. 382–5.
34. Thom, *Rhymes*, p. 18.
35. Bennett, *History of Burnley*, vol. 3, p. 385.
36. Elliott, *David Whitehead*, p. 75.
37. *Preston Advertiser*, 15 April 1826.
38. Grimshaw evidence to Select Committee, 1833, p. 748.
39. *Preston Pilot*, 25 March 1826.
40. Thom, *Rhymes*, p. 28.
41. Ibid., p. 48.
42. *Preston Chronicle*, 15 April 1826.
43. *Blackburn Mail*, 19 April 1826.
44. Hammond, *Skilled Labourer*, p. 124.
45. *Blackburn Mail*, 22 February 1826.

Chapter Two

1. The King's actual birthday was 12 August.
2. The official title of the regiment was The 2nd, or Queen's, Regiment of Dragoon Guards. Since 1766 the regiment had been mounted on bay horses exclusively; therefore they were more commonly known as the 'Queen's Bays'.
3. Eckersley to Hobhouse, 24 April 1826, P.R.O., H.O. 40/19 (Henry Hobhouse was Permanent Under Secretary of State for the Home Office from June 1817 to July 1827.)
4. *Wheeler's Manchester Chronicle*, 29 April 1826. The description of the dinner is taken from the report published in this newspaper.
5. Major General William George Harris of the 73rd Regiment (Highlanders), a Waterloo veteran, was commander of the Northern District from 1825 to July 1828. Major General Sir John Byng was commander of the Northern District from 1816 to 1825. His experience of industrial disorder in the north made him the expert, so he was temporarily recalled in May 1826.
6. Lieutenant Colonel Bunbury, commander of the 60th (Duke of York's Own) Rifle Corps. since 1824, was an eccentric character. When asked by an inspecting General if there was any gambling amongst his officers he said, 'No Sir, for I have won all their money'. (See L. Butler, *Annals of the King's Royal Rifle Corps.*, vol. 2, 1923.)
7. The stagecoach left the Star Inn,

Deansgate, Manchester at 5 p.m. each day and arrived at the Old Bull Inn, Church Street, Blackburn at approximately 8.30 p.m.

It was easy for a mob to provide themselves with stones. The streets in the area were loosely paved with water-worn cobble stones collected from local rivers.

8. Whinney Hill was a popular and convenient meeting place. Enfield lay at the junction of the roads from Blackburn, Burnley, Whalley, Clitheroe, Haslingden and Accrington.
9. It became a common feature of the riots that only powerlooms and their ancillary fixtures, e.g. driving shafts, reeds and healds, were destroyed. Factory doors were broken down only when locked or when demands to open them were refused. This consensus can only have come from the meeting. Obviously windows suffered in the general excitement.

   The name 'Captain' was one given to themselves by the mob leaders.
10. B. Hargreaves, *Recollections of Broad Oak* (Bowker, 1882) p. 142.
11. Thomas Duckworth, 'Reminiscences of a Nonagarian', *Haslingden Gazette*, 2 March 1901.
12. Ibid.
13. Lord Ribblesdale's Craven Legion Yeomanry had suppressed riots in Burnley and Clitheroe in 1808.
14. Thomas Duckworth, 'Reminiscences'.
15. James Clough, deposition, P.R.O., 27/10, part 1.
16. Ann Lonsdale, deposition, P.R.O., 27/10, part 1.
17. James Bury, deposition, P.R.O., 27/10, part 1.
18. There were, however, claims that Mary Rigby, landlady of the Bay Horse Inn, Salford Bridge, was compelled to give rioters food and drinks. As her inn was a popular resort of manufacturers, it is possible that this was a form of 'tit for tat'.
19. The Riot Act 1 Geo. 1, st.2 c.5, 1714: 'That if any persons to the number of twelve or more, being unlawfully riotously and tumultuously assembled together, to the Disturbance of the Publick Peace – and being required or commanded by any one or more Justices of the Peace – where such assembly shall be, by Proclamation in the King's Name – continue together for the space of one hour after such Proclamation – the Offenders therein shall be adjudged Felons and shall suffer death as in case of Felony without benefit of Clergy'.
20. Soldiers, constables, onlookers and rioters alike were injured by stones, and threats were made, but this was one of only two unprovoked personal assaults by a rioter in three days of rioting. Simeon Wright claimed in court that he was 'much confused' by an earlier fall and did not know how he came to commit the assaults.
21. John Houghton stated at Entwistle's trial that he had employed him for the past three years. He had seen him at his work at half past one on the day of the riot. Obviously, when Houghton closed the factory, Entwistle joined the rioters.
22. In a touch of irony, the *Blackburn Mail*, two days later on 26 April, published a list of subscribers to the fund for unemployed weavers of Blackburn. Amongst the contributions was: 'From persons employed in the Jubilee Cotton Works – £3 6s. 3½d.'
23. G. C. Miller, *Blackburn Worthies of Yesterday: a Biographical Galaxy*, (Blackburn Times, 1959) p. 313.
24. Later, as Houghton recovered at home from his wounds, the high constable arranged for a Thomas Brady to keep watch on Houghton 'for twenty days at 2/6d per day', to prevent his escape. See 'An Account of Extraordinary Expenses incurred in various cases of Tumult, Riot and Felony', dated 18 October 1826; Lancashire Record Office (L.R.O.), QSP 2870/76.

Chapter Three

1. *Manchester Guardian*, 29 April 1826.
2. Eckersley to Hobhouse, 25 April 1826, P.R.O., H.O. 40.19.
3. Ann Seed, deposition, P.R.O., P.L. 27/10, part 1.
4. Built in 1824 on the site of previous factories, Bowling Green was also known locally as Pall Mall factory.
5. William Carr, deposition, P.R.O., P.L. 27/10, part 1.
6. Some at least of Over Darwen's hand-loom weavers were troubled by the lawlessness. In May 1826 a group sent a memorial protesting their innocence to the Home Office and blaming the destruction on outsiders.
7. James Garsden, deposition, P.R.O., P.L. 27/10, part 1.
8. Middle Mill was a five-storey building built in 1822. As the name indicates, it was one of three in Helmshore owned by William and Ralph Turner.
9. Coincidentally, Clegg's predecessor as £200 *per annum* cashier, Helmshore man, Thomas Dunn, at the time of the riot lay in the New Bailey Prison, Salford, awaiting transportation to New South Wales, Dunn had been convicted of embezzling £50 from William Turner and Co.
10. St James's Church, Haslingden, stands 845 feet above sea level. From its doorway there is a panoramic view covering several miles of the area.
11. It is ironic that the vestry meeting was to appoint thirteen 'substantial householders and occupiers for the care and management of the concerns of the poor of the township', among whom were William Turner and Richard Emmett (see L.R.O., PR 3016/6/1).
12. L. Shaw, letter to *Blackburn Mail*, 3 May 1826.
13. Ibid.
14. Timothy Jones, deposition, P.R.O., P.L. 27/10, part 1.
15. Harry Holt, ibid.
16. James Heys, ibid. Heys stated a part-truth; the looms wove woollen cloth.
17. *Blackburn Mail*, 23 August 1826.
18. L. Shaw, letter to *Blackburn Mail*, 3 May 1826.
19. Harry Holt and W. T. Clegg, depositions, P.R.O., P.L. 27/10, part 1. This was the second instance of unprovoked physical violence to a person (see Chapter Two).
20. See Appendix 4.
21. *Preston Pilot*, 19 August 1826.
22. James Barker, deposition, P.R.O., P.L. 27/10 part 1. Mary Hindle paid the heavy price of transportation for life for her bet. Although probably only 'tavern talk', and hardly evidence of a prearranged plot, the authorities took the matter very seriously.
23. Harry Holt, deposition, P.R.O., P.D. 27/10, part 1.
24. Samuel Hamer, ibid.
25. Joseph Woods, ibid.
26. There is no record of Thomas Emmett's being arrested at Middle Mill. He was, however, kept under such close observation the following day that it is very possible that he was, and his name taken by Turner's men.
27. John Wolstenholme, deposition, P.R.O., P.L. 27/10, part 1.
28. L. Shaw, letter to *Blackburn Mail*, 3 May 1826.
29. The name was changed to the 'New Inn' because the previous inn, the 'Old Thorn', was converted into cottages and a new inn built on adjoining land. The name reverted to the 'Thorn' in the mid nineteenth century. After extensive alterations in 1980 it was re-named the 'New Thorn'.
30. By law Mr Townsend, Haslingden's petty (parish) constable was responsible for the prisoners. In this unprecedented situation neither the Reverend Gray nor Colonel Kearney seems to have consulted Mr Townsend.
31. *Blackburn Mail*, 16 March 1827.
32. Ibid., 3 May 1826.
33. John Haslem, deposition, P.R.O., P.L. 27/10, part 1.

Chapter Four

1. The Whitehead brothers, Thomas, David and Peter, started in business as spinners in 1815. They were also putters-out to hundreds of handloom weavers throughout Rossendale and beyond. In 1822 they bought land at Lower Booth, Rawtenstall, on which a new factory was completed in November 1824. Ninety-six powerlooms for weaving cotton were installed. Benjamin, the youngest, then joined the business.
2. Major Eckersley, as Northern District representative and liaison officer, was present as an observer to report events to the Home Office.
3. See detailed discussion of the dispute between the Reverend Gray and Colonel Kearney in Chapter Eight.
4. Eckersley to Hobhouse, 26 April 1826, P.R.O., H.O. 40.19.
5. *Preston Pilot*, 29 April 1826.
6. John and Lawrence Haslem, depositions, P.R.O., P.L. 27/10, part 1.
7. Ibid.
8. Elliott, *David Whitehead*, p. 57.
9. Anonymous letter, *Blackburn Mail*, 10 May 1826.
10. Ibid.
11. Ingham and Rostron were also acquitted of entering a factory at Carr Hall nearby. There are no further details and no compensation claims for this factory, so it is not known if there was any damage or if, indeed, the main mob attacked the building.
12. Named after the owner's father, Richard Rostron. As a putter-out to Rochdale handloom weavers, Rostron together with W. Turner demanded – and got from those in dire need – work done at one third less than the agreed standard rate: hence 'Pinch Dick'. In 1824 other local putters-out banned both men from putting out work in Rochdale.
13. Ann Ingham, however, later received three months' imprisonment for breaking machinery at Waterbarn, Rossendale.
14. The 60th (Duke of York's Own) Rifle Corps. had been in Manchester since December 1825, with detachments in Blackburn, Bury, Middleton, Hyde and Ashton-under-Lyne. Lieutenant Fitzgerald's detachment had come from Manchester to Ramsbottom at short notice – presumably at Colonel Kearney's request.
15. H. Martineau, *The Rioters, or A Tale of Bad Times* (Houlston, 1827) p. 50. Although written as fiction, Harriet Martineau's graphic account is based on the events at Chatterton.
16. *The Manchester Courier*, 29 April 1826.
17. Ibid, 29 April 1826.

Chapter Five

1. The 60th (Duke of York's Own) Rifle Corps. was formed in North America in 1755 as the 62nd Royal American Regiment. On 19 June 1824 they became the 60th (Duke of York's Own) Rifle Corps. In 1830 they were renamed the 60th, or King's Royal Rifle Corps. In 1966 the regiment became part of The Royal Greenjackets.
2. For example, in Dublin in 1820 Major General Sir C. Grant expressed his 'entire approbation of this excellent Corps'. 'The manner in which the Regiment is mounted reflects very great credit on Colonel Kearney, and strongly evinces the attention which he has paid to this most essential part of the duty of a Commanding Officer'. (See F. Whyte and A. H. Atteridge, *A History of the Queen's Bays, 1685–*

1929 (Jonathan Cape, 1930) p. 122.
3. Depositions, Aitken and Ratcliffe, P.R.O., P.L. 27/10, part 1.
4. *Wheeler's Manchester Chronicle,* 3 May 1826.
5. Eckersley to Hobhouse, 26 April 1826, P.R.O., H.O. 49.19.
6. *Manchester Courier,* 29 April 1826.
7. Quoted in *A Second Bacup Miscellany* (Lancashire Library, 1975) p. 43.
8. Deposition, Ratcliffe, P.R.O., P.L. 27/10, part 1.
9. *Blackburn Mail,* 28 March 1827.
10. *Preston Pilot,* 24 September 1826.
11. Edenfield's parish constable, who watched the riot at Dearden Clough, and who possibly accompanied Whatacre and Leech to Chatterton, also ran away. He hid in a pigsty, from which he was ignominiously pulled by the riflemen.
12. *Manchester Mercury*, 30 May 1826.
13. Mrs Upton, aged 28, had been a widow just three weeks. Her husband, William, was buried in Edenfield parish churchyard on 3 April 1826.
14. The sword bayonet of the Baker rifle was commonly used as a short sword. It would be the work of a moment to withdraw it from its scabbard.
15. *Manchester Mercury*, 30 May 1826.
16. In a letter to the *Manchester Mercury* of 23 May 1826 Edmund Sagar, the inquest jury foreman, claimed Mrs Upton was genuinely ignorant of how the rioter, an Accrington man, had got upstairs: 'No doubt he got there unnoticed during the tumult'. This, however, conflicts with the story of the barred door. Whether the riflemen found the rioter by chance or saw him enter is not known.
17. *Manchester Mercury*, 30 May 1826.
18. P.R.O., H.O. 40.19.
19. No-one knows how many shots were fired at Chatterton. Major Eckersley, in a note to Hobhouse on 26 April 1826, stated: '. . . an incessant firing was kept up for quarter of an hour. Five or six hundred shots were fired'. This is feasible. Twenty riflemen firing an average of two shots per minute for fifteen minutes totals six hundred shots. Even though the total wounded is unknown – 'a considerable number' – it is very likely that many shots were fired into the air. At such close range, skilled riflemen could surely, if they wished, have turned the 'Chatterton Fight' into a bloodbath.

   For over 150 years, cottage walls at Chatterton bore the marks of rifle balls. Sadly, these disappeared when the walls were sand-blasted in the late 1970s.

Chapter Six

1. Richard Hamer, deposition, P.R.O., P.L. 27/10, part 1.
2. David Hamer, ibid.
3. *Leeds Mercury*, 19 August 1826.
4. M. Gray, *History of Bury from 1660 to 1876* (Bury Times, 1970), p. 164.
5. Sgt William Hamilton, deposition P.R.O., H.O. 40.19; *Leeds Mercury*, 19 August 1826.
6. The prisoners at Bury, twenty-three in all, including some taken at Chatterton, were later remanded on bail to appear at the August assizes at Lancaster. Three only were remanded in custody. Escorted by a troop of Bolton Yeomanry, they went by chaise to Lancaster Castle two days later (Friday). It is very possible that the three were Melling, Yates and Buskey.
7. There is a tradition in the Dewhurst family of Edenfield that rioters were given temporary shelter in the family farm at nearby Chatterton Hey.
8. Baize: a coarse woollen fabric with a long nap, used for box linings, coverings, etc. Bocking: named after the vil-

lage of Bocking in Essex. A similar, coarser baize used for floor coverings and table cloths.

9. Ann Entwistle is the only person of the Middle Mill/New Inn group known to have been at Chatterton. She was seen by witnesses W. T. Clegg and John Wolstenholme, 'going towards Mr Aitken's mill at Chatterton (P.R.O., P.L. 27/10, part 1).
10. Samuel Haworth, deposition, P.R.O., P.L. 27/10, part 1, and *Preston Pilot*, 29 July 1826.
11. Listed as a scribbled note on an inquisition prepared for Lancaster Assizes, August 1826.
12. Mary Crabtree, deposition, P.R.O., P.L. 27/10, part 1.
13. Ibid. Lawrence Hardman paid for his impetuous call with transportation for life.
14. Samuel Lord, deposition, P.R.O., P.L. 27/10, part 1.
15. The usual duties of a petty constable were to patrol his district regularly and visit ale-houses once a week to check on excessive drinking and unlawful gaming. In time of riot he was supposed to 'repair instantly to the spot with his stave and there put himself under the direction of the magistrate in attendance'. The onerous nature of the constable's work, the lack of any pay, plus the risks involved, made it the most unpopular of all the parish duties.
16. George Ormerod, deposition, P.R.O., P.L. 27/10, part 1.
17. John Sutcliffe, ibid.
18. Samuel Lord's evidence sent Emmett to Botany Bay. Lord was remarkably active in his undercover duties. His evidence also sent Baldwin to Botany Bay. Three others, including Betty Cunliffe, got twelve months' imprisonment, but six others that he named were acquitted for lack of evidence.
19. John Pickup, deposition, P.R.O., P.L. 27/10, part 1.
20. Nelson Hoyle, ibid., and *Preston Pilot*, 19 August 1826. As Nelson Hoyle was twenty, he was almost certainly named after England's national hero of Trafalgar in 1805.
21. John Pickup, deposition, P.R.O., P.L. 27/10, part 1.
22. *Wheeler's Manchester Chronicle*, 29 April 1826, and *Blackburn Mail*, 3 May 1826.

Chapter Seven

1. J. Aikin, *Description of the Country from Thirty to Forty Miles Around Manchester* (Stockdale, 1795), pp. 228–9.
2. Henry Sudell of Mellor, near Blackburn, was east Lancashire's foremost textile merchant. In addition to being a putter-out to thousands of handloom weavers, his textile business activities were worldwide. In 1826 he was reputed to be a millionaire. In 1827 he was unexpectedly declared bankrupt.
3. William Hall, the leader of a 'turn-out' (strike) at the Water Street factory in January 1824. (See William Hall's *Vindication of the Chorley Spinners*, dated 23 November 1824, reprinted in the *Chorley Standard*, October 1885, for a detailed description of a dispute which resulted in violence, coercion and legal actions by both sides.)
4. *Blackburn Mail*, 26 April 1826.
5. *Blackburn Mail*, 19 April 1826.
6. Robert Butterworth, deposition, P.R.O., P.L. 27/10, part 1.
7. James Chambers was not to realise the irony of the place-name Botany Bay. For his actions at Water Street and his earlier ones at Blackburn and Oswaldtwistle, he was transported for life to the other Botany Bay in New South Wales. The origin of the Chorley Botany Bay is obscure. There are no local references to the name before 1790, yet it

was in common use by the early 1800s. The most likely explanation is that the canal, wharfs and cottages were built at about the time that convicts were first transported to Botany Bay in New South Wales in 1788. The canal's route through comparatively remote countryside, plus, perhaps, difficult working conditions, possibly inspired a typically Lancashire sardonic, humorous comparison between the two 'settlements'. (The author is indebted to Mr James Heyes, the Deputy District Librarian of Chorley, for his opinion on the matter.)

8. William Blades, deposition, P.R.O., P.L. 27/10, part 1. The Gillibrand Arms, then a coaching inn, was demolished in 1879 and Chorley Town Hall was built on the site.
9. Thomas Ellison, deposition, P.R.O., P.L. 27/10, part 1, and *Preston Pilot*, 29 April 1826.
10. *Preston Advertiser*, 29 April 1826.
11. Ibid.
12. Article in *Chorley Standard*, 31 May 1865, author unknown.
13. *Preston Advertiser*, 29 April 1826.
14. In August 1826 Henry Sudell successfully sued the Hundred of Leyland (in which Chorley stood) for £408 compensation – his valuation of one hundred looms. (See *Lancaster Gazette*, 26 August 1826.) Some references quote the sum of £483. It is open to speculation that Sudell, for compensation purposes, 'over estimated' the actual numbers.
15. A. Prentice, *Historical Sketches of Manchester and Personal Recollections* (Parkes, 1851) p. 278.
16. Ibid., p. 278.
17. Ibid., p. 279.
18. Ibid., p. 279.
19. Just one month later Samuel Mottershead received £39 12s. 4d. compensation for his broken windows. Thomas Harbottle received £24 18s. 10d. (See County Treasurer's Accounts, Annual General Session, Lancaster, June 1826.)
20. See T. Bramwell, *About Gargrave* (Yorkshire Dales Tourist Trust, 1980).
21. Diaries of William Rowbottom, vol. 4, 1822–30 (Oldham Local History Library).
22. James Taylor, aged twenty-four, of Rochdale, was acquitted at Lancaster August Assizes of destroying machinery at J. Clegg's factory.
23. Diaries of William Rowbottom, vol. 4.
24. *Blackburn Mail*, 10 May 1826.
25. Ibid., 21 June 1826.

Chapter Eight

1. Kearney to Harris, 26 April 1826, P.R.O., H.O. 40/19.
2. *Manchester Mercury*, 2 May 1826.
3. Ibid.
4. *Manchester Guardian*, 6 May 1826.
5. This decision is inexplicable. Only the first few hundred yards could be described as 'steep'.
6. *Blackburn Mail*, 10 May 1826.
7. *Manchester Guardian*, 13 May 1826.
8. Colonel Kearney's meaning is unclear but he can hardly be saying that the magistrate was under the orders of the military. As senior officer present at Chatterton, Colonel Kearney gave Lieutenant Fitzgerald the order for the riflemen to fire.
9. Rather strangely, Reverend Gray's letter of 30 May contained many phrases used in the anonymous letter to the *Blackburn Mail* on 10 May (see note 6). The conclusion can only be that the Reverend Gray either colluded with the author or, for reasons of his own, wrote the letter himself.
10. Reverend Gray, as magistrate for the County of Lancashire, was responsible to the then Lord Lieutenant of the

County, the 12th Earl of Derby.

11. Gray to Derby, 31 May 1826, P.R.O., H.O. 40/19.
12. There were many precedents for military reluctance to be at the scene of a disturbance or riot, e.g. after the 1812 Westhoughton riots, Dr Taylor of Bolton pointed out '. . . the military did not proceed to Westhoughton by the direct route . . . but wasted time by going the longer way in order not to give the alarm and so catch the rioters red-handed'. (See C. H. Saxelby (ed.), *Bolton Survey* (S.R. Publishers., 1971), p. 68.)
13. In England in 1826 some 85,000 veterans of the Napoleonic Wars drew an army pension. Although old age and wounds incapacitated many, there were still approximately 20,000 fit pensioners at an average age of 31. At times of economic distress and unrest, however, the army pensioner had much in common with the poor. Pension rates were low, and in most instances inadequate, especially for those with families. Ex-soldiers with a grievance, therefore, could even be amongst the rioters.
14. Watkins to Peel, 30 April 1826, P.R.O., 40/19.
15. Letter to *Wheeler's Manchester Chronicle*, 3 May 1826. Unfortunately no copy exists of the *Bolton Chronicle* issue in which the article appeared. Lieutenant Colonel Bunbury's reply, published in *Wheeler's Manchester Chronicle*, is the only reference.
16. Watkins to Peel, 30 April 1826, P.R.O., 40/19.
17. *Manchester Mercury*, 30 May 1826.
18. Letter to *Bolton Chronicle*, 16 May 1826 (copy in *Manchester Mercury*).
19. H. F. Wood, *The King's Royal Rifle Corps: the 60th Regiment of Foot* (Hamish Hamilton, 1967) p. 28.
20. Lieutenant Fitzgerald later served in Portugal, Gibraltar, Malta, Corfu, Zante, Limerick and Cork until 1840, when he was at Woolwich and Windsor. He returned to Lancashire as Captain in 1841, when he was at Bolton at another time of riot and civil disorder.
21. Ferrand to Home Office, 5 June 1826, P.R.O., H.O. 40/20. Service in Lancashire was unfortunate for the 60th Regiment. While serving with a detachment in Burnley in November 1841, Rifleman Robert Morris murdered his officer, Lieutenant William O'Grady, and a local girl with whom both were involved, then stabbed himself to death.

Chapter Nine

1. The Tupling Papers, Manchester University (by courtesy of C. Aspin).
2. The full title was 'The Society for Preventing and Prosecuting for Felonies and Misdemeanours within the Forest of Rossendale, the Township of Spotland, the Parish of Bury and the Township of Haslingden'. (See Nick Dunnachie, 'A Rossendale Society to Prosecute Felons', *Red Rose Magazine*, October 1991. Also Haslingden Library Local Collection 364/715.)
3. John Fowden Hindle was a barrister and county magistrate who lived at Gillibrand Hall.
4. 'An Echo of Loom-breaking Days', article, sections 66/67, newspaper cuttings book (undated), Accrington Library Local Collection.
5. *Blackburn Mail*, 13 September 1826.
6. Elliott, *David Whitehead*, p. 79.
7. *Manchester Mercury*, 6 June 1826. An anonymous correspondent to the *Blackburn Mail* of 14 June 1826 poured scorn on the *Mercury*'s report and supported the magistrate's action as necessary. He did not, however, deny any of the details.
8. This did not stop the Queen's Bays from taking part in the Manchester

Race Meeting: 'The Garrison Stakes for horses the property of officers of the 2nd Dragoon Guards – over one mile – gentlemen riders'. Entrants were Captain Ferguson's bay mare *Mary Rose*, Captain Copeland's bay gelding *Jemmy*, Mr Griffith's bay gelding *Rapid*, and Captain River's un-named bay mare. (*Manchester Mercury*, 23 May 1826.)

9. Eckersley to Lieutenant General Sir John Byng, 4 July 1826, Eckersley Letterbook, National Army Museum (N.A.M.), 8510/37. Lieutenant General Byng was temporarily in command of the Northern District.
10. Elliott, *David Whitehead*, p. 79.
11. Ibid., p. 79.
12. The high constable's expenses offer a clue. John Gibbs, 'a spy', and George Walmsley, 'a spy', were paid respectively 5s. and 6s. for a journey from Blackburn to Bolton (no date). Also 'Horses for scouts to Rawtenstall and Padiham and other places out all night, paid £1 0s. 0d.' (23 May 1826). (See L.R.O., QSP 2870/76.)
13. Eckersley to Byng, 22 July 1826, N.A.M. William Cobbett (1763–1835), author, reformer and radical, stood unsuccessfully as a Radical candidate at Preston in the April 1826 elections. Sir Thomas Beevor, a Norfolk squire and ardent supporter of Cobbett, had organised a fighting fund in his support.
14. Eckersley to Byng, 13 July 1826, N.A.M.
15. Eckersley to Byng, 15 July 1826, N.A.M. As long ago as February 1811 Colonel Fletcher spoke of the 'want of employment amongst cotton weavers as the means of supplying the Jacobins with great opportunities of instilling disaffection amongst the lower orders'. (See P.R.O., H.O. 42/114.)
16. Eckersley to Byng, 20 July 1826, N.A.M.
17. Ibid.
18. Whittaker to Eckersley, 16 April 1826, P.R.O., H.O. 40/19.
19. Quoted in Eckersley to Byng, 19 August 1826, N.A.M.
20. Reference in a letter dated 29 April 1826 from a Mr J. S. Penny, a businessman in Manchester, to an associate, Mr T. Parker, in Carlisle (quoted by courtesy of Mr Fergus Read).
21. See Barrack Master's Return, 6 May 1826, Eckersley Papers, Wigan Record Office, DDZ A74/55.
22. Eckersley to Byng, 4 July 1826, N.A.M.
23. S. Bamford, *Walks in South Lancashire* (1844, reprinted Harvester Press, 1972) p. 217.
24. Ibid., p. 221.
25. Deposition, June 1826, P.R.O., H.O. 40/20. Howson gave remarkably precise numbers of people expected to join the uprising: 'from Blackburn 257, Mellor 39, Tockholes 39, Darwen 478, Accrington 378 and Haslingden 284'. In contrast, making his reliability more suspect, he did not name a single individual.
26. Eckersley to Byng, 6 July 1826, N.A.M.
27. Ibid.
28. Ibid., 13 July 1826.
29. The first troops to be so quartered was a detachment of the 53rd Regiment (Northamptonshire). Before the end of the year the 36th Regiment (Herefordshire) replaced them.
30. Eckersley to Byng, 20 July 1826, N.A.M.
31. *Manchester Courier*, 3 May 1826.
32. L.R.O., PR 2863/4/2 (Adamson papers).
33. L.R.O., PR 2863/4/2 (Replies to interrogatories, London Relief Committee).
34. Ibid.
35. L.R.O., PR 2863/4/2 (Adamson papers).
36. Ibid. John Laudon MacAdam (1756–1836), 'the macadamiser of roads', later built and improved many roads in east Lancashire.
37. L.R.O., PR 2863/4/2 (Adamson papers).
38. G. C. Miller, *Blackburn: The Evolution of a Cotton Town* (Blackburn Times,

1951) p. 112.
39. *Blackburn Mail*, 22 November 1826.
40. Haslingden Parish Church of St James Register. From December 1826 to March 1827 a total of 156 people were buried at St James's, 111 of whom were under fifteen years old.
41. Bennett, *History of Burnley*, vol. 3, p. 387.

Chapter Ten

1. R. Hindle, *An Account of the Expenditure of the County Palatine of Lancaster for a period of 23 years, 1819 to 1842, with Remarks* (Whittaker, 1843), p. 46.
2. J. Howard, *The State of the Prisons in England and Wales* (1777), p. 435.
3. M. De Lacey, *Prison Reform in Lancashire, 1700–1850*, Chetham Society, 3rd Series, vol. 33 (1986) p. 173.
4. Hindle, *Account*, p. 62.
5. Ibid., p. 64.
6. De Lacey, *Prison Reform*, p. 176.
7. S. Bamford, *Passages in the Life of a Radical*, vol. 2 (1844, reprinted Fisher, Unwin, 1905) p. 7. As far as is known, Bamford remained in Lancaster for seven months until his trial at York. The Radicals' leader, Henry 'Orator' Hunt, arrested at the same time, also commented that his cell was 'most infamously close'. He, however, was released on bail the next morning.
8. The prison authorities needed to supply new clothing. Most prisoners arrived in rags which were dirty and possibly harbouring parasites (fleas, lice, etc.), which would encourage typhus and similar diseases. (In the 1820s, working-class women did not wear knickers. They came into common use only in the 1840s.)
9. Hindle, *Account*, p. 51.
10. Ibid., p. 57.
11. The manner in which judges were met depended on the individual High Sheriff. In 1834 the High Sheriff met Judge Baron Alderson with eighty persons, all on grey horses, in a coach drawn by six greys, with seven outriders also on greys. (See E. S. Turner, *May it Please your Lordship* (Michael Joseph, 1971) p. 178.)
12. Similar cells with similar conditions in 1612 held the 'Lancashire Witches'; in 1664 George Fox, the founder of the Quaker movement; and in 1812 the Lancashire 'Luddites', of whom eight were hanged.
13. J. Corry, *The History of Lancashire* (Whittaker, 1828) p. 602.
14. Members of the county's landed gentry served on the Grand Jury. In this particular one were at least five who were also county magistrates.
15. 52 Geo. 3, c.130, 1812: '. . . if any persons, unlawfully and tumultuously assembled, should demolish and pull down, or begin to demolish and pull down . . . any building or engine for the purpose of carrying on the manufacture of goods, every such act should be a felony without benefit of clergy'.
16. *Leeds Mercury*, 12 August 1826.
17. Petty Juries were treated rather differently from Grand Juries. The law allowed a Petty Jury to be 'kept without meat, drink, fire or lodging' until they returned a unanimous verdict. In November 1835 Mr Justice Park was to threaten to lock a jury in their room from Saturday to Monday until they returned a conviction. (See *Quarterly Review*, February 1836.)
18. As early as 1649 a member of the House of Commons said that a person charged with a felony should be allowed a defence lawyer in the same way as a person charged with a misdemeanour could be represented. It was 1836 – by which time England and Wales were the only countries in the

world still to have the rule – that a defence lawyer was allowed for all felonies.

19. In December 1830 Mr Justice Park rebuked a barrister attempting to screen his own client at the expense of a defendant: 'Sir, that . . . I shall not be so negligent of my client's [the defendant's] interest as to allow you or anyone else to hang one of my clients to save one of your own'. (*The Times*, 30 December 1830.)
20. Character witness were regarded by defendants as highly important. An employer, neighbour or friend could tell the court about a defendant's character and background. Defendants had to make their own arrangements for this. In past years men had been hanged for lack of a character witness.
21. It says much for John Houghton that he acted as a character witness for Entwistle. Entwistle was later given six months' imprisonment for breaking powerlooms in Houghton's own factory.
22. Samuel Lord acted on the instructions of the Rossendale Society for Prosecuting Felons. His evidence resulted in transportation for life for Emmett, Baldwin and Hoyle. Three others, including Betty Cunliffe, got twelve months' imprisonment. Six others he named were, however, acquitted.
23. *Blackburn Mail*, 23 August 1826.
24. *Leeds Mercury*, 19 August 1826.
25. *Manchester Courier*, 19 August 1826.
26. Wakefield finally appeared before the spring assizes in March 1827 after he voluntarily returned to Lancaster.
27. *Blackburn Mail*, 23 August 1826. The congestion was so great that it was later decided that 'a passage be made behind the Bar [dock] to . . . secure the Bar from pressure when the court is crowded and to accommodate witnesses attending trials'. (See L.R.O., QAL/1/1, 13 March 1827.)
28. *The Times*, 22 December 1830.
29. *Lancaster Gazette*, 26 August 1826.
30. There is some evidence from newspaper reports that rioters were arrested at Chatterton and bailed to appear at the assizes. They never appeared. In March 1827, when public interest in the riot – and the military's involvement – had waned, just one man arrested after Chatterton appeared at the assizes and was acquitted. Another man arrested and charged in October 1826 never appeared in court, the charges dropped.
31. *Lancaster Gazette*, 30 September 1826.

Chapter Eleven

1. See Annual General Report of Lancaster Gaol, Surgeon's Report, October 1826, L.R.O., QAL 1/1.
2. It was to cost the County £52 8s. 6d. or £7 9s. 9½d. per convict, to send Emmett and his group to Chatham. (See Accounts from the Annual General Sessions 1826–7 L.R.O., QTG/1 – hereafter A.G.S.).
3. From 1794 to 1842 a total of 4,291 persons, including 534 women, were transported from Lancaster Castle – an average of 93 *per annum*. (See Hindle, *Accounts*, p. 118.) In addition many thousands were transferred, in chains, to and from other prisons in Lancashire. Chained convicts were, therefore, a common sight to the public.
4. There is no documentary evidence detailing Emmett's journey by stage to the hulks, therefore this account is based on various contemporary accounts and information from directories, timetables, etc. (See also A.G.S. 1827, L.R.O., QTG/1.)
5. Thomas de Quincey, *The English Mail Coach and other Essays* (Dent, 1912, reprinted 1970), p. 4.

6. Each coach had a coachman (driver) and a guard. The guard's duties were numerous. As stagecoaches had no brakes, at the top of every hill it was necessary for the guard to place a drag-shoe (shaped like a shovel and fixed to a chain) under the real wheel to prevent it from turning. This provided a braking effect. He also sounded the posthorn to give tollbar keepers, inn landlords etc. warning of the coach's approach. He was also responsible for the general safety of passengers and baggage.
7. Passing Royal Mail coaches had absolute priority over other road traffic. On the narrow roads of the day, stage-coaches were obliged to pull over and stop to let the 'Mail' go through. Toll-bar keepers risked a fine if they delayed the Royal Mail.
8. Thus the expression, 'going up to London and down to the country'.
9. Mr Hepworth Dixon, quoted in H. Mayhew and J. Binny, *The Criminal Prisons of London* (1862), p. 588.
10. John Henry Capper, in a letter to Lancaster Castle, complained that prisoners lodging overnight in Newgate 'had led to considerable inconvenience'. He asked that 'arrangements be made to proceed direct to the hulks'. (See L.R.O., QTG/1.)
11. '. . . we saw the black hulk lying out a little way from the mud of the shore, like a wicked Noah's ark. Cribbed and barred and moored by massive rusty chains, the prison ship seemed in my young eyes to be ironed like the prisoners.' Pip describing a hulk, probably the *Dolphin*, in *Great Expectations* by Charles Dickens (Dent, 1971 edn.), p. 37.
12. From 1825 to 1832, 28,258 men and women were transported; a rate of 4,037 *per annum* (Select Committee Secondary Punishments, P.P. 1831–32 (547), vii.559).
13. G. Rosenberg (ed.), *The Adventures of Ralph Rashleigh, a Penal Exile in Australia 1825–1844* (Jonathan Cape, 1929), pp. 60–1.
14. W. Branch–Johnson, *The English Prison Hulks* 2nd edn. (Phillimore, 1970) p. 93.
15. Evidence by a former prisoner to the Select Committee on Secondary Punishments, P.P. 22/6/1832 (hereafter S.C.S.P. 1832).
16. Branch–Johnson, *English Prison Hulks*, p. 137.
17. P. MacDougall, *The Chatham Dockyard Story* (Rochester Press, 1982) p. 177.
18. The Hulks Act, 16 Geo. 3 c.43, 1776).
19. *Ralph Rashleigh,* p. 44.
20. Evidence by William Brett to S.C.S.P. 1832.
21. Evidence by Thomas Knight to S.C.S.P. 1832.
22. Quoted in Branch–Johnson, *English Prison Hulks*, p. 120.
23. Evidence by Thomas Dexter to S.C.S.P. 1832.
24. Prisoners were allowed one visitor every three months. It is unlikely that the east Lancashire men received any. The expense of travelling to Kent and staying the three days allowed (visitors from the north and Scotland only) would be prohibitive to their families.
25. On his discharge from the *Dolphin* Emmett was described by the Overseer: '. . . former character and connections not known. Has behaved well in gaol.' Simeon Wright was similarly described. John Hoyle, however, earned: 'Convicted once before. Character and connections bad.' (Dolphin Hulk Returns, 31 March 1827, P.R.O., H.O. 9/1/184.)
26. Coincidentally, the Arctic explorer William Parry started his journey of exploration in the *Hecla* from off Sheerness on the same day.
27. E. M. Butler (ed.), *A Regency Visitor: the English Tour of Prince Puckler–Muskau, Described in His Letters, 1826–1828* (1832, reprinted Collins, 1957) p. 191.

Chapter Twelve

1. *The Quarterly Review*, 28 (1828), quoted in A. G. L. Shaw. *Convicts and the Colonies* (1966, reprinted Melbourne U.P., 1981), p. 143.
2. *Liverpool Mercury*, 4 May 1827, quoted in Shaw, *Convicts and the Colonies*, p. 143.
3. Two east Lancashire examples: 1. John Towers of Blackburn, in January 1824, for stealing a pair of clogs, property of John Baron, transported for seven years; 2. Edward Clegg, in July 1824, for stealing at Oswaldtwistle £25 7s. 0d. in cash, the property of Benjamin and Robert Walmsley, transported for seven years. (See L.R.O., QJC/2.)

   40% of transported male English convicts had no previous convictions. (See R. Hughes, *The Fatal Shore* (Collins, Harvill, 1987) p. 163.)
4. Thomas Holden letters 1812–16, L.R.O., DDX HO/7.
5. Ibid.
6. The *Manlius* later made two other voyages, in 1828 and 1830, both to Hobart, Van Diemen's Land (now Tasmania).
7. P. Cunningham, *Two Years in New South Wales* (1827, reprinted Angus & Robertson, 1966) p. 212.
8. For example, in 1827 twenty-five convict ships took 3,685 male and female convicts to Van Diemen's Land and New South Wales. Thirty-six died en route – less than one per cent. (See C. Bateson, *The Convict Ships, 1787–1868* (Brown, 1959).)
9. D. Conway Ship's Surgeon's Journals, P.R.O., ADM 101/48/1.
10. See Report of the Select Committee on Transportation, P.P. 1837 (518) xix.1 (hereafter S.C.T.) appendix 20, for the 46-paragraph 'Instructions for Surgeon Superintendents on Board Convict Ships'.
11. Ibid.
12. Details of ship, name, trade and sentence from census of New South Wales, November 1828.
13. Cunningham, *Two Years in New South Wales*, p. 241.
14. Hughes, *Fatal Shore*, p. 154.
15. Ibid, p. 154.
16. In the absence on board of a clergyman, the Surgeon Superintendent was required 'to read the church service to the convicts every Sunday, and also a sermon, or some well selected parts from the religious tracts supplied to him'. Paragraph 31, 'Instructions for Surgeon Superintendents on Board Convict Ships'. S.C.T. 1837, appendix 20.
17. Conway, P.R.O., ADM 101/48/1.
18. Ibid.
19. Quoted in Shaw, *Convicts and the Colonies*, p. 112.
20. Cunningham, *Two Years in New South Wales*, p. 213.
21. From 1801 to 1835, 472 convict ships sailed to Australia. Only five complaints about short rations were received by the authorities, and one of these was the *Harmony* (see Chapter Thirteen). (See Shaw, *Convicts and Colonies*, pp. 114–15.)
22. Conway, P.R.O., ADM 101/48/1. Conway's conclusion about a cause of dysentery gives some idea of his medical knowledge. In 1827, however, little was known by the medical profession in general about the causes of such diseases as dysentery, typhus, cholera and scurvy.
23. M. Clarke, *For the Term of his Natural Life* (1874, reprinted Angus & Robertson, 1985) p. 53, referring to Rufus Dawes, the convicted felon, on board the *Malabar* in 1826.
24. Sydney Opera House now stands on Bennelong Point.
25. Bateson, *Convict Ships*, appendix 1.

Chapter Thirteen.

1. Proceedings of the Court of Annual General Session for the County Palatine of Lancaster, 28 June 1827 (hereafter A.G.S. 1827). Report for quarter ending March 1827.
2. Report to the County Magistrates, A.G.S. 1827.
3. In a system not uncommon in late eighteenth-century Lancashire, a Building Club of up to, say, twenty persons bought land on which to build a row of houses. Houses were allocated by ballot. As each house was completed, the person with the appropriate balloted number occupied the house.
4. L. L. Robson, *The Convict Settlers of Australia* (Melbourne U.P., 1965) pp. 185 and 187.
5. E. Foss, *The Judges of England, 1066–1870* (John Murray, 1870) p. 497.
6. P.R.O., H.O. 17/35, part 2, and H.O. 11/107 VL.
7. Surgeon's Report, A.G.S. 1827.
8. Report, A.G.S. 1827.
9. Phoebe Tomlinson of Nook, Oswaldtwistle, married John Grimshaw, a fellow rioter, at St James's, Church Kirk, on 26 May 1828.
10. *Lancaster Gazette*, 24 March 1827.
11. Ibid.
12. Heys was prosecuted at the expense of the Rossendale Society for the Prosecution of Felons at a cost of £12 0s. 2d. John Kay received £4 for his expenses.
13. *Lancaster Gazette*, 24 March 1827.
14. 4 Geo. 4 c.64, 1823, rule 19, Lancaster Prison Rule Book (courtesy of Mr D. M. Sailor).
15. Hindle, *Accounts*, p. 53, and L.R.O., QSP 2286/6. 217 cows' heads at 1s. 6d. each were purchased in one quarter of 1827. (See A.G.S. 1827).
16. 'An Order to Remove Female Convicts', Lancaster Public Library Local History Collection.
17. Ibid.
18. L.R.O., QSP 2286/6.
19. 'An Order to Remove Female Convicts'.
20. The cost of this clothing was borne by the County of Lancashire. The master of the female convict ship *Grenada*, when receiving fourteen convicts from Lancaster on 24 July 1826, charged the County £1 5s. 0d. for repair to 'the County Clothing' somehow damaged by fire on the journey.
21. Robson, *The Convict Settlers*, p. 186.
22. P.R.O., H.O. 11/6.
23. Home Office regulations stated: 'Children whose ages do not exceed, if Boys, six years, and Girls, ten years, will be allowed to accompany their Mothers'. ('An Order to Remove Female Convicts'.)
24. Hughes, *Fatal Shore*, p. 458.
25. Ibid, p. 458.
26. Bateson, *Convict Ships*, p. 50.
27. Surgeon John White, 1790, quoted in Shaw, *Convicts and the Colonies*, p. 125.
28. Bateson, *Convict Ships*, pp. 205–7.
29. Ibid., p. 207.
30. P.R.O., ADM 101/32.
31. Ibid.
32. Ibid.
33. Ibid.
34. *Sydney Gazette*, 28 September 1827. The *Gazette* wrongly stated that 180 female convicts (instead of eighty) had arrived.
35. Bateson, *Convict Ships*, p. 208.

Chapter Fourteen

1. Sir Ralph Darling (1775–1858), Governor Chief Executive of New South Wales, November 1825–December 1831.

2. A.D.M. 101/48/1.
3. *The Sydney Gazette and New South Wales Advertiser*, 13 August 1827. The *Manlius* brought 174 prisoners (see NSW 4/4012, reel 397).
4. The detailed description was necessary to establish the identity of a convict in case of escape. It is noteworthy that part of Hardman's first finger on his left hand was missing. It is quite possible that he lost this while wrecking the powerlooms.
5. Between 1800 and 1849, about 1,000 people were transported from England to New South Wales and Van Diemen's Land for political or protest crimes. Luddites were sent in 1812–13, food rioters from East Anglia in 1816, fourteen of the 'Pentridge Rising' group were sent in 1817. Radical weavers from Scotland and Yorkshire in the 1820s and the east Lancashire rioters in 1827. Most of the rest, however, came after 1830 including 457 'Swing' rioters in 1831, the Tolpuddle Martyrs in 1834 and Chartists between 1839 and 1848. (See *Fatal Shore*, pp. 195–6.)
6. Slade, evidence, S.C.T.
7. Cunningham, *Two Years in New South Wales*, pp. 46–7.
8. Ibid., p. 46.
9. Macarthur, evidence, S.C.T.
10. See A.O. NSW 4/4012, reel 397, Convict Indents.

    Isaac Hindle and John Hoyle who arrived on the *Guildford* on 25 July 1827 were also described as 'Farmsman'. Hindle was assigned to Captain Rossi, the Chief Superintendent of Police, who had a 2,560-acre holding near Goulburn. Hoyle went to John Philip Webster's 3,280-acre (222 cattle, 1,674 sheep) farm at Redhill, Paterson's Plains. James Chambers arrived on the *Marquis of Hastings* in 1828, but his future remained unrecorded. There is no reference to Simeon Wright on any NSW Convict Indent or Index, therefore his fate remains unknown.
11. An analysis of the 1828 census of New South Wales traces 116 *Manlius* convicts out of 174 landed in 1827 (67%). A further breakdown indicates that, of these 116, twenty were in prison, penal camps or on the *Phoenix* hulk in Lavender Bay, near Sydney, awaiting transportation to Moreton Bay or Norfolk Island penal camps; 22 were in road gangs or 'iron gangs' (in permanent chains where discipline was harsher); 47 were on farms in rural areas; 11 were servants in Sydney; 15 were with the Australian Agricultural Company, and one was in hospital.
12. C. Sweeney, *Transported in Place of Death* (Macmillan, 1981) p. 66.
13. Lang, evidence, S.C.T. 1837.
14. Anley, appendix 9, S.C.T. 1837.
15. Macarthur, evidence, S.C.T. 1837.
16. Ibid.
17. C. H. M. Clarke, *A History of Australia*, part 3 (Melbourne U.P.) p. 245.
18. P. A. Pemberton, *Pure Merinos and Others: the Shipping Lists of the Australian Agricultural Co.* (Australian National University, 1986) p. 1.
19. Stroud, and later Gloucester and the River Avon, were named after the intended destination in England of the Company's output of wool.
20. Conditions at Newcastle were similar to Moreton Bay. Convict miners worked twelve hours a day, in leg-irons, a hundred feet underground in almost total darkness. Conditions were made almost unbearable by brutal overseers, rock falls, bad air and seepage from the sea above. In 1831 the Australian Agricultural Company took over the coal mines and conditions improved.
21. A. A. Co. Superintendents' Reports, April and May 1826, October 1827. Quoted in John Perkins, 'Convict Labour and the Australian Agricultural Company', in *Convict Workers: Interpreting Australia's Past*, p. 175.

Chapter Fifteen

1. It was Parry's ship the *Hecla* which left the Medway for the Arctic on the same day in 1827 as the *Manlius*, and Emmett, left for Sydney.
2. Clarke, *A History of Australia*, part 3, p. 247.
3. Ibid., p. 247.
4. Letter from P. Pemberton, 1987.
5. A.O. NSW 4/4099, T.O.L. No. 35/722.
6. Pemberton, *Pure Merinos and Others*, table vi, p. 98.
7. A.1218, p. 540, G. Gipps' despatch, 1838.
8. Sir William Parry, evidence, S.C.T. 1837.
9. Pemberton, *Pure Merinos and Others*, table vi, p. 98.
10. Letter from J. Peasley, 1986.
11. A.O. NSW 4/4443 Conditional Pardon No. 43/348.
12. Copy of burial certificate, issued Sydney 1976, courtesy of J. Peasley.
13. Sir William Parry, evidence, S.C.T. 1837.
14. Pemberton, *Pure Merinos and Others*, table vi, p. 98.
15. Clarke, *A History of Australia*, part 3, p. 153.
16. M. T. Place, *Gold Down Under: the Story of the Australian Gold Rush* (Collier–Macmillan, 1969) p. 33.
17. R. Boldrewood, *Robbery Under Arms* (O.U.P., 1949) pp. 194–5.
18. This information, and all succeeding family names and dates, is from the Peasley family tree, courtesy of J. Peasley.
19. *Australian Encyclopaedia* (Halstead Press, 1965) p. 320.
20. Bushrangers such as Frank Gardiner, Ben Hall and 'Captain Thunderbolt' operated in the area, stealing gold and holding up stagecoaches. They later became folk heroes in Australian song and story. Henry Lawson, a 'bush balladeer' and writer of short stories on life in rural Australia, was born in Grenfell in 1867.
21. G. C. Mundy, *Our Antipodes: or, Residence and Rambles in the Australian Colonies . . .*, 3 vols. (London, 1852), p. 369.
22. Maria Jane Emmett later married a James Hamilton Norris, and her tenth child, Hilda Ethel May, was born in 1888. Maria Jane Norris died aged 48, a true pioneer woman, in Adelong, New South Wales, in 1894.

Chapter Sixteen

1. Ann Entwistle is also described as a 'Protestant' on the *Harmony* convict indent (A.O. NSW 4/4012), yet as 'Catholic' in the 1828 census of New South Wales.
2. Ullathorne evidence, S.C.T. 1837, quoted in Hughes, *Fatal Shore*, p. 348.
3. An analysis of the 1828 census of New South Wales traces 56 *Harmony* convicts out of 80 (70%). A further breakdown indicates 23 in the Female Factory at Parramatta; ten servants in rural areas; thirteen servants in Sydney, and ten with occupation not stated.

   A Mary Thompson was assigned as servant to George Milner Slade, the Australian Agricultural Company's accountant at Carrington. One speculates whether she told Thomas Emmett about Mary Hindle and Ann Entwistle.
4. Ann Entwistle was with the Hazards for at least one month. Employers paid to the government a bond of 40 shillings to guarantee employment for at least that period.
5. Martineau, *The Rioters*, p. 63.
6. Shaw, *Convicts and the Colonies*, p. 241.
7. A. Salt, *These Outcast Women: The Parramatta Female Factory 1821–*

1848 (Hale & Iremonger, 1984) p. 69.
8. Thomas Reid, *Two Voyages to New South Wales and Van Diemen's Land* (London, 1822) quoted in Hughes, *Fatal Shore*, p. 256.
9. Parramatta Female Factory Records, A.O. NSW, reel 2278, shelf 2/8211.
10. J. F. O'Connell, *A Residence of Eleven Years in New Holland and the Caroline Islands* (Boston [Mass.], 1836) quoted in Hughs, *Fatal Shore*, pp. 256–7.
11. Convict Marriage Banns, St John's Church, Parramatta, pre-1856 microfiche (courtesy of J. Peasley).
12. A.O. NSW 4/4015 T.O.L. No. 36/1094.
13. Appendix to Report of S.C.T. (P.P. 1837 (518) xix.1), quoted in para. H.34, 'Select Documents in Australian History 1788–1850'.
14. Convict Marriage Banns (place not stated), pre-1856 microfiche (courtesy of J. Peasley).
15. A.O. NSW 4/4443 Convict Pardon No. 44/37; also Gibbs despatch A.1231, p. 519.
16. Convict Deaths Register, N.S.W., on microfiche (courtesy of J. Peasley).
17. See John Wolstenholme, deposition, P.R.O., P.L. 27/10, part 1.
18. See Harmony convict indent 1827, Ann Entwistle, A.O. NSW/4012, reel 397.
19. Evidence, E. A. Slade S.C.T. 1837.
20. George Hindle paid a total of 9s. 6d. rates for his house and property in Pleasant Street, Haslingden, in 1829 (see 1829 Rate book, Haslingden Public Library). There are no further references to George Hindle, or Elizabeth, in either directories or church records; therefore, it is possible that Hindle left Haslingden shortly after 1829.
21. Sweeney, *Transported in Place of Death*, p. 141. Some husbands, however, committed offences to be with their wives. For example, the husband of Mary Jones, transported in the *Harmony*, stole a pair of stockings just to be transported himself (p. 93).
22. Petitions A.O. NSW 4/2425.
23. I am grateful to the Society of Australian Genealogists, Sydney, N.S.W., for this information.
24. Hughes, *Fatal Shore*, p. 244.

Chapter Seventeen

1. Elliott, *David Whitehead*, p. 57.
2. Ibid., p. 57.
3. *Lancaster Gazette*, 26 August 1826.
4. Elliott, *David Whitehead*, p. 57.
5. Calculations based on evidence of James Grimshaw to the Select Committee on Manufacturing, Commerce and Shipping 1833; 1831 census returns; and the published list of Hundred Township Contributions, *Blackburn Mail*, 7 June 1826.
6. *Blackburn Mail*, 19 April 1826.
7. Great Harwood Parish Records, L.R.O., PR163.
8. Handlooms were always described as a 'pair' (as in a pair of scissors, trousers, etc.).
9. Oswaldtwistle Poor Law Overseers' Accounts, L.R.O., PR2674/4.
10. Jon Elliott (ed.), *My Life and Times: Moses Heap of Rossendale 1824–1913* (Rawtenstall Local History Library) p. 2. Sad-cake was a pastry mix of flour, fat and water, rolled out approximately half an inch thick and baked on a hot plate over a fire. Ideally, it was eaten hot with butter.
11. Evidence of William Fielden to House of Commons Select Committee on Emigration from the United Kingdom, PP 1826 (404) iv.1 (hereafter S.C.E.).
12. Ibid.
13. *Blackburn Mail*, 12 July 1826.
14. Evidence, William Fielden, S.C.E.
15. *Hansard*, vol. xvi, House of Commons, 9 February 1827, p. 412.
16. Thomas Rogerson, *Statement of Facts Relative to the Taking Down and Re-*

building of the Parish Church (Blackburn, 1827).

17. Ibid.
18. Evidence, William Hulton, S.C.E.
19. Ibid.
20. Ibid.
21. Evidence, Reverend J. W. Whittaker, S.C.E.
22. Evidence, The Right Reverend Bishop of Chester, S.C.E.
23. G. Hull, *The Poets and Poetry of Blackburn (1793–1902)* (Toulmin, 1902) p. 23.
24. Report, House of Commons Select Committee on the Causes of Increase in the Number of Criminal Commitments in England and Wales, 1828 (545) vi.419.
25. Ibid.
26. See B. Dobson, *Policing in Lancashire 1838–1989* (Landy, 1989) p. 15.
27. L.R.O., PR 166.
28. Lyons, *Lancashire Cotton Industry*, p. 167.
29. John Ashworth, evidence to House of Commons Select Committee on Handloom Weavers' Petitions 1835, P.P. 1835 (341) xiii.1. On 8 May 1826 Ashworth resigned from the Rossendale Society for Prosecuting Felons in protest at the prosecution of rioters. He was one of at least four members who were against the introduction of machinery.
30. William Greg, evidence to House of Commons Select Committee on Manufacturers, Commerce and Shipping, P.P. 1833 (690), vi.
31. L.R.O., QSP 2841/29 (Preston Sessions, Epiphany 1825).
32. Ibid.
33. Hopwood, *History of the Lancashire Cotton Industry*, p. 65.
34. L. Pritchard (ed.), *England and America: A Comparison of the Social and Political state of both Nations* (1833); *The Collected Works of Edward Gibbon Wakefield* (Collins, 1968) p. 344 Paul Louis Courier (1772–1825) was a French pamphleteer, anti-Monarchist and anti-cleric.
35. B. Inglis, *Poverty and the Industrial Revolution* (Hodder, 1971) p. 330.
36. *Northern Star*, 1 January 1842, quoted in D. Bythell, *The Handloom Weavers: a Study in the English Cotton Industry During the Industrial Revolution* (C.U.P., 1969) p. 227.
37. Elliott, *David Whitehead*, p. 83.
38. Bythell, *The Handloom Weavers*, p. 267.
39. *Darwen Gazette*, 30 December 1911.
40. Bythell, *The Handloom Weavers*, p. 267.
41. G. H. Tupling, *The Economic History of Rossendale*, Chetham Society, New Series, vol. 86 (1927) p. 222.

Dramatis Personae

Principal persons mentioned in the text

Adamson, Sanford John Cyril, 1799–1873

Parson, Padiham Parish Church of St. Leonard's. Third of six children of the Reverend John Adamson. In 1823 Sanford Adamson succeeded his father at Padiham after serving two years at St. James's Church, Altham, near Accrington. The Reverend Adamson cared deeply for his parishioners, inheriting from his father a strong dislike of all other faiths. He founded National Schools in Padiham, and in nearby Simonstone, Higham and Hapton. During the 1862–3 Cotton Famine he provided meals for the distressed at his own expense.

He was outspoken and controversial on many local and church issues, and was much loved or hated accordingly. He retired in 1863. In 1865, a year after the death of his wife, Nancy, he moved to Moorside House, Altham, where he died in 1873. They had no children.

Aitken, Thomas, 1799–1858

A tablet inside Haslingden St. James's Church records: 'In memory of Thomas Aitken of Edenfield, Formerly Chatterton, who died on the 5th of March 1858, aged 68 years. Also his wife Jane who died 4th of March 1856, aged 67 years. Erected by their children as a token of affectionate remembrance'. The Aitken family vault is but a few yards away from the family grave of Richard Lund, killed at Chatterton.

After 1826 Thomas Aitken continued at Chatterton and also opened a factory at nearby Irwell Vale. After his death his family extended the Irwell Vale factory to become manufacturers of cotton sailcloth and also felt for paper-making. Throughout the nineteenth century, the Aitken family were generous public benefactors in Ramsbottom. The Chatterton factory was demolished in 1896. In 1923 the factory and lodge area was landscaped and presented by the then owner to Chatterton as a recreation ground.

Bamford, Samuel, 1788–1872

Born Middleton, near Manchester, son of a handloom weaver. He was educated at Manchester Grammar School. Whilst working as a handloom weaver, he became a prominent Radical and agitator for Parliamentary reform.

In 1826 he became correspondent of a London newspaper, because of which he became unpopular and distrusted by some of his fellow Lancashire men. He was, however, always sympathetic to the causes of the poor. In 1851 he became a messenger at Somerset House, London. After a few years he became disenchanted with London life and returned to Middleton to take up again his trade of handloom weaving. He died at Harpurhey, Manchester, in 1872. During his life Samuel Bamford published many works of poems and prose including *Passages in the Life of a Radical*, and *Early Days*.

Byng, Sir John, 1772–1860

Born in Middlesex, he enlisted as an ensign in the 33rd Regiment in 1793 and served in Flanders and Ireland. By 1804 he was a Lieutenant Colonel in the third Guards (later Scots Guards). He served as a Major General throughout the Peninsular Wars. From 1819 to 1825 he was Commander of the Northern District. He was then appointed Commander-in-Chief of the forces in Ireland, but because of the riots returned in 1826 to take temporary command of Northern District. In 1831 he became M.P. for Poole. In 1833 he became Baron Strafford; in 1841 promoted to General; in 1855 to Field Marshall. He died at his London home in 1860.

Duckworth, Thomas, 1811–1903

Born at Torside Farm, Musbury, he was the youngest of fourteen children. He started work at six years old, partly as a nurse (looking after a child whilst its parents worked), partly as a bobbin winder. He later became a handloom weaver. From 1833 to 1839 he worked as a weaver in Manchester. He then worked in Holland as a tackler (loom maintenance man) until about 1845. Afterwards he took a similar position in France. He returned to Manchester to take a beerhouse. He retired in 1873 to Crumpsall, near Manchester.

Dugdale, Adam, 1770–1838

Fifth and youngest son of John Dugdale (1722–1791), a shoemaker of Great Harwood. After his apprenticeship to the calico printing trade he became an expert calico print pattern designer. In 1811 he went into partnership with Thomas Hargreaves, his brother-in-law, at Broad Oak printworks, Accrington. Dugdale, however, spent much of the time representing the firm's interests at their Manchester office.

On the death of Thomas Hargreaves in 1821 Dugdale continued as partner with Thomas's sons, Benjamin and John. After an early retirement because of ill-health, he lived at Liverpool where he died after a long illness. He built and endowed St. John's Church, Knotty Ash.

Eccles, Bannister, 1794–1842

Eldest son of John Eccles, whose forebears moved to Lower Darwen from Pickup Bank in the eighteenth century and settled there. In the 1770s John Eccles started business as a cotton spinner. By 1818 Bannister, and his brother Joseph, owned two small mills employing sixty persons. In 1820 they erected

Jubilee Factory in Blackburn, on the site of an old brewery of that name. From that time Bannister became prominent in Blackburn civic life and became a magistrate. He married in 1825 and had three daughters. He was a Methodist of the 'Independent persuasion'.

Eckersley, Sir Nathaniel, 1779–1837

Born Hindley, near Wigan, the son of a wealthy manufacturer. In 1795 he enlisted as a private in the 10th, Prince of Wales Own, Light Dragoons. By 1800 he was adjutant of the 1st (King's) Dragoon Guards. He later transferred to the 60th Regiment and served in the Peninsular War and in Paris with the Army of Occupation. He was promoted Major in 1817. Between 1819 and 1827 he was at Manchester as Northern District Brigade Major. In 1827 he went, as Lieutenant Colonel, to the Leeward and Windward Islands where he was Deputy Quartermaster General. He returned to his native Hindley in 1833, his health broken. He died in 1837. He was unmarried.

Fielden, Sir William, 1772–1850

The Fieldens had been landowners in Blackburn since the sixteenth century when a Henry Fielden was trustee of an estate given by the Earl of Derby. The Fieldens were described in the seventeenth and eighteenth centuries as 'almost exclusively traders in the special class of fabrics (Checks and Greys) produced in Blackburn'.

William Fielden began his business career as a putter-out. After the invention of Arkwright's Water Frame, he was a pioneer of the factory system, building several mills in the Blackburn area. He became east Lancashire's most influential merchant and manufacturer. He was a friend and admirer of Sir Robert Peel and, in 1832, became an M.P. for Blackburn. He was an M.P. for fourteen years. On his retirement from the House of Commons he was awarded a baronetcy.

Fitzgerald, David, 1807–?

Enlisted in the 60th Regiment in 1825. As a Lieutenant he later served in Lisbon, Limerick, Cork, Gibraltar, Malta, Corfu and Zante until 1840 when he was at Woolwich and Windsor. He returned to Lancashire as a Captain in late 1841 when he was at Bolton during the period of the Plug Riots.

Ferrand, Thomas, 1764–1845

Son of James Ferrand of Marland, near Rochdale, and Susan, his second wife, the daughter of a wealthy Rochdale woollen merchant. Thomas Ferrand practised as an attorney and coroner in Rochdale and Manchester for over fifty years. In 1843, when he was seventy-nine, Slater's Directory of Manchester described his as 'Attorney and Steward of the Lord of the Manor'. He died unmarried and is buried in Rochdale Parish Church.

Ferrand received much publicity and notoriety by his handling, as coroner, of the inquest of a victim of Peterloo in 1819. In an alleged attempt to prevent publicity damaging to Manchester magistrates, he expelled newspaper reporters from the courtroom. Subsequently, because of other legal irregularities, the proceedings were declared null and void. Many Radicals complained that Ferrand, 'by omitting to observe the law, placed himself above the law'.

Fletcher, Ralph, J.P., 1757–1832

Only son of John and Mary Fletcher of Bolton. He became a magistrate in 1797. In 1805 he married Jane Grundy, who died, aged 78, in 1856. In 1808 he became Colonel of the Bolton Regiment of Loyal Volunteer Infantry. He was for many years prime mover and director of a heartily detested anti-Radical spy system in Lancashire (for example Colonel Watkins' involvement in Rossendale in 1826). Ralph Fletcher had a 'firm belief in the absolute ascendancy of the Orange or Protestant interest' (*Bolton Chronicle*, 22nd December 1832). He is buried in Bolton Parish Churchyard.

Garnett, Jeremiah, ?–1853

The second son of Jeremiah Garnett of Otley, Yorkshire, owner of the Wharfeside Paper Mill, Otley. Jeremiah's (senior) daughter Sarah was the wife of Timothy Horsfall, a worsted spinner and manufacturer of Bingley, Yorkshire. In 1799 the Garnett and Horsfall families bought Low Moor factory, near Clitheroe, and appointed Jeremiah Garnett (junior) as a managing partner. The factory was modernised and extended during Garnett's life-time, particularly in 1810, 1824 and 1834. By 1824, after powerlooms were introduced, 2,500 pieces of cotton goods and 14,000lbs. of cotton yarn were produced weekly.

Gray, William, J.P., M.A., 1785–1847

Parson, Haslingden Parish Church of St. James from 1813 until his death. He was a native of Bootle, Cumberland, and formerly curate at Heysham, near Lancaster, before coming to Haslingden. From his appointment in 1826 until 1842 he was the only magistrate in Haslingden. From that date he shared the bench with William Turner. Gray, 'a genial and kind-hearted man', with old-fashioned values of service to home, family and people, was in complete contrast to the autocratic capitalism of William Turner. (Moses Heap made the laconic comment in his diary: 'He [Gray] sat on the bench with William Turner and I daresay Mr Gray would have to sanction many things he did not like'.)

On Sunday, 17th October 1847 Gray, in a state of deep depression caused by the death of two friends in Bootle, committed suicide by cutting his throat with a razor.

Grant, William, J.P., 1769–1842

Eldest of four sons of William Grant (1733–1817) who came to Bury from Strathspey in 1783. A Mr Dinwiddie of Hampson Mills, Bury, found employment for the Grants and William (the younger) was apprenticed to calico printing. In 1806 the brothers William, Daniel, John and James purchased the Ramsbottom calico print works of Haworth, Peel and Yates and founded the firm of William Grant and Brothers.

The brothers became prosperous employers and landowners in Ramsbottom and William was appointed a Justice of the Peace in 1824. He, with his brothers, built houses, schools and churches in the Ramsbottom area and were known for their diligence and strict sobriety. William and Daniel are reputed to be the originals of the Cheeryble brothers in Charles Dickens' *Nicholas Nickleby.*

Hamer, Richard, 1770–1850

Son of Edward Hamer of Summerseat, a fustian manufacturer and dealer in Blackburn Greys. He started work at six years old as a tier boy at Haworth, Peel and Yates' calico print works at Bury (owned by Robert Peel, his uncle William Haworth, and William Yates, a local publican). Hamer went on to become a cotton buyer, then a supervisor of the firm's five small spinning mills in Summerseat. In 1812 Haworth, Peel and Yates sold their Summerseat interests to a group of the firm's supervisors, including Hamer. In 1824 he bought out his partners' interests for himself and his son Daniel (1792–1844).

On Richard Hamer's death in 1850 the properties were left to his three married daughters. The youngest, Mary, was the wife of John Robinson Kay, son of Thomas Kay of Longholme, Rawtenstall. The Hamers and the Kays were devout Methodists. After his death, Richard Hamer's descendants dominated the religious, social and industrial life of Summerseat for over a hundred years.

Hobhouse, Henry, 1776–1854

A solicitor with H.M. Customs from 1806 to 1812, he then became solicitor to the Treasury. He was Permanent Under Secretary of State for the Home Office from June 1817 to July 1827, when he retired. He was also keeper of the state papers (the public records) from May 1826 until his death. Henry Hobhouse was responsible for the development of the Public Record Office into one of the finest, most complete archives of government and court records in Europe. He was married with eight children.

Heap, Moses, 1824–1913

His grandfather, John Heap, a farm labourer, came from Marsden (now Nelson) to Brex, Newchurch-in-Rossendale, in the late eighteenth century. John's son, William (1800–1867), a jenny spinner, married Ann Lord at Bacup in 1823. Moses Heap, born at Doals, near Bacup, was the eldest of eight sons and three daughters. He started factory work at the age of five and worked at many factories in the Rossendale area until 1874, when he became a yeast merchant. His notebook/diary entitled 'My Life and Times' was in the family's possession until 1961, when it was presented to Rawtenstall Library. Moses Heap was a Baptist.

Hindle, Christopher, 1777–1847

Eldest son of Christopher and Elizabeth Hindle. The Hindle family originated in Great Harwood. At the end of the eighteenth century they moved to Highercroft, Lower Darwen, on their purchase of the mansion and estate. Hindle was high constable of the Lower Division of Blackburn Hundred. He died, unmarried, in Higham, Kent in 1847.

Hindle, John Fowden, J.P., 1757–1831

Son of John Hindle, a Blackburn chapman and linen dealer. Educated at

Manchester Grammar School. His first house was in King Street, Blackburn and he later moved to Gillibrand Hall, near Chorley. In 1831, on the bankruptcy of Henry Sudell, he purchased Woodfold Hall and estate. He died shortly afterwards. He was married with five sons and four daughters. In addition to being a magistrate, Hindle was a Deputy Lieutenant of the County of Lancaster.

'Huncoat Jack', c.1790–?

Known to history only as 'Huncoyt Jack',* he was described by the 'oldest inhabitant in Accrington' in an interview in the *Accrington Observer* of 20th December 1890 as a captain of the 1826 rioters. His description of Huncoat Jack fits many of those normally law-abiding handloom weavers driven to riot by hunger and frustration:

> He was between thirty and forty years of age. He was no reckless rowdy; no village bully . . . he never drank intoxicants, never provoked a quarrel; he was a loving husband; an indulgent parent; a genial neighbour. He was, however, a principal agitator in the riots. Jack was born to be a leader of men for good or evil. He had a vast amount of moral courage combined with mental energy; he was deeply religious, nay, even devoutly pious. His speech at Whinney Hill [the day the riots started] was a fine example of his ability to arouse the passions and to give counsels of prudence and moderation at the same time.

Huncoat Jack went on trial at Lancaster, together with fifteen other local 'loomoclasts', but unfortunately there is no clue to his identity.

Hutchinson, James, 1785–1861

Youngest of four sons of William Hutchinson (1741–1806), a Bury landowner and wool merchant. Although his brothers continued in the woollen industry James, in about 1816, was a cotton spinner. He was known as a good employer. In 1816 he employed 143 people in two mills at Woodhill. A factory inspector's report in that year described his 46 child employees under fourteen as 'clean and healthy', and his factories as 'very clean'.

The Hutchinson family was Anglican. James, together with his brothers, was active in the religious and social life of Bury. At the time of the riots James was high constable of the Bury and Bolton Division of Salford Hundred. He retired to Cheltenham, where he died aged 76. He was unmarried.

Kay, John, ?–1834

A butcher by trade, he became Blackburn's full-time constable in 1809. For many years he was not paid by the town, his income coming from the 'unsolicited board and lodging' paid by his prisoners in the town lock-up. From

---

* It is not surprising that Jack's surname is unknown. At that time descriptive nicknames were freely, and permanently, given. East Lancashire was, to quote L. O. Shaw in *The Duel*:

Where nicknames fit the men so tight on
That scarce a fellow knows his right one.

1824, after complaints by local people to the Select Vestry, he was paid a fixed salary. He was respected in Blackburn as a highly efficient, intelligent and painstaking police officer. For twenty-five years he policed the town with the help of just two 'Runners', or assistants, Thomas Morten and Thomas Woodhall.

Kearney, James, 1777–1846

At seventeen he was a Lieutenant in the 9th Regiment of Dragoons, at nineteen a Captain in the 29th Regiment of Light Dragoons. In 1802 he transferred to the 12th (Prince of Wales) Light Dragoons and in 1805 to the 2nd Queen's Dragoon Guards (Queen's Bays). He served with the Bays as Major from 1805; Acting Lieutenant Colonel from 1810; Lieutenant Colonel from 1814 and Colonel from 1819. In 1830 he became a Major General; in 1835 a Knight Commander of the Royal Hanoverian Guelphic Order (K.C.H.). In 1841 Sir James became a Lieutenant General and, from 1842 until his death, he was Honorary Colonel of the 7th (The Queen's Own) Regiment of Light Dragoons (Hussars).

In addition to service in England and Ireland, he spent several years in the East Indies. He was in the Walcheren Expedition of 1806 and at Flushing in 1809. He also served in France in 1816.

Park, James Alan, 1763–1838

Son of James Park, an Edinburgh surgeon. In 1791 he married Lucy Atherton, daughter of a Preston woollen draper. They had two sons. Park was called to the Bar in 1784. In 1791 he became Vice-Chancellor of the Duchy of Lancaster, in 1795 Recorder of Preston. In 1799 he became a King's Counsel. In 1802 he was promoted to Chief Justice on the Northern Circuit. In 1816 he was knighted on his appointment as a Judge of the Common Pleas.

Park was a pious churchman and he wrote and published religious tracts. 'With no particular eminence as a lawyer he proved himself by his good sense and strict impartiality as well as by the respectability of his character' (*The Judges of England*, p. 497).

Peel, Sir Robert, 1788–1850

Born near Bury (some three miles from Chatterton), the eldest son of Robert (afterwards Sir Robert) Peel (1750–1830) of Oswaldtwistle. At the age of ten he moved with his family to Drayton Manor, Tamworth, Staffordshire. In 1801 he went to Harrow, then Oxford, and in 1809 entered Parliament as M.P. for Cashel. From 1812 to 1818 he was Secretary for Ireland. He was Home Secretary from 1822 to 1827. When Home Secretary, Peel reorganised the London police force (hence 'Peelers', or 'Bobbies'). In 1834 he was for four months Prime Minister, and in 1841 became Prime Minister again.

He was M.P. for Tamworth from 1833 until his death. In 1841 he abandoned his support of the Corn Laws and eventually carried the repeal laws in 1846. In 1850 he was badly injured in a riding accident, and died three days later. The 120-foot high Peel Tower at Holcombe was erected in his memory.

Shaw, Lawrence Ormerod, 1788–1851

Solicitor and magistrates' clerk at Haslingden. He was married with three daughters and two sons. Shaw was also a versatile writer and publisher of poetry. He held no high opinion of local people, or of the area, and his caustic observations often got him into trouble. In *The Duel; A Satirical Poem*, first published in 1815, he described Haslingden as:

> Where children swear with so much grace
> You'd think 'Old Clootie' [the devil] farmed the place
> Where publicans repose in quiet
> Whilst beerhouse keepers strive in riot . . .

He lived in Haslingden and practised as an attorney until his death.

Silvester, John, J.P., *c*.1765–1827

A member of a Yorkshire family (he was baptised in Rotherham), he married Joanna Threllfall of Chorley in 1788. They had five sons and three daughters. John Silvester was a landowner, a magistrate and a Colonel of Militia. He lived in Hollinshead Street, Chorley. An 1818 directory lists the family as bankers in Chorley, with other business interests in Manchester.

John Silvester was one of the few magistrates who escaped criticism for their involvement in the events at St. Peter's Field in 1819 (Peterloo). He courageously went into the crowd to read the Riot Act, but unfortunately he was pushed down and trampled on by the milling crowd. In 1826, at Water Street factory, he again deliberately went amongst the crowd to read the Riot Act, but again was unsuccessful.

Sudell, Henry, 1764–1856

Son of Henry, a Blackburn chapman who died before his son was born. The Sudell family was one of the oldest in Blackburn, dating back to a John Sudell who held chantry lands in Oozebooth, Blackburn, in 1548. In 1785 Henry Sudell inherited the joint fortune of his uncles, John and William, and soon became the most important and influential merchant and putter-out in east Lancashire. For forty years he was 'leader of the elite, patron of every local charity and arbiter of the destiny of a whole generation of handloom weavers'.

Although by repute a millionaire, in 1827 Sudell was declared bankrupt. Just before the news broke, Sudell and his family secretly left his mansion and settled in Bath, where he lived for almost thirty years. The family name is preserved in the Sudell Cross area of Blackburn.

Throp, William, ?

Born in Preston. He came to Blackburn in 1818 and set up business as a cotton spinner in premises in King Street. He erected King Street Factory in 1820. In 1828 he went into partnership with William Fielden and William Townley. The partnership was dissolved in 1835. From that date nothing is known about his life.

Turner, William, 1794–1852

Son of James Turner of Martholme, Great Harwood. In 1824 William, with his brother Ralph, took control of the family firm in Helmshore. This was founded in 1789 by his father, his father's two brothers and three cousins.

William Turner was described as a 'martinet' by his friends, and an 'arrogant autocrat' by his enemies. As an employer and magistrate (appointed 1842) he imprisoned employees for bad workmanship and for leaving work without notice. After one particularly unjust case of three months' imprisonment for a spinner who persisted in spinning 'thick', many local people protested to the Home Secretary, who had the sentence quashed. He did, however, build houses and a school for his workers and paid £2,000 towards the cost of building St. Thomas's Parish Church, Helmshore. His chief passion was tulip growing, and in his search to grow the elusive 'black' tulip would often pay £100 for a single bulb. He was married with eleven daughters.

He employed over 2,000 people in his factories in Helmshore. Many of these had no alternative but to leave the district when the firm ceased production on his death.

Wakefield, Edward Gibbon, 1796–1862

Born in London of Quaker parents. In May 1827 Wakefield received three years' imprisonment in Newgate for abducting and marrying Ellen Turner. The prison experience changed his life. In Newgate, he wrote a critical study of English criminal law which, when published, considerably influenced future changes in the legal system. His study of emigration as a benefit to the poor aroused his interest in Australasia. He believed Britain was over-populated by paupers and 'systematic colonisation' would answer the problem. The colony of South Australia was founded in 1834 on Wakefield's principles.

Wakefield also contributed to Canada's self-government and, in 1839, to the colonisation of New Zealand. He emigrated to New Zealand and died, almost forgotten, in Wellington in 1862.

There is no doubt that Wakefield's knowledge of, and visits to, east Lancashire influenced his later ideas on criminal law and emigration.

Whitehead, David, 1790–1865

Born near Gambleside, Rossendale, the son of John Whitehead and his second wife, Ann. He had four brothers and three sisters. By 1802 he was working in a cotton factory. His business career began in 1813 when he and his brothers Thomas and Peter agreed to be partners as handloom weavers. In 1815 they expanded into spinning. At the same time the brothers became putters-out to many handloom weavers in the Rossendale area.

In 1822–24 they built, at Springside, Lower Booths (Rawtenstall) a factory for powerloom weaving, at which time the youngest brother Benjamin joined the business. In 1830 the firm of David Whitehead and Brothers became textile merchants, establishing a house in Montreal, Canada. During the Victorian era the firm rapidly expanded, dominating industrial life in Rawtenstall.

David Whitehead was a devout Wesleyan Methodist who expected his employees to be the same. He was, however, a good employer. He built houses, schools and chapels for his workers and encouraged community activities in music, drama and learning. He encouraged thrift with the use of saving schemes. He also expected sobriety. David Whitehead married Betty Wood of Clitheroe in 1818 and they had eleven children. His diary is in the possession of Rawtenstall Library.

Whittaker, James, J.P., 1789–1855

Of Broadclough Hall, Bacup (the home of the Whittaker family from 1525–1923). He was a prominent landowner and influential figure in Rossendale life. Better known as 'Justice Whittaker' after his appointment as Rossendale's first magistrate on 29th April 1824 at the age of thirty-five. He was born in 1789 and married Harriet Ormerod at Newchurch on 2nd November 1826. He died on 19th April 1855 and is buried at St. John's Church, Bacup.

Whittaker, John William, D.D., 1791–1854.

Vicar of Blackburn Parish Church of St. Mary from 1822 until his death. His wife was the daughter of William Fielden. They had six sons and four daughters. He was an excellent scholar and the author of numerous controversial theological tracts and treatises. He became a Doctor of Divinity in 1830.

Appendix 1

East Lancashire factories and their owners involved in the riots.

O.S. Ref.*	Ref. No.	Situated at	Owned/ Occupied by	Date visited	Looms destroyed
729 419	A	Low Moor, Clitheroe	Garrett & Horsfall	24 April	Not attacked
763 282	B	Grange Lane, Accrington	R. & T. Sykes	24 April	60
760 277	C	Woodnook, Accrington	J. Marquis	24 April	4
751 272	D	Fern Gore, Accrington	B. & R. Walmsley	24 April	20
735 278	E	White Ash, Oswaldtwistle	J. & W. Bury	24 April	94
683 279	F	Jubilee Street, Blackburn	B. Eccles	24 April	212
686 273	G	Park Place, Blackburn	J. Houghton	24 April	25
677 277	H	King Street, Blackburn	W. Throp	24 April	None
				Sub-total:	**415**
729 419	I	Low Moor, Clitheroe	Garrett & Horsfall	25 April	Not attacked
696 211	J	Bowling Green, Darwen	W. H. & G. Carr	25 April	16
696 211	K	Bowling Green, Darwen	J. Garsden	25 April	6
696 212	L	Bobbin Hall, Darwen	J. Garsden	25 April	16
716 235	M	House, Hoddlesden	J. Garsden	25 April	14
779 212	N	Middle Mill, Helmshore	W. & R. Turner	25 April	106
				Sub-total:	**158**
814 231	O	Lower Booth, Rawtenstall	D. Whitehead	26 April	96
811 225	P	Longholme, Rawtenstall	T. Kay	26 April	20
806 223	Q	New Hall Hey, Rawtenstall	Hoyle & Ashworth	26 April	3
802 189	R	Dearden Clough	L. & J. Rostron	26 April	56
793 187	S	Chatterton	Aitken & Lord	26 April	46
792 146	T	Summerseat	R. & D. Hamer	26 April	38
796 116	U	Woodhill, Elton	J. Hutchinson	26 April	49
829 218	V	Holt Mill, Waterfoot	J. & D. Ashworth	26 April	20
844 216	W	Waterbarn, Stacksteads	G. & J. Ormerod	26 April	50
848 218	X	Tunstead, Stacksteads	G. & J. Ormerod	26 April	28
869 228	Y	Irwell Mill, Bacup	Hargreaves & Hardman	26 April	28
873 259	Z	Old Clough, Bacup	R. & J. Munn	26 April	52
				Sub-total:	**486**
587 181	a	Water Street, Chorley	Lightoller & Harrison	27 April	80
				Sub-total:	**80**
				Total looms destroyed:	**1139**

Factories and their owners involved in other riots:

O.S. Ref.*	Ref. No.	Situated at	Owned/Occupied by	Date visited	Looms Destroyed
984 850	1	Great Ancoats St., Ancoats	J. Kennedy	27 April	None
985 853	2	Jersey Street, Ancoats	H. Beaver	27 April	Not known
989 843	3	Miller Street, Manchester	S. Mottershead	27 April	None
989 840	4	Long Millgate, Manchester	Clegg, Norris & Co.	27 April	None
983 855	5	Pollard Street, Ancoats	J. Clarke & Sons	27 April	None
983 855	6	Pollard Street, Ancoats	T. Harbottle	27 April	None
935 542	7	Middle Green, Gargrave	J. Mason	27 April	20
940 089	8	Higher Crompton, Shaw	J. Clegg	30 April	28
929 079	9	Luzley Brook, Royton	Milne & Travis	30 April	None
938 051	10	Lees Road, Oldham	Collinge & Lancashire	30 April	None

* Ordnance Survey Landranger Series, Scale 1:50,000, Sheets 102, 103 and 109.

Appendix 2

The Rioters and their Sentences

Name (men)	Age	Known to be present at	Sentence	Commuted to
Josiah Baldwin	22	W, X, Y, Z	Death	Transported for life
James Chambers	55	E, F, G, H, a	Death	Transported for life
Joseph Clayton	29	Y , Z	Death	Transported for life
Thomas Emmett	22	N, O, W, X, Y, Z	Death	Transported for life
Lawrence Hardman	37	W	Death	Transported for life
Isaac Hindle	35	E, F, G, H	Death	Transported for life
John Hoyle	27	Z	Death	Transported for life
Simeon Wright	27	F, G, H	Death	Transported for life
Thomas Dickenson	19	F, G, H	Death	18 mths' imprisonment
Thomas Leaver	26	G	Death	18 mths' imprisonment
Thomas Sharples	24	F, G, H, a	Death	18 mths' imprisonment
William Winder	27	F, G	Death	18 mths' imprisonment
George Ashworth	21	W, Y, Z	Death	12 mths' imprisonment
John Ashworth	22	Y	Death	12 mths' imprisonment
Robert Butterworth	30	a	Death	12 mths' imprisonment
Mark Cockerill	29	W, Y, Z	Death	12 mths' imprisonment
John Howarth [1]	27	F	Death	12 mths' imprisonment
William Sutcliffe	22	F	Death	12 mths' imprisonment
Michael Tomlinson	28	E	12 mths' imprisonment (not commuted)	
Thomas Ashworth [2]	27	O	Death	6 mths' imprisonment
James Aspden	23	N, H, a	Death	6 mths' imprisonment
James Crawshaw	19	T	Death	6 mths' imprisonment
Richard Entwistle	18	E, F, G, N	Death	6 mths' imprisonment
Edward Houghton [3]		G	Death	6 mths' imprisonment
Richard Kay	17	F	Death	6 mths' imprisonment
James Latham	18	F	Death	6 mths' imprisonment
James Leaver [4]	20	F, G	Death	6 mths' imprisonment
James Ormerod	18	F	Death	6 mths' imprisonment

Name (men)	Age	Known to be present at	Sentence	Commuted to
James Shorrock	23	L, M, N	Death	6 mths' imprisonment
Thomas Greenhalgh	20	T	Death	3 mths' imprisonment
James Howarth	25	F	Death	3 mths' imprisonment
Thomas Lomax	30	T	Death	3 mths' imprisonment
Henry Melling	21	U	Death	3 mths' imprisonment
Alexander Norris	17	E, N	Death	3 mths' imprisonment
John Orrell	25	N	Death	3 mths' imprisonment
James Riding	29	F	Death	3 mths' imprisonment
William Almond	25	N	Acquitted	
Thomas Bolton	27	F, I	Acquitted	
James Buskey	16	U	Acquitted	
William Charnley [5]	29	F	Acquitted	
William Cockerill	23	W, X, Y, Z	Acquitted	
Patrick Gibbons	35	W, X, Y, Z	Acquitted	
Aaron Gregson	17	R	Acquitted	
James Grundy	27	F, G	Acquitted	
Anthony Harrison	17	R	Acquitted	
John Holt	20	W, X, Y, Z	Acquitted	
John Ingham	19	P, Q	Acquitted	
Richard Rawsthorne	20	W, X, Y, Z	Acquitted	
James Rostron	21	P, Q	Acquitted	
Richard Tattersall	30	W, X, Y, Z	Acquitted	
James Taylor	29	W, X, Y, Z	Acquitted	
William Taylor	20	N	Acquitted	
Edward Yates	18	U	Acquitted	

1. Wounded in shoulder at Jubilee Street.
2. Died in Lancaster Castle, 26th September 1826.
3. Wounded in neck and mouth at Park Place.
4. Wounded at Park Place.
5. Wounded in arm at Jubilee Street (arm removed).

Name (women)	Age	Known to be present at	Sentence	Commuted to
Ann Entwistle	46	N, S	Death	Transported for life
Mary Hindle	27	N	Death	Transported for life
Betty Cunliffe	25	W, X, Y, Z	Death	12 mths' imprisonment
Johanna Oldham	20	E	12 mths' imprisonment (not commuted)	
Phoebe Tomlinson	27	E	12 mths' imprisonment (not commuted)	
Betty Marsden	35	N	Death	6 mths' imprisonment
Alice Grimshaw	18	E	12 mths	3 mths' imprisonment
Betty Howorth	17	F, N	Death	3mths' imprisonment
Ann Ingham	29	R, W	Death	3 mths' imprisonment
Margaret Yates	17	N	3 mths' imprisonment (not commuted)	
Alice Lord	19	O	Acquitted	
Peggy Lord	20	O	Acquitted	

The following were tried and sentenced at the March 1827 assizes at Lancaster Castle:

Name	Age	Known to be present at	Sentence	Commuted to
George Heys	28	N, O	3 mths' imprisonment (not commuted)	
William Barnes	57	S	Acquitted	
John Fairbrother	23	U	Acquitted	
Lawrence Rostron	30	O	Acquitted	

N.B. Some prisoners were acquitted of offences at one factory, and found guilty for offences at another.

Appendix 3

Persons killed at Chatterton, Wednesday 26 April 1826

Name	Age	Occupation	Home town	Date buried	Place buried	Remarks
John Ashworth	27	Handloom weaver	Haslingden	30 April	St. James's C. of E., Haslingden*	Shot in abdomen
James Lord	26	Fulling Miller	Mill End, Newchurch-in-Rossendale	30 April	St. Nicholas's C. of E., Newchurch	Shot in body and head.
Richard Lund	23	Blacksmith	Haslingden	29 April	St. James's C. of E., Haslingden*	Shot in abdomen
James Rothwell	22	Handloom weaver	Hutch Bank, Haslingden	30 April	ditto*	Shot in heart
Mary Simpson	23	Handloom weaver	Clough End, Haslingden	30 April	ditto*	Shot in thigh (verdict: 'Accidental death')
James Waddicar (or Whatacre)	40	Dresser (powerloom)	Ramsbottom	30 April	Emmanuel C. of E., Chapelry of Holcombe	Shot in abdomen (verdict: 'Murder by rifleman unknown')

* Annotated in Register: 'Shot in a mob'.

Appendix 4

Persons arrested but not proceeded against (Blackburn only)
April/May 1826

1. Arrested for rioting at Grange Lane, Accrington (B)

John Bentley

2. Arrested for rioting at White Ash, Oswaldtwistle (E)

Jacob Balmer
Joseph Barnes
Benjamin Fish
Joseph Harwood
John Preston
Ellen Grimshaw

3. Arrested for rioting at Jubilee Street, Blackburn (F)

John Cook
John Crompton
James Duckworth
Thomas Entwistle
John Hartley
Thomas Leaver
John Lewis
Christopher Norris
Richard Pearson

4. Arrested for rioting at Middle Mill, Helmshore (N)

Thomas Almond
William Almond (the elder)
Henry Baron
Henry Cook
Thomas Duckworth
Christopher Duckworth
Benjamin Fish (see also [E])
John Gibson
Jabez Green
John Hirst
William Hurst
Henry Orrell
Thomas Sutcliffe
Abraham Wade
John Yates
Margaret Hadcroft
Nancy Marsden
Lydia Taylor

5. Arrested for rioting at Chatterton (S)

William Ratcliffe
William Rawcliffe
William Rishton (November 1826)

Appendix 5

Address of the Weavers' Union Society of Blackburn to the Right Honourable Secretary of State for the Home Department.

To the Right Honourable Robert Peel

Sir,

We, the operative handloom weavers of Blackburn presuming upon that public spirit and love of justice which distinguishes your political character, have ventured in the unadorned language of British Mechanics to lay before you a statement of a part of our numerous grievances in the firm persuasion that His Majesty's Government need only be informed of the sufferings of the people, for full and complete justice to be applied to them. It is well known that the cotton weavers received for many years wages sufficient to procure all the necessities of life and thus were placed on a footing of equality with the rest of the community; but within the last eleven years we have experienced repeated reductions in the price of our labour; and often when there was not the least reason, until at this time we cannot procure more than one or two meals per day. Our dwellings are totally destitute of every necessary comfort. Every article of value has disappeared either to satisfy the cravings of hunger or to appease the clamour of relentless creditors: our homes where plenty and contentment once resided are now become the abodes of penury and wretchedness. This, however, is only a faint picture of those who are *fully* employed. No adequate idea can be formed of the sufferings of those who are unemployed of whom there are upwards of seven thousand in this town and neighbourhood. Thousands who were once possessed of an honest independence gained by laborious industry, are now sunk in the lowest depths of poverty.

Thousands who once looked forward with confidence to a decent competence to support themselves in old age are now reduced to the melancholy alternative of subsisting on casual charity or becoming the inmates of a workhouse.

Were the humane man, Sir, to visit the dwellings of four fifths of the weavers and see the miserable pittance sixteen hours' hard labour can procure, even of those fully employed, divided between the wretched parents and their starving little ones, he would sicken at the sight and blush for the patience of humanity!

The principal causes, Sir, which in our opinion have conspired to produce that wretchedness and misery, which reign universally amongst the weavers are the Corn Laws and the Introduction of Power Loom Weaving. The former, by enhancing the price of provisions, afforded a pretext to avaricious manufacturers to reduce the wages of their workmen in order that their quantum of profits might still be the same and all the others were soon necessitated to follow their example and by preventing the admission of foreign grain they contributed effectively to deprive us for ever of thousands of our best foreign customers by forcing them in retaliation to manufacture for themselves. But whatever may have been the evils inflicted by the operation of the Corn Laws, they vanish into nothing when compared with those which followed the adoption of the Power Loom. This was the grand blow which struck at the root of our domestic happiness – this completed what the Corn Laws had begun - and like the tenth Egyptian plague, this exceeded all the commercial evils which had ever visited this once happy country. This machine produced a new epoch in our manufactures. One boy or girl was able to perform as much work as several Hand Loom Weavers – immense numbers in consequence were thrown out of employment. The Hand Loom manufacturers were forced to reduce their wages, that they might be able to meet their rivals in the market – reduction followed reduction until at this time our wages are eighty to ninety percent less than they were twenty to twenty-five years ago. The Power Loom has done incalculable injury to the country – it has forced thousands to the workhouse – the land has been taxed to support them – rents have consequently risen – and, we venture to assert, that three fourths of that opposition which has been manifested towards any alteration in the Corn Laws may be traced to the Power Loom, and the recent improvements in machinery, as its parents. Were land the common property of all, then any improvement in machinery, which would tend to abridge human labour, would be a national benefit; but while every new discovery in the art of diminishing manual labour, tends only to enrich those by whom the improvement was introduced, and to spread an equal proportion of poverty amongst the working classes, we cannot refrain from protesting against such innovations, as calculated to sap the foundations of society, and to transform a happy, well-fed and independent peasantry into a race of grovelling, mean-spirited paupers.

We are aware of the slippery ground on which we stand when we address persons in office in the language of simple truth: but when we reflect that almost all the officers of His Majesty's Government have had their salaries advanced, and in many cases, more than doubled, upon the plea of an advance in the price of provisions: whilst for the same reason, amongst many others, we have had our wages repeatedly reduced, until they are now no more than three or at most five shillings per week, when we contrast our present circumstances with what they once were, and when we look upon our starving wives and children, and have no bread to give them – we should consider ourselves still more degraded than we are – as undeserving the name of Englishmen, were we to withhold our complaint from His Majesty's Government, or to abstain from speaking in proper terms of the causes of the present unparalleled distress which exists amongst the weavers, and we implore you, Sir, by all the ties which bind the patriot to his country – by that anxiety for the welfare of England, which you have frequently evinced – to use that influence which you possess with His Majesty's Government; towards procuring an amelioration of the condition of the most injured and oppressed of His Majesty's subjects.

by order of the Committee of
the Weavers' Union Society
John Lancaster, Secretary.

April 12th 1826

Appendix 6

To our Truly and Wellbeloved our Justices of Gaol Delivery for the Northern Circuit, The High Sheriff of the Courts of Lancaster and all others.

signed by Royal Command
Robt. Peel

Richard Shorrock et al
Pardon George R

Whereas the following persons were at the General Sessions of Assize of Oyer and Terminer and General Gaol Delivery held at the Castle of Lancaster in and for the County Palatine of Lancaster on Tuesday the eighth day of August last tried and convicted of the crimes hereafter mentioned and had judgement of death recorded against them for the same viz:-

Robert Shorrock of Rape, James Bridge of Burglary, Will Lancaster, James Grosvenor, James Winterbottom and Oliver Collins severally of stealing in a dwelling house the value of 40/– and upwards. Daniel Guinan, John Kelly, Thomas Fitzgerald, Michael Bonnell, Peter Walton and John Ketland, severally of Highway Robbery. Patrick Blake having pleaded guilty of the like offence. Richard Sumner and James Anderson severally of horse stealing. James Chambers, Simeon Wright, Isaac Hindle, Joseph Clayton and John Hoyle severally of feloniously with divers persons riotously and tumultuously assembled breaking into Cotton Mills and wilfully and maliciously demolishing certain Machines and Engines employed in the Weaving of Cotton Cloth. Thomas Emmett, Mary Hindle, Ann Entwistle, Josiah Baldwin and Lawrence Hardman severally of feloniously with divers persons unlawfully and riotously and tumultuously assembled breaking into Woollen Mills and wilfully and maliciously demolishing certain Machines and Engines employed in the Weaving of Woollen Cloth.

We in consideration of some circumstances humbly represented unto us, are graciously pleased to extend our Grace and Mercy unto them and to Grant them our Pardon for the said crimes on condition of their being transported to New South Wales or Van Diemen's Land or some one or other of the Islands adjacent thereto, for and during the term of their respective Natural Lives. Our Will and Pleasure therefore is that you do give the necessary directions accordingly. And for so doing on 8th of September 1826.

Robert Peel
(signature)

Appendix 7

The Apprenticeship Indenture of John Hartley

This Indenture made the fourteenth day of August in the Year of our Lord one Thousand eight Hundred and five Between Thomas Astley, John Astley, Joseph Margerison and George Clayton Overseers of the Poor of the Township of Blackburn in the County of Lancaster of the one Part, and Richard Aspden of the Township of Blackburn aforesaid Weavers –

Witnesseth, That the said Overseers, by the Assent of two of his Majesty's Justices of the Peace (One of the Quorum) of and for the said County of Lancaster, Have put, placed, and bound, and by these Presents Do put, place and bind John Hartley, a poor Boy of the Age of eight years – belonging to the said Township of Blackburn as an Apprentice to the said Richard Aspden, with him to cohabit and dwell after the Manner of an Apprentice, from the Day of the Date hereof until the said John Hartley shall attain the Age of twenty-one Years. During which time his said Master he shall faithfully serve, his Secrets keep, his lawful Commands obey. At Cards, Dice, or any unlawful Game he shall not play, or exercise himself therein. Alehouses, Taverns, or evil company he shall not frequent. Fornication or Adultery he shall not commit during the said Term: Neither shall he consume, waste, or lend the Goods of his said Master to anyone without his knowledge and consent: Damage he shall not do to his said Master or suffer the same to be done by others: but shall endeavour to prevent the same, and give Notice thereof to his said Master: Neither shall he absent himself from the Service of his said Master by Day or Night, during the whole Term of his Apprenticeship, but in all things behave himself to his said Master and all his Family as becometh a faithful Apprentice, during the said Term.

In consideration of which said intended Service, and of the Sum of two Pounds and two Shillings in hand paid to the said Richard Aspden by the said Overseers of the Poor as and for an Apprentice fee with him the said John Hartley at or before the sealing and delivery hereof, the Receipt as hereof is hereby acknowledged. And also in consideration that the said Overseers of the Poor have provided suitable clothing for the said apprentice, the said Richard Aspden doth for himself his Executors and Administrators, covenant, promise and agree to and with the said Overseers of the Poor and their Successors, that he the said Richard Aspden, his Executors and Administrators, or some of them shall and will teach and instruct the said John Hartley or cause him to be well taught and instructed in the Art, Mystery and Occupation of a Weaver and find and provide for him all Manner of Wearing Apparel, and wholesome and sufficient Meat, Drink, Washing and Lodging, during the said Term and all other things useful and proper for such an Apprentice.

Provided always, that the said last-mentioned Covenant on the Part of the said Richard Aspden, his Executors and Administrators, to be done and performed, shall

continue to be in Force for no longer time than three Calendar months next, after the Death of the said Richard Aspden in case the said Richard Aspden shall happen to die, during the Continuance of such Apprenticeship: according to the Provisions of an Act passed in the Thirty-second Year of the Reign of King George the Third instituted 'An Act for the further Regulation of Parish Apprentices'. In Witness whereof, the said Parties to these Presents, have hereunto set their Hands and Seals the Day and Year above written.
Sealed and delivered by all parties in the presence of us –
John Haworth
Jno. Haworth Jnr.

Thomas Astley – seal

John Astley – seal

Joseph Margerison – seal

George Clayton – seal

The mark of
Richard X Aspden – seal

We, whose Names are hereunto subscribed Two of his Majesty's Justices of the Peace (Quorum Unus) in and for the County of Lancaster, do consent for the above-named John Hartley to be put forth Apprentice according to the true Intent and Meaning of the Indenture above-written.

Thomas Clayton.
R. H. Beaumont.

John Hartley was born in Blackburn on 24 January 1797, the seventh child of nine born to Thomas and Betty Hartley. On 14 August 1805, aged eight, he was apprenticed as a handloom weaver to Richard Aspden of Blackburn. He completed his apprenticeship in 1818. In 1824 he married Susannah Woods, and they had seven children. John worked as a handloom weaver in Blackburn all his life. He died around 1877.

There is a family tradition (1992) that John was involved in the 1826 riots. A John Hartley was arrested at Jubilee Street, Blackburn, but was not proceeded against (see Appendix 4).

(Source: L.R.O., PR 1558/1/328, and Hartley family.)

Select Bibliography

Primary Sources

Public Record Office:

a) Chancery Lane
Palatinate of Lancaster, depositions P.L. 27/10 parts 1 & 2.

b) Kew
ADM Admiralty Medical Journals; ADM 101/32 & 48.
HO Quarterly Returns, Prison Hulks; HO8, HO9
HO Transporation Registers; HO11/6
HO Warrants for Pardons and Reprieves; HO13
HO Criminal Petitions and Registers; HO19/4
HO Criminal Registers; HO27/31
HO Correspondence, Disturbances 1812–1855; HO40/19 & 20.

Lancashire County Record Office:

Adamson Papers PR 2863/4/2.
Blackburn Hundred Accounts 1826, QSP 2870/76.
Calendars of Crown Prisoners, QJC.
Great Harwood Poor Law Accounts, PR 157; 163/2 & 166.
Hartley Apprenticeship, PR 1558/1/328
Haslingden Parish Vestry Book, PR 3016/6/1.
Lancaster Castle Minutes 1826, QAL 1/1; 1827, QTG/1.
Lancaster Castle 1826, QSP 2869/25 & 2286/6.
Oswaldtwistle Poor Law Accounts, PR 2675/4.
Preston Sessions, Epiphany 1825, QSP 2841/29.
Thomas Holden Letters, 1812–16, DDX 140.

National Army Museum:

Eckersley Papers, 8510/37

New South Wales Archive Office:

Convict Records, AONSW 4/4012,4/4015 & 36/1094.
Convict Petitions, AONSW 4/2425 & 4/443.
Convict Pardons, AONSW 44/37.
Parramatta Female Factory Records, AONSW, reel 2278/2/8211.

Wigan Record Office (Leigh):

Eckersley Papers, D/DZ A74/55.

Parliamentary Papers

1826/27 – S.C. on Emigration from the United Kingdom. 1826 (404) iv.1
1828 – S.C. on Cause of Increase in Number of Criminal Commitments and Convictions in England and Wales. 1828 (545) vi.419.
1832 – S.C. on Secondary Punishments. 1831–32 (547) vii.559.
1833 – S.C. on Manufactures, Commerce, and Shipping. 1833 (690) vi.
1835 – S.C. on Hand Loom Weavers' Petitions. 1835 (341) xiii.1.
1837 – S.C. on Transportation. 1837 (518) xix.1.

Diaries/Manuscripts

Moses Heap: My Life and Times 1824–1913, introduction by Jon Elliott (held in Rawtenstall Local History Library).
William Rowbottom: The Diaries of an Oldham Hand Loom Weaver, volume 4, 1822–30 (held in Oldham Local History Library).
William Varley: The Household Accounts and Diary of a Higham Hand Loom Weaver, *History of Burnley*, volume 3: 1659–1850 (Burnley Express, 1949).
David Whitehead of Rossendale, 1790–1860, edited by Jon Elliott (Rawtenstall Local History Library).

Miscellaneous

Army List 1826, 1827 et seq.
Docton, K.H. (ed.), Returns and Correspondence, Lancaster Castle Scrapbooks 2 & 5, Box 30a (Lancaster Library).
Hall, W., *A Vindication of the Chorley Spinners* (1824; Chorley Standard reprint 1885).
Haslingden St. James's Church Parish Registers, 1826–1827.
Hansard, 1826, 1827.
Lancaster Castle Prison Rules 1785 and 1824–1844 (courtesy of Mr D.M. Sailor).
Stephenson Papers, R.C. 942 Ross (Rawtenstall Local History Library)

Journals and Newspapers

Annual Register.
Blackburn Mail
Blackburn Standard.
Bolton Chronicle.
Chorley Standard.
Darwen Gazette.
Haslingden Gazette.
Lancaster Gazette.
Leeds Mercury.
Manchester Courier.
Manchester Guardian.
Manchester Mercury.

Preston Advertiser.
Preston Chronicle.
Preston Pilot.
Quarterly Review
Sydney Gazette.
The Times.
Wheeler's Manchester Chronicle.

Secondary Sources

Abram, W.A., *History of Blackburn, Town and Parish* (Blackburn Times, 1877).

Aikin, J., *A Description of the Country from 30 to 40 miles around Manchester* (Stockdale, 1795).

Ashmore, O., 'Low Moor, Clitheroe: A Nineteenth-Century Factory Community', *Trans. of the Lancs. and Ches. Antiq. Soc.*, vol. 73–74 (1963/64).

Aspin, C., *Lancashire: The First Industrial Society* (Helmshore Local History Society, 1969).

Aspin, C., *The Turners of Helmshore and Higher Mill* (Higher Mill Museum Trust, 1970).

Aspin, C., *James Hargreaves and the Spinning Jenny* (Helmshore Local History Society, 1964).

Baines, E., *History of the Cotton Manufacture in Great Britain* (Fisher, Fisher & Jackson, 1835).

Baines, E., *History Directory and Gazetteer of the County Palatine of Lancaster* (Longman Hurst, 1824).

Bamford, S., *Passages in the Life of a Radical* and *Early Days*, two volumes (Fisher Unwin, 1905)

Bamford, S., *Walks in South Lancashire and on its Borders* (1844, reprinted Harvester Press, 1972).

Barnard, M., *A History of Australia* (Angus & Robertson, 1962).

Barton, B. T., *A History of the Borough of Bury and Neighbourhood* (1874, reprinted Morten, 1973).

Bates, A., *Directory of Stage Coach Services 1836* (David & Charles, 1958).

Bateson, C., *The Convict Ships 1788–1868* (Brown, Son & Ferguson, 1959).

Bennett, W., *The History of Burnley. vol. 3: 1650–1850* (Burnley Express, 1949).

Branch-Johnson, W., *The English Prison Hulks*, 2nd rev. edn. (Phillimore, 1970).

Bramwell, T., *About Gargrave* (Yorkshire Dales Tourist Trust, 1980).

Butler, E. M. (ed.), *A Regency Visitor: The English Tour of Prince Puckler-Muskau Described in His Letters, 1826–1828* (1832; reprinted Collins, 1957).

Butler, L., *Annals of the King's Royal Rifle Corps. vol. 2.* (John Murray, 1923).

Butterworth, E., *Historical Sketches of Oldham* (John Hirst, 1856).

Bythell, D., *The Handloom Weavers: A Study in the English Cotton Industry during the Industrial Revolution* (C.U.P., 1969).

Chapman, S. D., *The Cotton Industry in the Industrial Revolution* (Macmillan, 1977).

Clark, C. H. M., *Select Documents in Australian History, 1788–1850* (Angus & Robertson, 1950).

Clark, C. H. M., *A History of Australia, vol. 3: the Beginnings of an Australian Civilisation 1824–1851* (Melbourne U.P., 1979).

Clarke, M., *For the Term of his Natural Life* (1874; reprinted Angus & Robertson, 1985).

Clarke, S., *Clitheroe in the Old Coaching Days*, 2nd edn. (Clitheroe Advertiser, 1929).

Cole, G. D. H. and Postgate, R., *The Common People 1746–1938* (Methuen, 1938).

Corry, J., *The History of Lancashire* (Whittaker, 1825).

Cunningham, P., *Two Years in New South Wales* (1827; reprinted Angus & Robertson,

1966).
Darvall, F. O., *Popular Disturbances and Public Order in Regency England* (O.U.P., 1934).
De Lacy, M., *Prison Reform in Lancashire 1700–1850* Chetham Society, 3rd series, vol. 33 (1986).
Dobson, B., *Policing in Lancashire 1839–1989* (Landy Publications, 1989).
Elbourne, R., *Music and Tradition in Early Industrial Lancashire 1780–1840* (Brewer, 1980).
Elliot, W.H., *The Country and Church of the Cheeryble Brothers* (Elliot Stock, 1894).
Fishwick, H. (ed.), 'Lancashire Church Survey, 1650, Blackburn Hundred', *Trans. of the Lancs. and Ches. Record Soc.*, vol. 1 (1878–79).
Foss, E., *The Judges of England 1066–1870* (John Murray, 1870).
Foster, D., *The Changing Social and Political Composition of the Lancashire Magistrate 1821–1851* (unpublished Ph.D. thesis, Lancaster University, 1972).
Fox, K. O., *Making Life Possible* (privately published, 1982).
Gibbings, R., *John Graham: Convict 1824: an Historical Narrative* (1937, reprinted White Lion, 1975).
Gooderson, P. J., *A History of Lancashire* (Batsford, 1980).
Gray, K., *Some Contributions to the Early History of Nonconformity in Rossendale* (unpublished M.A. dissertation, University College of Wales, 1942).
Gray, M., *History of Bury from 1660 to 1876* (Bury Times, 1970).
Gurney, J. J., *Notes made on a visit to some of the Prisons in Scotland and the North of England in Company with Elizabeth Fry* (Edinburgh, 1819).
Gurr, D., and Hunt, J. (eds.), *The Cotton Mills of Oldham* (Oldham Leisure Services, 1985).
Halevy, E., *The Liberal Awakening 1815–1830*, rev. ed. (E. Benn, 1949).
Halstead, D., *Annals of Haslingden* (Haslingden, 1916).
Hammond, J. L., and Hammond, B., *The Skilled Labourer 1760–1832* (1919; reprinted Chivers, 1965).
Hammond, J. L., and Hammond, B., *The Town Labourer 1760–1832* (1917; reprinted Longman, 1978).
Hargreaves, B., *Recollections of Broad Oak* (Bowker, 1882).
Hawkings, D. T., *Bound for Australia* (Phillimore, 1987).
Henderson, W. O., *Industrial Britain under the Regency: the Diaries of Escher, Bodmer, May & De Gallois* (Cass, 1968).
Hindle, R., *An Account of the Expenditure of the County Palatine of Lancaster for a Period of 23 years Commencing 1819 and Ending 1842* (Whittaker, 1843).
Hopwood, E., *A History of the Lancashire Cotton Industry and the Amalgamated Weavers Association: the Lancashire Weavers' Story* (A.W.A., 1969).
Hughes, R., *The Fatal Shore: a History of the Transportation of Convicts to Australia, 1797–1868* (Collins Harvill, 1987).
Hull, G., *The Poets and Poetry of Blackburn* (Toulmin, 1902).
Johnson, T. (ed.), *All about Lancaster Castle* (Blackburn, 1892).
Langshaw, A., *How Cotton came to Clitheroe* (Clitheroe Borough Printing Co., 1953).
Leigh, J., *Directory of Bury and Rochdale 1818* (reprinted Neil Richardson, 1982).
Lewis, B., *Life in a Cotton Town: Blackburn 1818–1848* (Carnegie, 1985).
Lyons, J. S., *The Lancashire Cotton Industry and the Introduction of the Power Loom 1815-1850* (unpublished Ph.D. thesis, University of California, Berkeley, 1977).
Macdougall, P., *The Chatham Dockyard Story* (Rochester Press, 1982).
Maclachlan, N. (ed.), *The Memoirs of James Hardy Vaux* (Heinemann, 1964).
Martineau, H., *The Rioters: or a Tale of Bad Times* (Houlston, 1827).
Midwinter, E., *Social Administration in Lancashire, 1830–1860* (Manchester U.P., 1969).
Miller, G. C., *Blackburn: The Evolution of a Cotton Town* (Blackburn Times, 1951).

Miller, G. C., *Blackburn Worthies of Yesterday: a Biographical Galaxy* (Blackburn Times, 1959).
Newbigging, T., *The History of the Forest of Rossendale*, 2nd edn. (Riley, 1893).
Newbigging, T., *Lancashire Characters and Places* (Brook & Chrystal, 1891).
Pemberton, P. A., *Pure Merinos and Others: The Shipping Lists of the Australian Agricultural Company* (Australian National University, 1986).
Pike, D. (ed.), *The Australian Dictionary of Biography, vols. 1 and 2, 1788–1850* (Melbourne U.P., 1967).
Place, M. T., *Gold Down Under: the Story of the Australian Gold Rush* (Collier–Macmillan, 1969).
Prentice, A., *Historical Sketches and Personal Recollections of Manchester* (Parkes, 1851).
Price, J., *Manufactory, Methodism and the Making of a Village: Summerseat 1700–1988* (Neil Richardson, 1989).
Radcliffe, W., *The Origins of the New System of Manufacture Commonly called "Power Loom Weaving"* (Stockport, 1828).
Robson, L. L., *The Convict Settlers of Australia* (Melbourne U.P., 1965).
Rosenberg, G. (ed.), *The Adventures of Ralph Rashleigh 1825–1844* (Jonathan Cape, 1929).
Rothwell, M., *Industrial Heritage: a Guide to the Industrial Archaeology of Accrington* (Author, 1979).
Rothwell, M., *Industrial Heritage: a Guide to the Industrial Archaeology of Oswaldtwistle* (Lancashire County Library, 1978).
Rudé, G., *The Crowd in History 1730–1848* (Wiley, 1964).
Rudé, G., *Protest and Punishment: The Story of the Social and Political Prisoners Transported to Australia 1788–1868* (Clarendon Press, 1978).
Sainty, M. R. and Johnson, K. A., *Census of New South Wales 1828*, rev. edn. (Library of Australian History, 1985).
Salt, A., *These Outcast Women: The Parramatta Female Factory* 1821–1848 (Hale & Iremonger, 1984).
Shaw, A. G. L., *Convicts and the Colonies: a Study of Penal Transportation from Great Britain . . .* (1966; reprinted Melbourne U.P. 1981).
Shaw, A. G. L., *The Story of Australia*, 5th edn. (Faber, 1983).
Shaw, J. G., *History and Traditions of Darwen and its People* (Toulmin, 1889).
Shaw, L. O., *The Duel: A Satirical Poem in Four Cantos, with other Poems* (Rogerson, 1815).
Smith, I., *A Warder's Experiences in Lancaster Castle* (Thomas & Son, n.d.).
Sweeney, C., *Transported in Place of Death* (Macmillan, 1981).
Thom, W., *Rhymes and Recollections of a Hand Loom Weaver* (Smith, Elder, 1845).
Timmins, J. G., *Handloom Weavers' Cottages in Central Lancashire* (University of Lancaster, Centre for North-West Regional Studies, 1977).
Thompson, E. P., *The Making of the English Working Class* (1963; reprinted Penguin, 1974).
T.U.C. General Council, *The Book of the Martyrs of Tolpuddle 1834–1934* (T.U.C. General Council, 1934).
Tupling, T. H., *The Economic History of Rossendale* Chetham Society New Series, vol. 86 (1927).
Turner, E. S., *May it please Your Lordship* (Joseph, 1971).
Walton, J. K., *Lancashire: A Social History 1558–1939* (Manchester U.P., 1987).
Warnes, A. W., 'Early Separation of Homes from Workplaces and the Urban Structure of Chorley 1780–1850', *Trans. of the Hist. Soc. of Lancs and Ches.*, vol. 122 (1970), pp 105–136.
Wearmouth, R. F., *Methodism and the Working Class Movements of England 1800–1850* (1937; reprinted Epworth Press, 1947).

Whyatt, C. B., *The Baptists and Political and Social Conditions in Lancashire 1760–1832* (unpublished M.A. dissertation, Manchester University, 1948).
Whyte, F., and Atteridge, A. H., *A History of the Queen's Bays 1685–1929* (Jonathan Cape, 1930).
Wood, L. S., and Wilmore, A., *The Romance of the Cotton Industry in England* (Oxford U.P., 1927).
Woodcock, T., *Haslingden: A Topographical History*, Chetham Society, 3rd Series, vol. 4 (1952).